Thomas Nelson and Sons Ltd
Nelson House
Mayfield Road
Walton-on-Thames
Surrey KT12 5PL
United Kingdom

© Ray Allan, Martin Williams 1999

First published by Thomas Nelson and Sons Ltd 1999
ISBN 0-17-431491-4
9 8 7 6 5 4 3 2 1
03 02 01 00 99

All rights reserved. No part of this publication may be reproduced, copied or transmitted in any form or by any means, electronic or mechanical, including photocopy, recording, or any information storage and retrieval system, without permission in writing from the publisher or under licence from the Copyright Licensing Authority, 90 Tottenham Court Road, London W1P 9HE.

Acknowledgements

The authors and publishers would like to thank the following for all their help and assistance in the preparation of this book:

Fran Ashworth, Consultant

Ashburton High School, Croydon; Bensham Manor School, Croydon; Bradon Forest School, Swindon; Breeze Hill School, Oldham; Edenham High School, Croydon; Farleigh College, Bath; Harold Hill Community School, Romford; Hollins High School, Accrington; Park View School, Birmingham; Parklands Middle School, Northampton; Pinner Wood Middle School, Harrow; Sacred Heart of Mary Girls' School, Upminster; South Halifax High School, Halifax; St. Angela's Ursuline Convent, Forest Gate, London; St. Anne's Catholic School, Palmers Green, London; St. Chad's School, Tilbury, Essex; The Minster School, Southwell, Nottingham; The Park School, Barnstable; William Brookes School, Salop.

Editor: Marie Lister
Design: Moondisks Ltd, Cambridge
Printed in China

Contents

Chapter		Page
1	Co-ordinates	4
2	Addition and Subtraction	14
3	Parallel Lines	22
4	Below Zero	28
5	Estimation	36
6	Area and Perimeter	42
7	Angles	50
8	Work Out 1 – The Airport	60
9	Multiplication and Division	66
10	Solid Shape	72
11	Fractions	78
12	Time	84
13	Data Handling	92
14	Large Numbers	100
15	Decimals	106
16	Algebra	114
17	Fractions, Decimals and Percentages	122
18	Rules	128
19	Work Out 2 – The Magic Shop	136

Chapter 1 Co-ordinates

Step-up 1

	Column A	Column B	Column C	Column D
Row 4	Pearl pin	Ruby earrings	Garnet pendant	Gold bracelet
Row 3	Gold ring	Gold locket	Gold brooch	Emerald ring
Row 2	Pearl earrings	Onyx ring	Diamond ring	Cross pendant
Row 1	Silver locket	Gold cuff links	St Christopher pendant	Sapphire brooch

Here is a tray of jewellery. Each item can be located by a **co-ordinate**.
For example the **emerald ring** is in square (**D, 3**).

> **Remember:** The first part of the **co-ordinate** tells you which **column** you are in.
> The second part tells you which **row** you are in.

1. What items will you find in column C?
2. What items will you find in the top row?
3. What item will you find in the bottom right-hand corner of the display?
4. What item will you find third from the left, in the second row from the bottom?
5. What will you find at these co-ordinates?
   - (a) (A, 2)
   - (b) (D, 4)
   - (c) (B, 3)
   - (d) (C, 1)
   - (e) (D, 2)
   - (f) (C, 4)
6. Give the co-ordinates for these items.
   - (a) Gold brooch
   - (b) Ruby earrings
   - (c) Gold cuff links
   - (d) Pearl pin
   - (e) Onyx ring
   - (f) Silver locket

Step-up 2

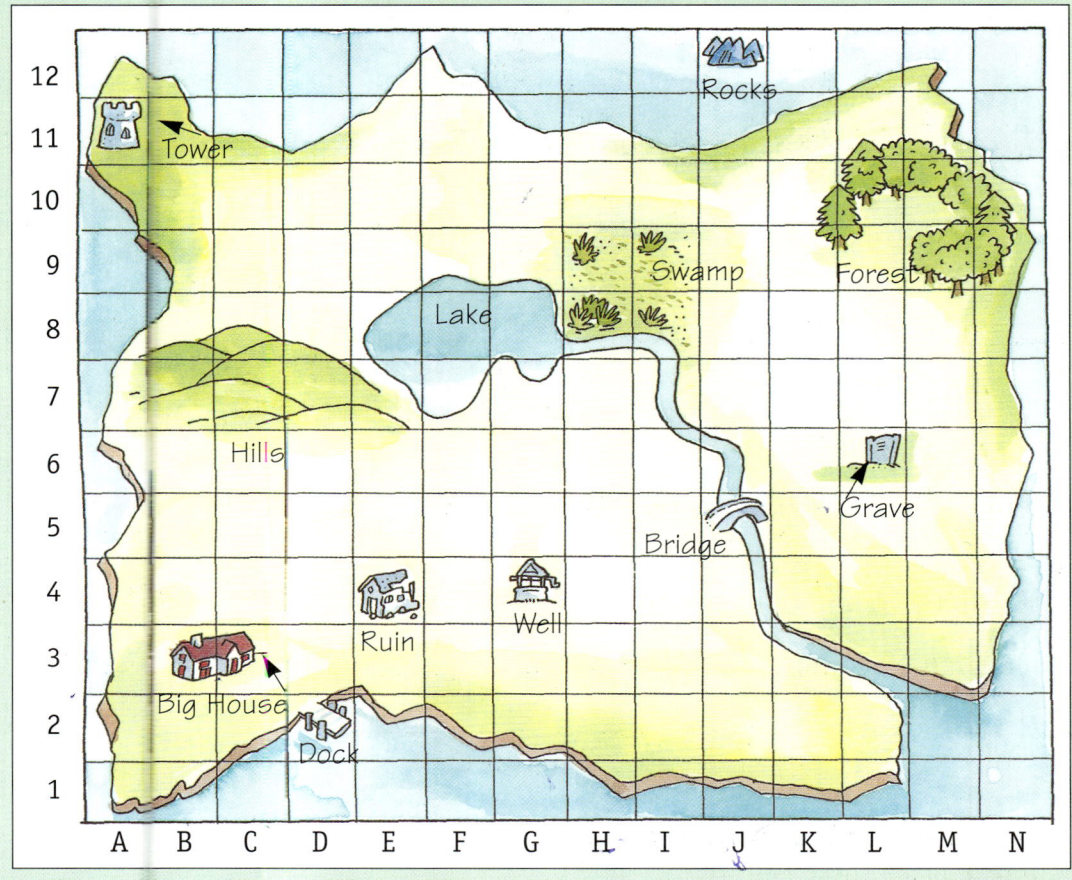

1 What will you find at these positions?
   (a) (L, 10)   (b) (C, 7)
   (c) (H, 9)   (d) (J, 5)

2 Give the co-ordinates for:
   (a) The grave
   (b) The tower
   (c) The rocks
   (d) The dock

3 In which two squares is the Big House?

4 If you move in a straight line from (E, 5) to (G, 10), what will you have to cross?

5 Give two co-ordinates that are in the sea.

6 Give two co-ordinates that the river passes through.

7 Using the map above, can you give co-ordinates to these pieces of the map?

(a)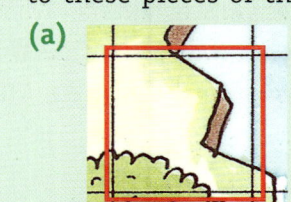

(b)

(c)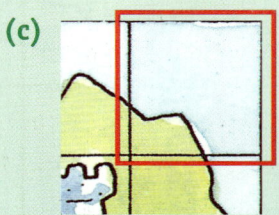

Co-ordinates 5

Co-ordinate pairs

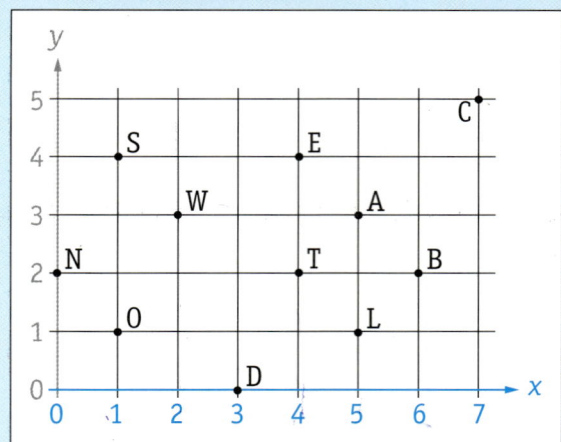

We find points on a grid using two directions: **horizontal** (across) and **vertical** (up).
We use numbered lines to give the exact position on the grid.

Lines are numbered along two **axes**: **x** and **y**.
The **x axis** goes across the page (horizontal).
The **y axis** goes up the page (vertical).

To find the letter 'A' on this grid, you go along the **x axis** to line 5. You then move up the **y axis** to line 3 – the co-ordinate pair for 'A' is **(5, 3)**.
Axes usually start from zero.

A is at **(5, 3)**   B is at **(6, 2)**   C is at **(7, 5)**

Exercise 1

Use what you know about co-ordinates and grids to answer these questions.

1 Use the grid above to complete these co-ordinates.
W is at (2, ?)   N is at (?, 2)   S is at (?, 4)
D is at (3, ?)   T is at (?, ?)   L is at (?, ?)

2 Use the co-ordinates on the grid to make these two words.
(2, 3) (4, 4) (5, 1) (5, 1)   (3, 0) (1, 1) (0, 2) (4, 4)

3 What is wrong about these statements?
(a) The **x axis** is the vertical axis.   **(b)** We look at the **y** co-ordinate first.
(c) Vertical means across.   **(d)** The **y axis** is horizontal.

Exercise 2

Think of five words of your own using letters on the grid.
Write each letter of the word as a co-ordinate.
See if your friends can decode them.

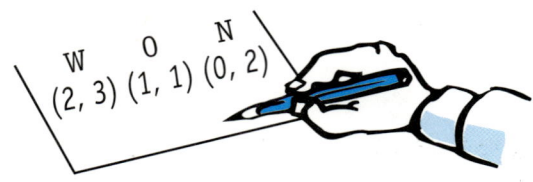

See how many words you can make from the letters in the grid. Put them into co-ordinates.

6   Chapter 1

Exercise 3

Complete these statements by using the co-ordinate grid and the **answer box**.

For example: to find the answer to Question 1:
Read the statement.
Go to the grid and find the co-ordinate given (8, 4).
At the co-ordinate you will find a letter (**C**).
In the **answer box** letter C = 2.12 kilometres so this answer will allow you to complete the statement:
A daisy chain made in Essex was *2.12* kilometres long.

1 A daisy chain made in Essex was (8, 4) long.

2 The Tyrannosaurus Rex was (2, 6) tall and weighed (3, 1).

3 The peregrine falcon can dive at a speed of (9, 7).

4 The Angel waterfall drops (7, 3).

5 At birth a baby Blue Whale weighs (3, 3).

6 The largest recorded iceberg was (0, 5) long and (6, 6) wide – larger than Belgium!

7 The ocean is deepest at Challenger Deep. It is nearly (9, 0) deep.

8 Robert Wadlow was the world's tallest person at (4, 5).

9 Jon Minnoch weighed (5, 0).

10 Mount Everest is (1, 3) high.

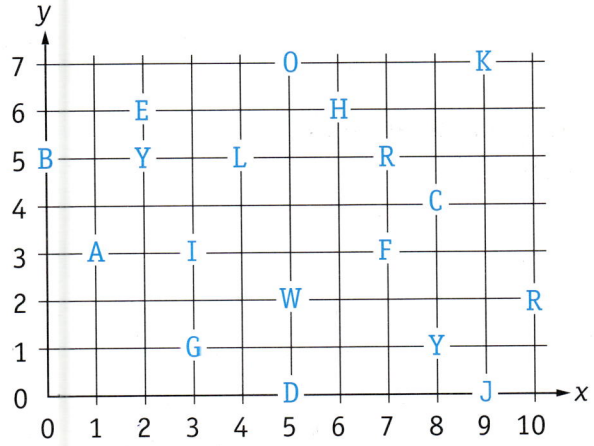

The answers
A = 8848 metres
B = 335 kilometres
C = 2.12 kilometres
D = 635 kilograms
E = 14 metres
F = 979 metres
G = 12 tonnes
H = 97 kilometres
I = 3 tonnes
J = 7 miles
K = 217 miles per hour
L = 272 centimetres

Exercise 4

Use the grid above to turn these co-ordinates into a tongue-twister.
(10, 2) (2, 6) (5, 0)   (4, 5) (5, 7) (7, 5) (10, 2) (8, 1)
(2, 5) (2, 6) (4, 5) (4, 5) (5, 7) (5, 2)   (4, 5) (5, 7) (10, 2) (7, 5) (2, 5)
Now say it quickly ten times!

Co-ordinates 7

Reflecting co-ordinates

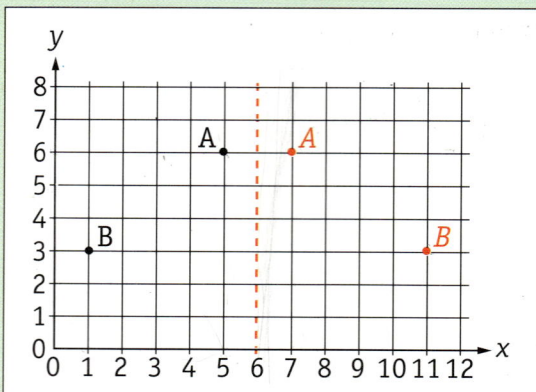

The red line on the grid acts like a mirror.

It reflects point A to *A* and B to *B*.

The co-ordinates for the letters are:

A (5, 6)   *A* (7, 6)

B (1, 3)   *B* (11, 3)

The points are reflected **horizontally**.

Exercise 5

Draw a grid on squared paper to complete this exercise.

1 Copy the points A and B. Use a colour to show the reflection.

2 Draw these three sets of co-ordinates: C (2, 1);   D (1, 8);   E (3, 5)

3 Use a colour to show the reflections of C, D and E (*C*, *D* and *E*).

4 Write down the co-ordinates of *C*, *D* and *E*.
   Write: '*C* (,)   *D* (,)   *E* (,).'

Exercise 6

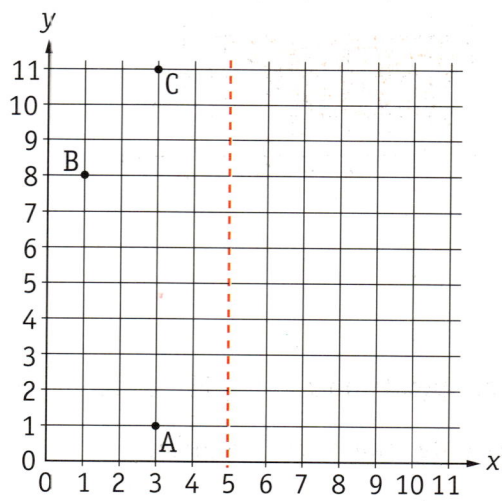

Draw a grid on squared paper to complete this exercise.

1 Draw the points **A** (3, 1) **B** (1, 8) and **C** (3, 11) onto the grid.

2 Put another point onto the grid so that you make a kite shape. Label it point **D**. Join the points.

3 Reflect the kite in the mirror line.

4 Give the co-ordinates of the four reflected corners.

5 What happens to point **D** when the shape is reflected?

Chapter 1

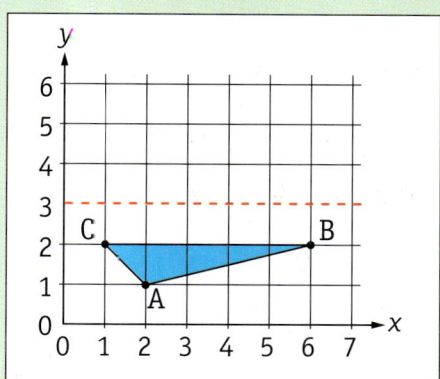

On this grid the mirror line is **horizontal**, so the reflection of the triangle will be vertical.

Exercise 7

Draw the grid above on squared paper to complete this exercise.

1. Reflect A. What are the co-ordinates of the reflection?
2. Reflect B. What are the co-ordinates of the reflection?
3. Reflect C. What are the co-ordinates of the reflection?

Exercise 8

Draw a grid on squared paper to complete this exercise.

1. Reflect A, B, C and D in the mirror line.
2. Join the reflected points to make a new shape.

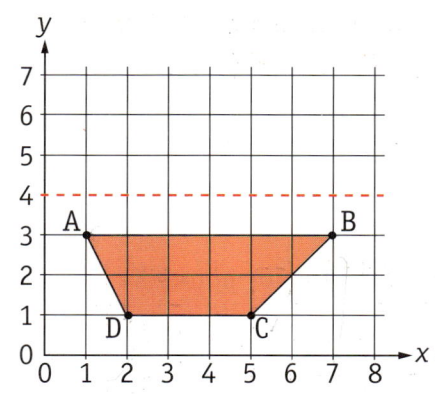

Exercise 9

Draw a grid on squared paper to complete this exercise.

1. Draw a mirror line from (4, 1) to (4, 7).
2. Draw these points onto the grid: (1, 1) (3, 7) (3, 3).
3. Join the points to make a triangle.
4. Draw the reflection of the triangle.
5. What are the co-ordinates of the three corners of the reflected triangle?

Co-ordinates   9

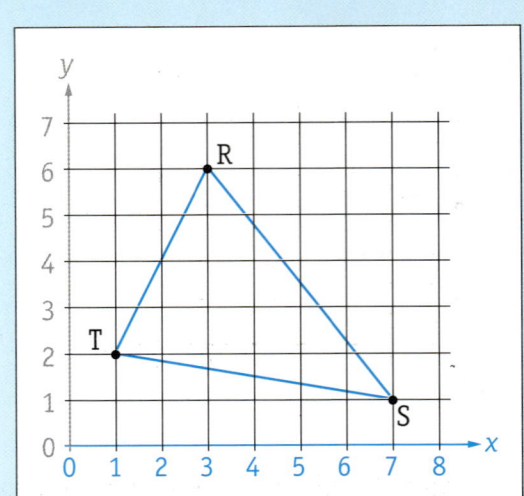

There are three points plotted on this grid, R, S and T.

The co-ordinates for R = (3, 6).

Co-ordinates for S = (7, 1).

Co-ordinates for T = (1, 2).

Exercise 10

1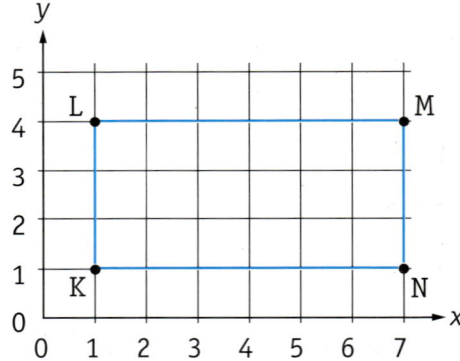

Give the co-ordinates for points K, L, M and N.

2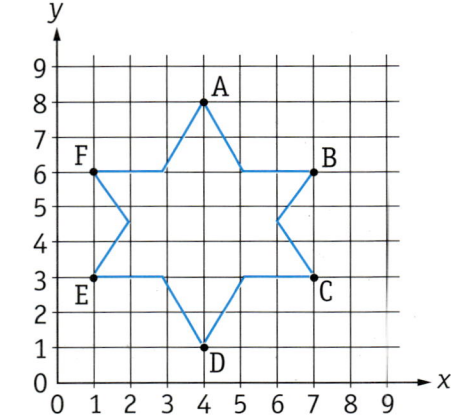

Give the co-ordinates for the six points of this star.

3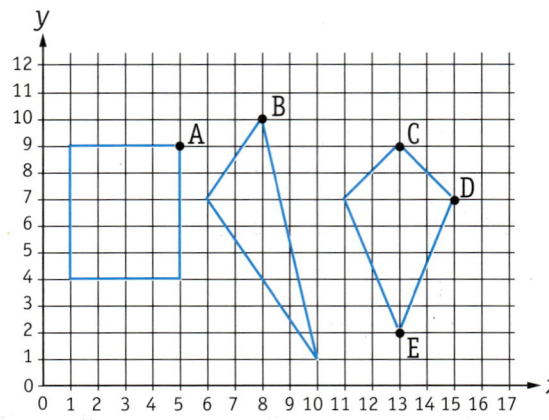

Give co-ordinates for the points A, B, C, D and E.

10 Chapter 1

4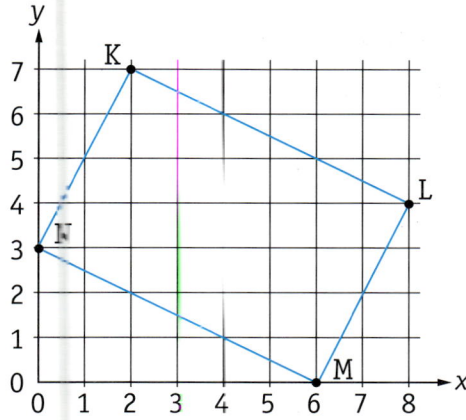

Give the co-ordinates for points K, L, M and N.

5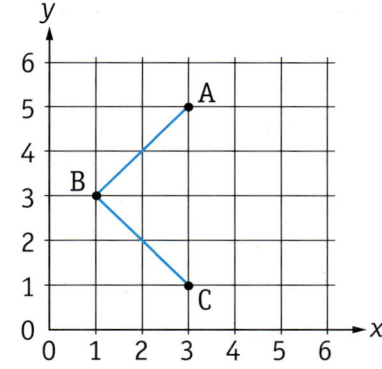

Point D is the missing corner of this square.
Give the co-ordinates for D.

6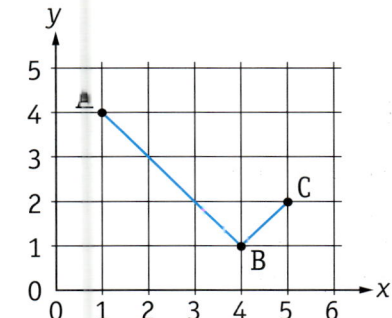

Point D is the missing corner of this rectangle.
Give the co-ordinates for D.

7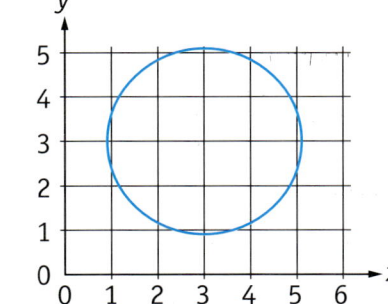

Give the co-ordinates for the centre of this circle.

8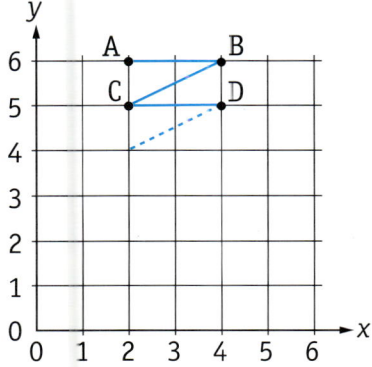

Give the next four co-ordinates for this pattern.

9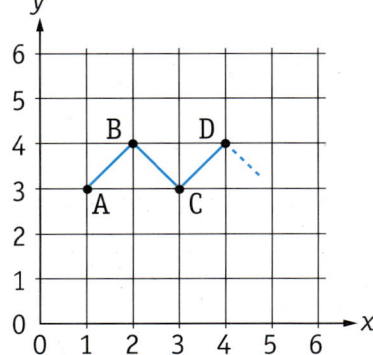

Give the next four co-ordinates for this pattern.

Co-ordinates 11

Exercise 11

For this work you will need Worksheet 4.

Class 8S is planning a school garden for their Technology Project.
Below is a picture of class 8S at work in their garden.

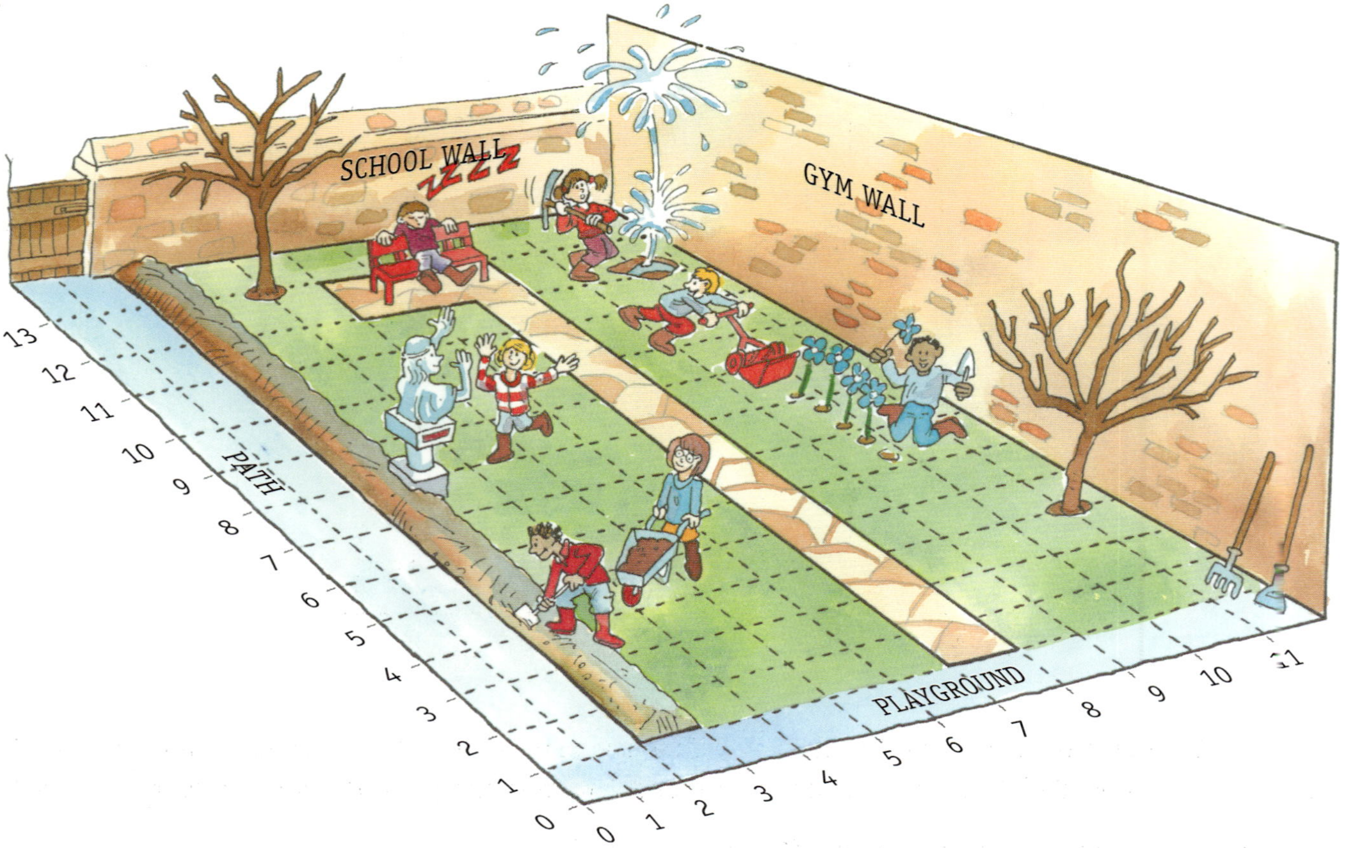

To help them with the project, a plan of the garden had to be made. You can see this plan on the next page. The plan shows: the school wall, the gym wall, the path and the playground.

1 Using the picture, and the plan, find the point where the gym wall and the school wall meet.
   What are the **co-ordinates** of this point?

2 In the picture find the sleeping boy. Which of these co-ordinates on the plan, is nearest to his position?
   (17, 8)   (12, 4)   (0, 0)   (7, 13)   (10, 10)

3 What will you find at co-ordinates (4, 13)?

4 What do you think happened at co-ordinates (10, 12)?

5 Daisy is pushing a wheelbarrow. Give co-ordinates for Daisy's position.

6 Rio is pushing a lawnmower. Give co-ordinates for Rio's position.

7 Copy out three co-ordinates that are in areas where there is grass growing.

Chapter 1

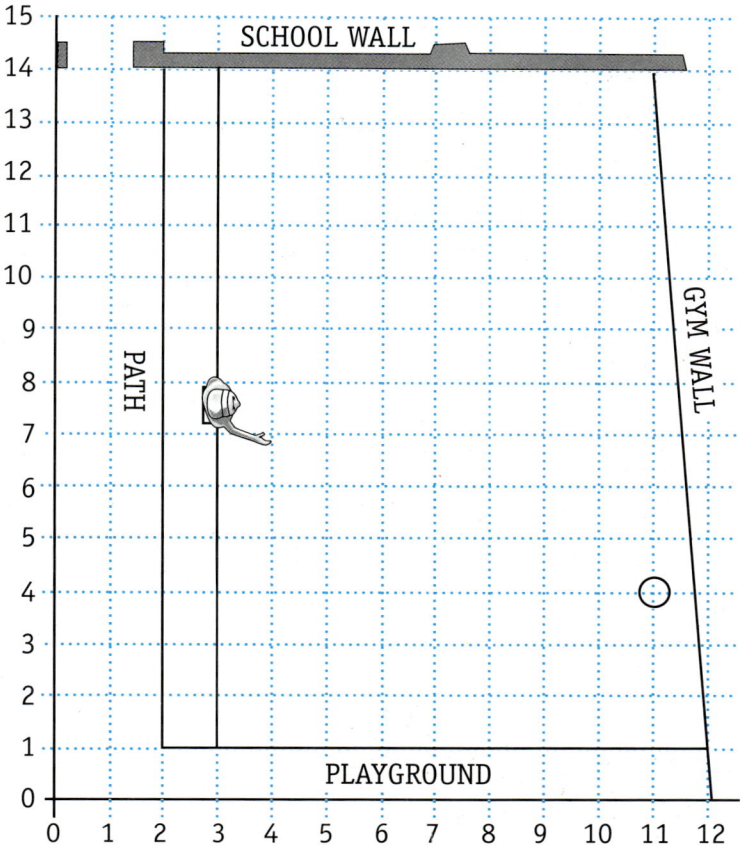

8 Look at (11, 4) on the plan. The circle shows where a tree stands. Give the co-ordinates for the other tree on the grid. It is planted 1 m from the school wall and 2 m from the path. (1 unit stands for 1 metre.)

9 The plan of the garden is drawn to scale. (1 unit : 1 metre.)
 (a) What is the widest part of the garden?
 (b) What is the length of the garden?

10 The flowerbed runs alongside the path. Give the co-ordinates of the four corners of the flowerbed.

11 Do you cross the path if you walk from (4, 1) to (6, 11)?

12 The statue stands about half-way down the flowerbed. Give its co-ordinates.

Key ideas

Co-ordinates These give the positions on a grid. They locate points two ways: horizontally and vertically.

Axes There are two **axes** on a graph: **x axis** and **y axis**.
 The x axis is **horizontal**, the y axis is **vertical**.

Co-ordinates   13

Chapter 2 Addition and Subtraction

Step-up 1

The four rules – **addition**, **subtraction**, **multiplication**, **division**.

As Megan works she comes across some number problems.
For each task below, work out which of the four rules (+, −, ×, ÷) she has to use, and give the answer to each problem.

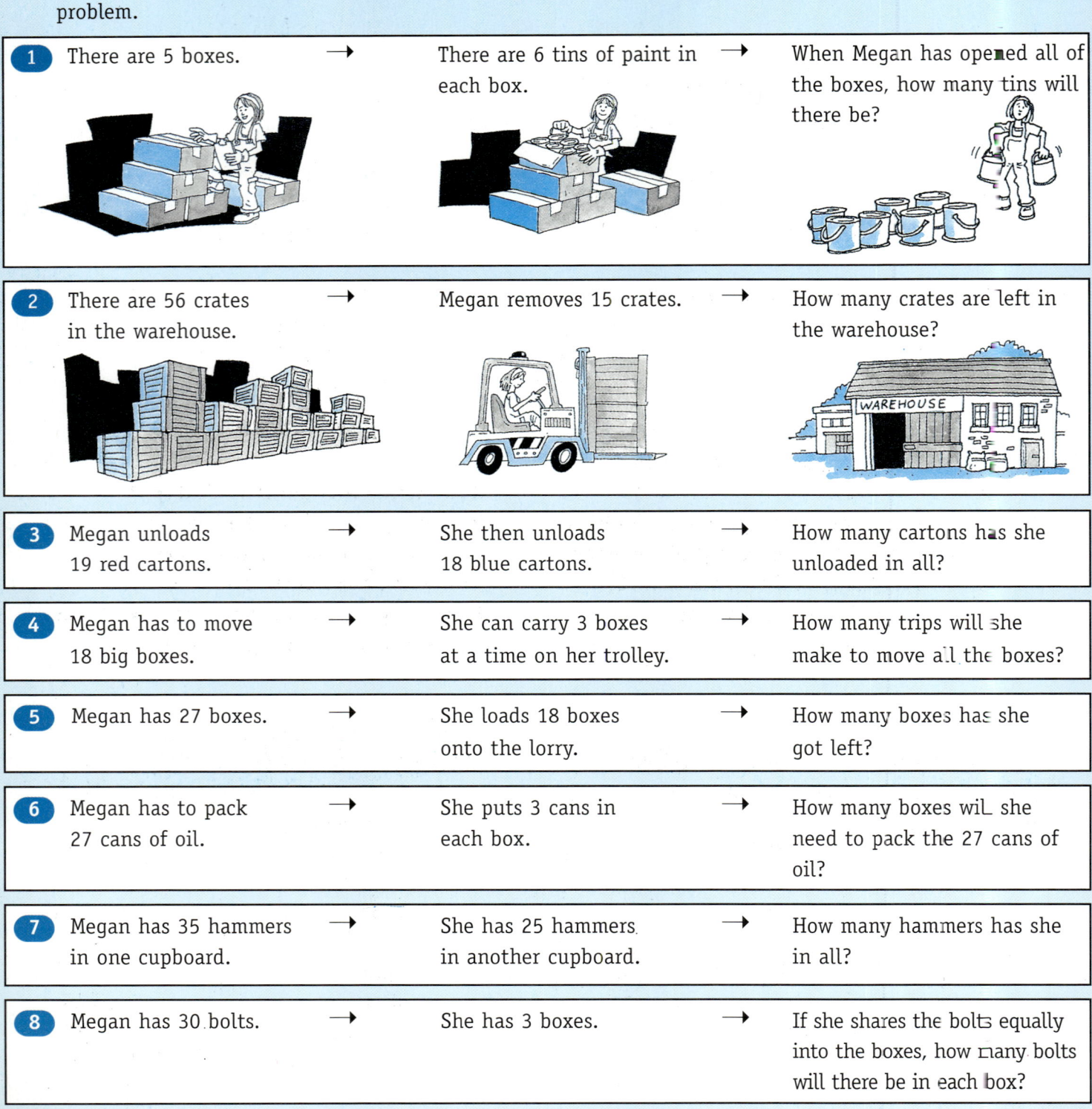

1. There are 5 boxes. → There are 6 tins of paint in each box. → When Megan has opened all of the boxes, how many tins will there be?

2. There are 56 crates in the warehouse. → Megan removes 15 crates. → How many crates are left in the warehouse?

3. Megan unloads 19 red cartons. → She then unloads 18 blue cartons. → How many cartons has she unloaded in all?

4. Megan has to move 18 big boxes. → She can carry 3 boxes at a time on her trolley. → How many trips will she make to move all the boxes?

5. Megan has 27 boxes. → She loads 18 boxes onto the lorry. → How many boxes has she got left?

6. Megan has to pack 27 cans of oil. → She puts 3 cans in each box. → How many boxes will she need to pack the 27 cans of oil?

7. Megan has 35 hammers in one cupboard. → She has 25 hammers in another cupboard. → How many hammers has she in all?

8. Megan has 30 bolts. → She has 3 boxes. → If she shares the bolts equally into the boxes, how many bolts will there be in each box?

Step-up 2

1 Answer these problems.
(a) 4 + 5 = ?
(b) 12 + 5 = ?
(c) 26 + 7 = ?
(d) 3 − 3 = ?
(e) 18 − 4 = ?
(f) 22 − 9 = ?
(g) 3 × 2 = ?
(h) 5 × 5 = ?
(i) 10 × 7 = ?
(j) 8 ÷ 4 = ?
(k) 12 ÷ 3 = ?
(l) 21 ÷ 7 = ?

2 Use one of the signs below to complete each problem.

| + addition | − subtraction | × multiplication | ÷ division |

(a) 2 ? 6 = 12
(b) 6 ? 7 = 13
(c) 9 ? 2 = 7
(d) 7 ? 3 = 4
(e) 6 ? 3 = 2
(f) 5 ? 3 = 15
(g) 11 ? 7 = 18
(h) 10 ? 5 = 2
(i) 3 ? 15 = 18

3 What figure is missing from each problem?
(a) 4 × ? = 12
(b) 8 ÷ 2 = ?
(c) ? + 6 = 14
(d) 10 − ? = 6
(e) ? × 7 = 14
(f) 12 ÷ ? = 4
(g) ? × 3 = 15
(h) 14 − ? = 12
(i) 8 + ? = 8

4 Answer these problems. Do them in your head.
(a) There are 4 boxes. Each box contains 11 cards. How many cards are there in total?
(b) There are 16 lorries in a lay-by. 9 lorries leave. How many are left in the lay-by?
(c) 3 children share 18 balloons equally between them. How many balloons do they each get?
(d) Ian has £13. His aunt then gives him £8. How much has Ian in total?
(e) 24 pencils are shared equally onto 4 tables. How many pencils are there on each table?
(f) 7 cars arrive. There are 4 people in each car. How many people are there in total?

Addition Card One

These involve 'carrying'.

1. 57
  + 25

2. 49
  + 43

3. 64
  + 38

4. 108
  + 277

5. 257
  + 528

6. 492
  + 270

Subtraction Card One

You will have to 'carry over' a ten or hundred.

1. 82
  − 26

2. 54
  − 17

3. 70
  − 25

4. 642
  − 318

5. 250
  − 228

6. 328
  − 155

Addition and Subtraction

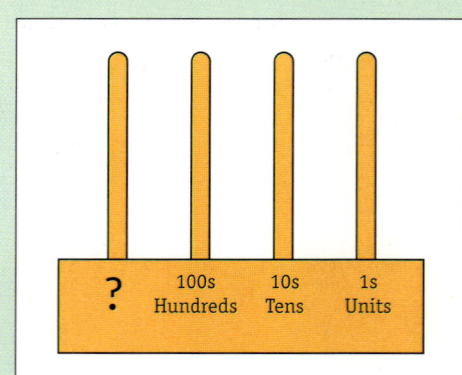

There are four spikes on this abacus.

Three of the spikes are labelled **Hundreds**, **Tens** and **Units**.

Remember, when we use the abacus to multiply by 10 the next spike on the left is always 10 times larger. The end spike should be labelled 10 times more than the hundreds spike:

100 × 10 = 1000 (one thousand).

Exercise 1

Write out these numbers as figures. The first is done for you.
1. Eight hundred and seventy-three. **873**
2. Seven hundred and ninety-two.
3. Four hundred and eighty.
4. Five hundred and fifty-five.
5. Nine hundred and sixty-nine.
6. One hundred and eleven.
7. Six hundred.
8. Nine hundred.
9. Three thousand eight hundred and fifty.
10. Six thousand five hundred and thirty-seven.
11. Eight thousand two hundred and seventy-three.
12. Five thousand three hundred and twenty-four.
13. Seven thousand seven hundred and seventy-seven.
14. Nine thousand eight hundred.
15. One thousand and thirty-three.

1000 – thousand	14 – fourteen
100 – hundred	13 – thirteen
90 – ninety	12 – twelve
80 – eighty	11 – eleven
70 – seventy	10 – ten
60 – sixty	9 – nine
50 – fifty	8 – eight
40 – forty	7 – seven
30 – thirty	6 – six
20 – twenty	5 – five
19 – nineteen	4 – four
18 – eighteen	3 – three
17 – seventeen	2 – two
16 – sixteen	1 – one
15 – fifteen	

Exercise 2

Write these numbers as words.
You can use the list of numbers to help you.
1. 226
2. 583
3. 931
4. 770
5. 4000
6. 6582
7. 1856
8. 3445
9. 8600
10. 5410
11. 2094
12. 9103

Exercise 3

1. Write out the **smallest** and **largest** numbers in these groups.
   (a) 1000, 1800, 990, 3000, 1500, 2500
   (b) 5500, 2300, 6100, 5200, 3200, 5900
   (c) 4100, 4660, 3600, 4550, 3250, 4450

2. Write the groups of numbers in order, smallest first.
   (a) 1100, 1650, 890, 2000, 950, 1900
   (b) 4500, 3950, 4700, 4550, 3550, 4000
   (c) 3443, 3600, 2980, 3500, 3000, 1950

16   Chapter 2

The jumps along this number line make a pattern. Each jump is 10 units long. Why does it always land on a '0'?

This pattern starts at 3. Every jump of 10 units lands on a number ending in 3. If the jumps were 10 units long and started at 7, what do you know about numbers where the jumps will land?

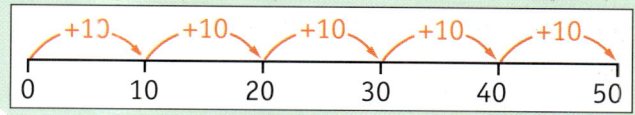
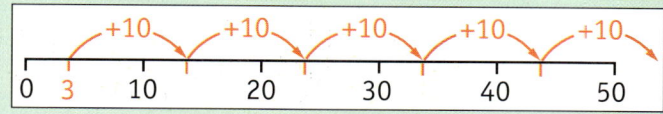

Exercise 4

Add ten to each of these numbers.

1 27   2 58   3 11   4 85   5 90   6 95

Exercise 5

Use the ideas above, or draw small number lines to add 'tens' to these numbers.

1 12 + 10 = ?   2 23 + 20 = ?   3 41 + 30 = ?   4 65 + 30 = ?
5 24 + 50 = ?

You can use the same idea for subtraction. The jump goes backwards to take away.

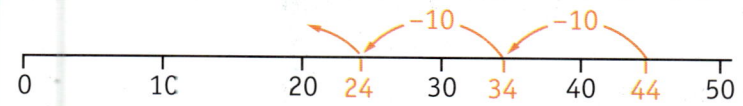

44 − 10 = 34
34 − 10 = 24

Exercise 6

Subtract 'tens' from these numbers.

1 37 − 10 = ?   2 78 − 10 = ?   3 31 − 20 = ?   4 59 − 40 = ?
5 77 − 50 = ?   6 45 − 40 = ?   7 83 − 70 = ?   8 110 − 90 = ?
9 150 − 50 = ?   10 150 − 60 = ?

To take 9 away from a number, take away 10, then add 1 back on.
43 − 9 → 43 − 10 = 33 → 33 + 1 = 34.

You can use this idea for other numbers:
25 − 7 → 25 − 10 = 15 → 15 + 3 = 18.

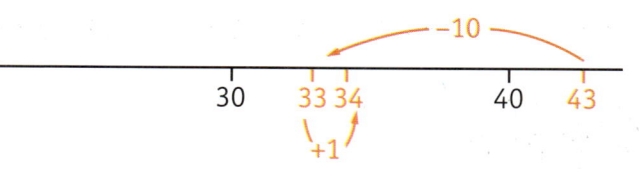

Exercise 7

Use the idea above to work these out in your head.

1 72 − 9 = ?   2 56 − 9 = ?   3 37 − 8 = ?
4 83 − 5 = ?   5 91 − 7 = ?   6 64 − 8 = ?

Addition and Subtraction

Subtraction – Finding the difference

Warren is running his first marathon. The total distance is a little more than 26 miles. Warren is at the 7 mile post. He works out how much further he has to run like this:

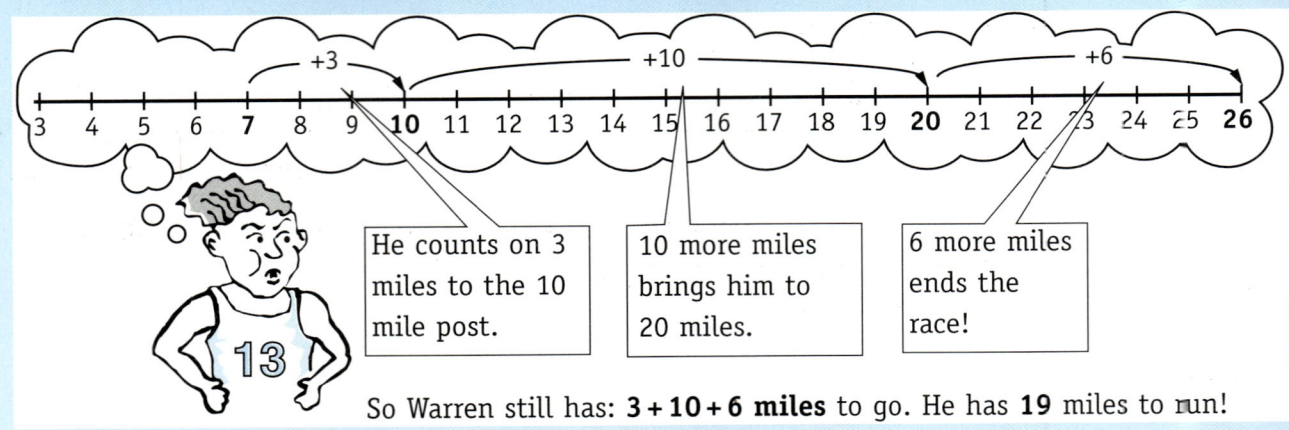

He counts on 3 miles to the 10 mile post.

10 more miles brings him to 20 miles.

6 more miles ends the race!

So Warren still has: **3 + 10 + 6 miles** to go. He has **19 miles** to run!

Exercise 8

Use the number line above to find how many more miles Warren has still to run.

1. 3 miles
2. 9 miles
3. 14 miles
4. 17 miles

Alex is painting lines on the 100 metre track.
He has painted 47 m so far in lane 1.
To calculate how much is left to paint, count on!

Alex counts 3 + 10 + 10 + 10 + 10 + 10 metres. He has 53 metres still to paint.
Can you find any shortcuts for these calculations?

Exercise 9

Calculate how much more painting Alex has to do to finish these 100 m lines.

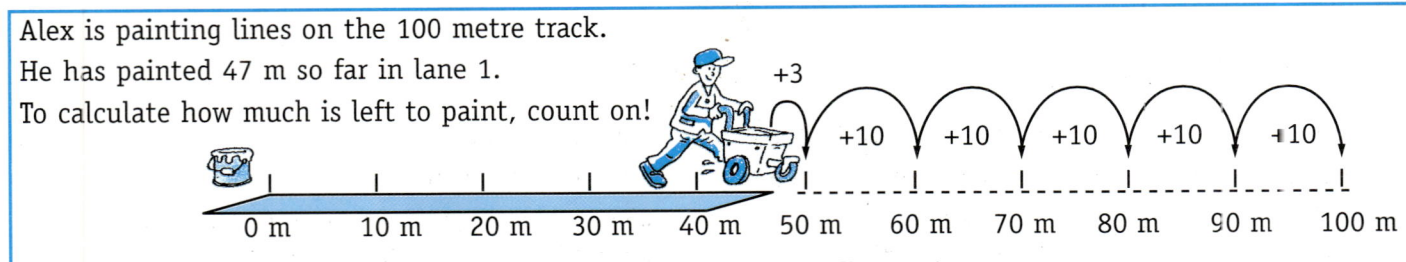

1. 0 m → 39 m
2. 0 m → 28 m
3. 0 m → 65 m
4. 0 m → 33 m
5. 0 m → 12 m
6. 0 m → 24 m

Chapter 2

Another way of using your own number line

Emma's family want to buy a new television. The TV costs £629. They have saved £376 so far. How much more must they save?

Make your own number line.

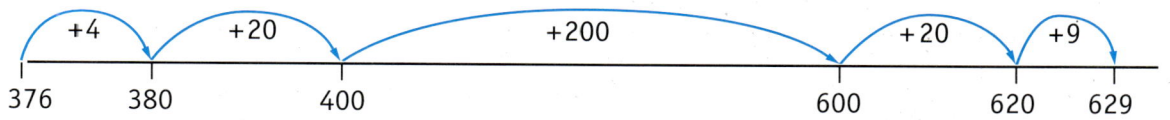

The family need to save: £4+£20+£200+£20+£9. They need to save £253. Talk to your teacher or partner, to find shortcuts that make your line simpler.

Exercise 10

Use these number lines to calculate the subtractions.

1 (a) 252 − 185 = ?

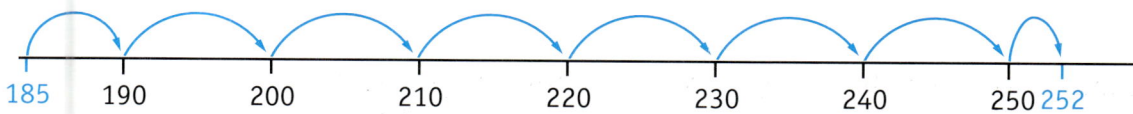

(b) Find a shorter way than this number line. Draw it and show it to your teacher.

2 (a) 724 − 367 = ?

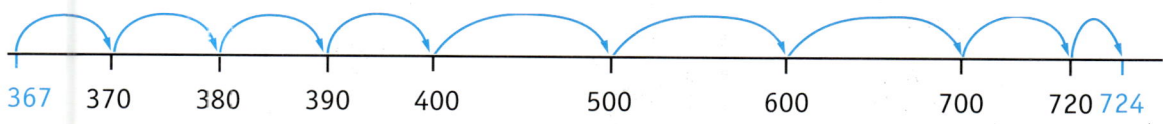

(b) This number line can be made simpler. Re-draw it in a simpler way.

Exercise 11

Use the number lines on Worksheet 10 to calculate these subtractions.
As you do more number lines you will be able to find more of your own shortcuts.

1 305 − 124 = ?   2 370 − 197 = ?   3 911 − 682 = ?   4 524 − 209 = ?
5 615 − 541 = ?   6 229 − 89 = ?   7 456 − 238 = ?   8 444 − 77 = ?

Exercise 12

Solve these problems. Write your own number line to help you.

1. Jenny is 182 cm tall. Jake is 87 cm tall. How much taller is Jenny than Jake?
2. Leroy has to write a 450 word essay. He has written 165 words so far. How many more words has he left to write?
3. Martin wants to buy a Yo-Yo that costs £5.75. He has £2.39 so far. How much is he missing?
4. Kim does 55 press-ups in her work-out. Today she stops at 27. How many press-ups has she missed?
5. Carl's record is 103 non-stop 'headers'. He has completed 49. How many more does he have to do to equal his record?

Addition and Subtraction

Time

There are 7 days in a week.

Exercise 13

Rewrite these times. Two of the problems have been done for you.

1. 1 week and 3 days = 10 days
2. 2 weeks and 2 days = ?
3. 2 weeks and 4 days = ?
4. 4 weeks and 2 days = ?
5. 3 weeks and 3 days = ?
6. 5 weeks and 1 day = ?
7. 11 days = 1 week and 4 days
8. 8 days = ?
9. 15 days = ?
10. 13 days = ?
11. 19 days = ?
12. 22 days = ?

Exercise 14

By turning weeks into days, solve these subtraction problems.
Try to work them out in your head.

1. Mary has a two week holiday. She spends four days travelling. How many days does she spend resting?
2. A painter says that it will take her 1 week and 4 days to decorate a house. After 5 days, how long has she left to finish the work?
3. Khalid goes away to scout camp. He should be away for 2 weeks and 2 days, but after 8 days he feels homesick and wants to go home. How much time will he miss?
4. Heather has her birthday in 3 weeks and 2 days. In 5 days' time it is her mother's birthday. How many days are there between the two birthdays?

Exercise 15

It will take 3 weeks and 1 day to sail around the island.

1. From the **Start** it takes:
   (a) 6 days for the ship to arrive at South Bay.
       How much longer should it take to finish the trip?
   (b) 1 week and 4 days to arrive at King's Point.
       If the ship is to complete the trip on time, how long is there left?
   (c) 2 weeks and 3 days to arrive at St Paul's.
       From St Paul's it will take another 6 days to finish the trip. Will the ship arrive on time?
2. How long did the journey from King's Point to St Paul's take?

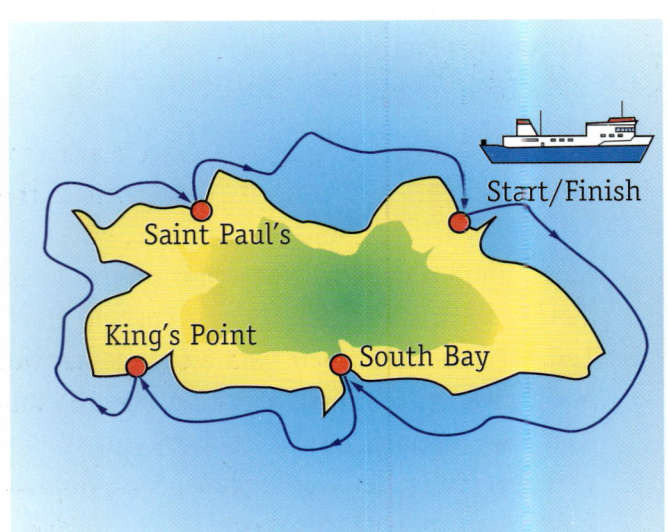

Making 9 – Investigation

You will need to make a set of cards like this:

You will need to make a set of cards with these operations:

Lay out the cards to make 9, like this:

   =9

3 cards

   =9

4 cards

1. Using 3 or 4 cards, make 9 in as many ways as you can.
2. Using any number of cards, find as many ways as you can to make 9.

Boxes – Investigation

Look at this box:

You can make 24 by using each of the numbers once, for example:

		or	
step 1	$5 \times 8 = 40$		$8 \times 3 = 24$
step 2	$40 \div 5 = 8$		$24 - 5 = 19$
step 3	$8 \times 3 = \underline{24}$		$19 + 5 = \underline{24}$

Make 24 from these boxes. Show your working out.

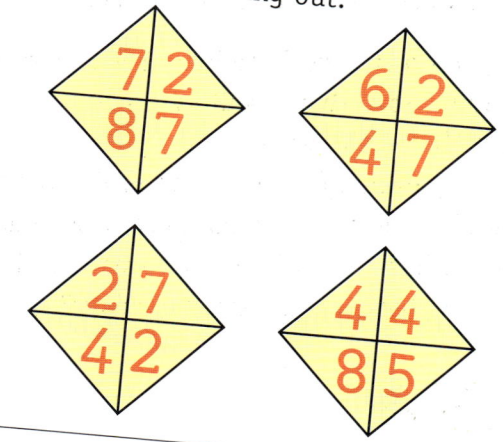

Key ideas

In our counting system each 'place' is worth ten times more than the place to its right. Beyond the **hundred** place, there is the **thousand** place. 2176 is written:

Thousands	Hundreds	Tens	Units
2	1	7	6

There are different ways to subtract numbers. Number lines are useful for counting on. You can find your own shortcuts to drawing number lines. The more you do, the quicker your shortcuts become.

287 +13→ 300 +300→ 600 +14→ 614

Addition and Subtraction

Chapter 3 Parallel Lines

Step-up

Look carefully at this street scene.
In real life some of the straight lines would be parallel, others would not be parallel.
Which sets of lines would be parallel?
Write: 'Lines ?, ? are parallel.'

Exercise 1

Answer these questions about tracks **A**, **B** and **C** above.

1. Which straight line track is safe for the train to use?
2. Discuss your reasons with your teacher or your friend.
3. Write your reasons in your book. Start like this:
   'Track ? is safe because ? .'

Exercise 2

1. Which straight line track is safe for the train to use?
   Write: 'Track **(a)** is safe,' or 'Track **(a)** is not safe.'

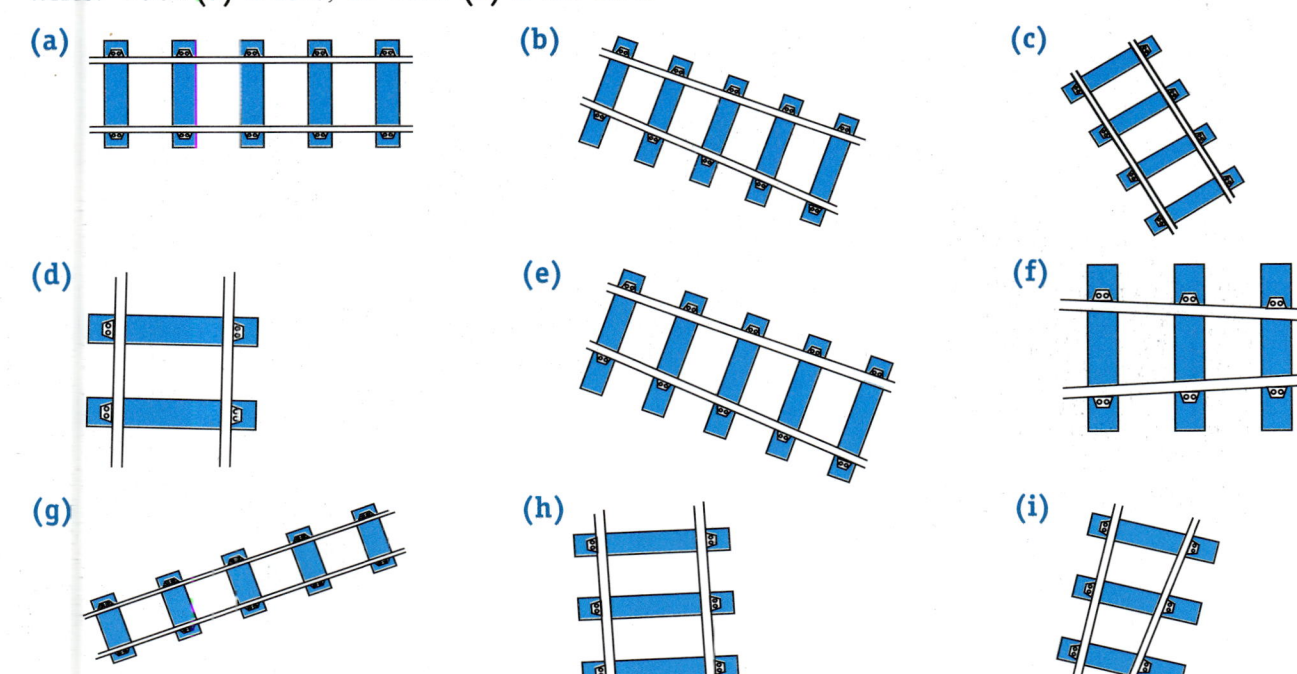

2. Copy and complete these sentences.
   The safe tracks have lines which stay the ? apart.
   The rails are ? lines.

Parallel Lines 23

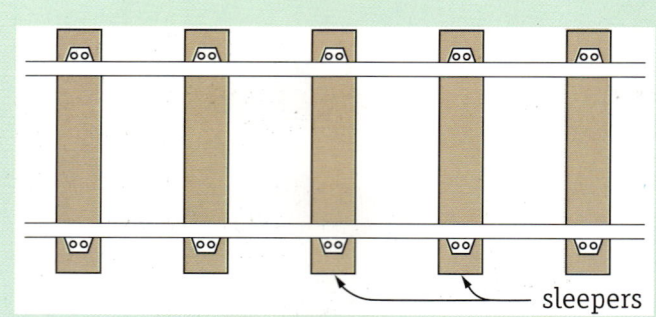

Sleepers keep the rails in position. They hold the rails the **same distance** apart right down the line.

The rails are ? cm apart all the way along.

Straight lines which stay the same distance apart are called ? lines.

sleepers

Exercise 3

1. Use your experience to say whether or not the red lines are parallel.
   Write: 'The lines are parallel,' or 'The lines are not parallel.'

   (a)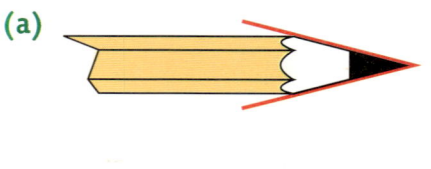

   (b)

   (c)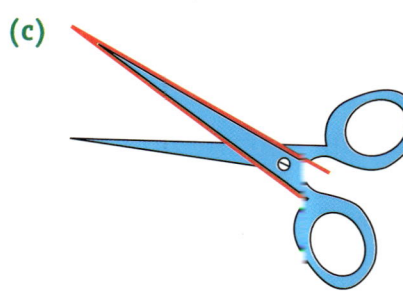

   (d)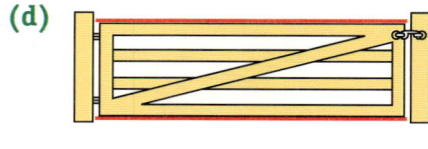

   (e)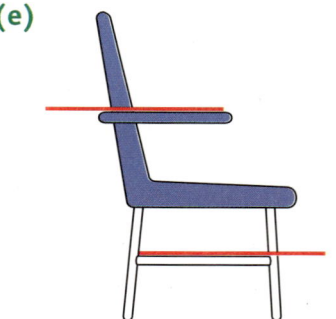

   (f)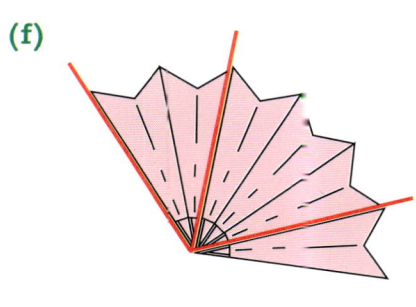

   (g)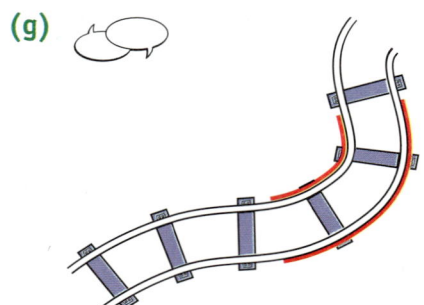

   (h)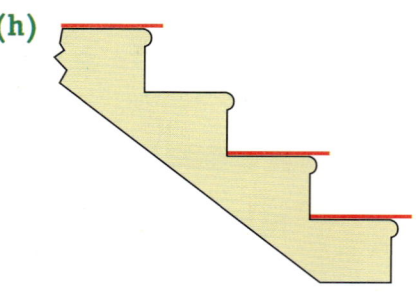

   (i)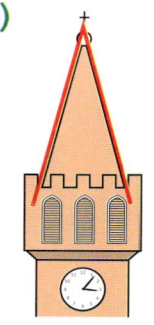

2. Why are the lines in drawing (g) not parallel?

24   Chapter 3

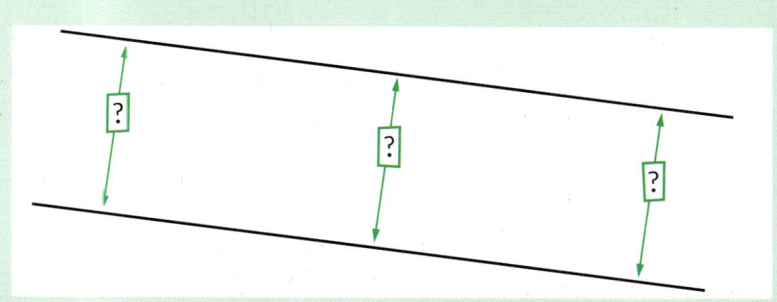

To check that these lines are **parallel** you can measure the distance between them in the middle and at the ends. If the distance stays the same then the lines are parallel.

Exercise 4

Which pairs of lines are parallel? Check by measuring.
Write: 'These lines are parallel,' or 'These lines are not parallel.'

Parallel Lines 25

Lines do not have to be side by side to be parallel. The lines below are parallel.

The two lines have been labelled. One line is called **AB** and the other line is called **CD**.

Exercise 5

Which of the lines below are parallel to each other. Use a ruler to help you.
Write: 'Lines EF and QR are parallel.'

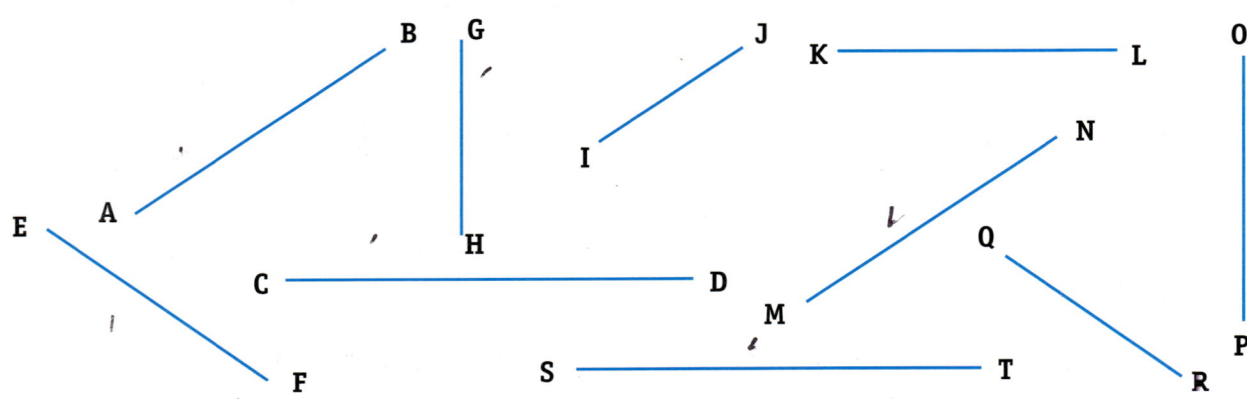

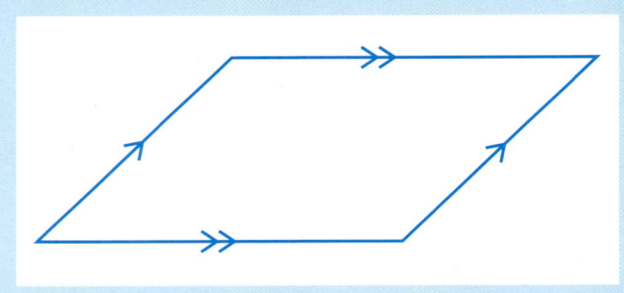

To show that lines are parallel with each other a small arrow (➤) is drawn on each line.

If there is another set of parallel lines two small arrows (➤➤) are drawn on each line.

Exercise 6

Draw these pairs of parallel lines. Use arrows (➤) to show that they are parallel.

1. Draw a line 12 cm long. Label the line XY. Draw another 12 cm parallel line 3 cm below it.
2. Draw a line 4 cm long. Label the line BC. Draw another 4 cm parallel line 3 cm below it.
3. Draw a line 6 cm long. Label the line AB. Draw another 6 cm parallel line 2 cm below it.
4. Draw a line 7 cm long. Label the line ST. Draw another 7 cm parallel line 4 cm below it.
5. Draw a line $8\frac{1}{2}$ cm long. Label the line DE. Draw another $8\frac{1}{2}$ cm parallel line $3\frac{1}{2}$ cm below it.

Exercise 7

Draw this shape.
Label it and copy the arrows
to show which sides are parallel.

Exercise 8

Which sides on each shape are parallel to each other?
Write: '1 Side AB is parallel with CD, and AC is parallel with BD.'

1

2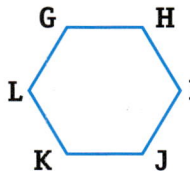

3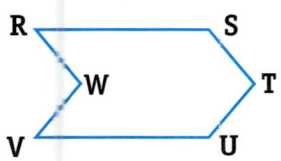

4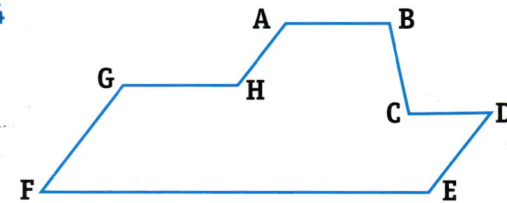

Exercise 9

How many parallel lines can you see in this pattern? There are three groups:
- horizontal lines (across the page);
- vertical lines (up and down the page);
- diagonal lines (from one top corner to the opposite bottom corner).

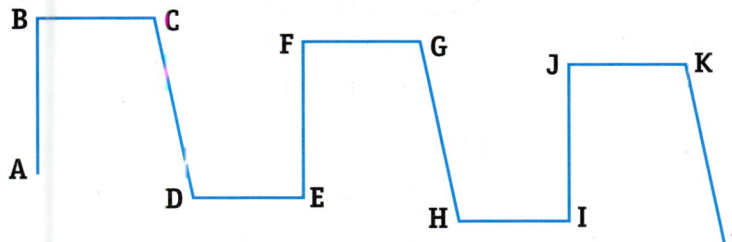

Key ideas

Parallel lines are straight lines that are the same distance apart.
Parallel lines do not have to be side by side.

To show that lines are parallel we mark them with **arrows**, pointing in the same direction.

Parallel Lines 27

Chapter 4 Below Zero

Step-up

1 (a) 9 take away 5 is ? (b) 8 minus 7 is ? (c) Take 7 from 11 ?
   (d) Subtract 8 from 15 ? (e) 14 minus 9 is ? (f) 21 take away 6 is ?

2 (a) 7 − 0 = ? (b) 6 − 6 = ? (c) 22 − 22 = ?
   (d) 15 − 0 = ? (e) 9 − 0 = ? (f) 12 − 12 = ?

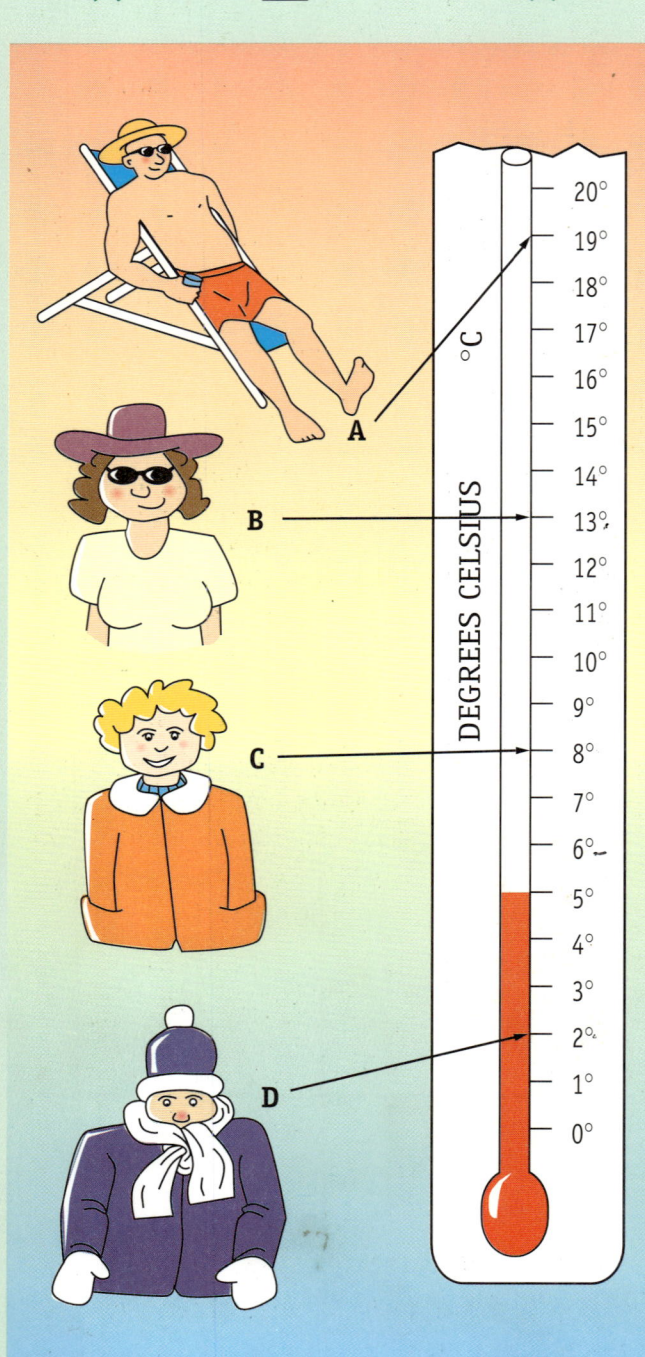

3 Use the thermometer to answer these questions. Remember to use **degrees Celsius** (°C).
   (a) What temperature does the thermometer show?
   (b) What is the temperature at **A**?
   (c) What is the temperature at **B**?
   (d) What is the temperature at **C**?
   (e) What is the temperature at **D**?

4 Say if the temperatures go **up** or go **down**.
   (a) Start at 3 °C, finish at 1 °C.
   (b) Start at 5 °C, finish at 7 °C.
   (c) Start at 2 °C, finish at 11 °C.
   (d) Start at 7 °C, finish at 6 °C.
   (e) Start at 13 °C, finish at 0 °C.

5 The temperature is 8 °C. The temperature **goes down** by 5 degrees.
   What is the new temperature?

6 The temperature is 17 °C. The temperature **goes down** by 9 degrees.
   What is the new temperature?

7 The temperature is 14 °C. The temperature **goes down** by 13 degrees.
   What is the new temperature?

8 The temperature is 9 °C. The temperature **goes down** by 9 degrees.
   What is the new temperature?

9 The temperature is 6 °C. How many degrees must the temperature **go down** to reach 0 °C?

10 The temperature is 11 °C. How many degrees must the temperature **go down** to reach 0 °C?

Temperatures can go **below zero**.
We call temperatures below zero **negative** temperatures.
⁻5 °C means 5 degrees **below** zero.

Exercise 1

Use the thermometer to answer these questions.

1 What temperature does the thermometer show?

2 The temperature starts at 4 °C and goes **down** to ⁻2 °C. How many degrees has the temperature gone down?

3 The temperature starts at 3 °C and goes **down** to ⁻5 °C. How many degrees has the temperature gone down?

4 The temperature starts at 0 °C and goes **down** to ⁻6 °C. How many degrees has the temperature gone down?

5 The temperature is 7 °C. It goes **down** by 11 degrees. What is the new temperature?

6 The temperature is 4 °C. It goes **down** by 9 degrees. What is the new temperature?

7 The temperature starts at ⁻5 °C and goes **up** to 8 °C. How many degrees has the temperature gone up?

8 The temperature starts at ⁻3 °C and goes **up** to 10 °C. How many degrees has the temperature gone up?

9 The temperature starts at ⁻8 °C and goes **up** to ⁻2 °C. How many degrees has the temperature gone up?

10 The temperature is ⁻6 °C. It goes **up** by 10 degrees. What is the new temperature?

11 The temperature is ⁻8 °C. It goes **up** by 15 degrees. What is the new temperature?

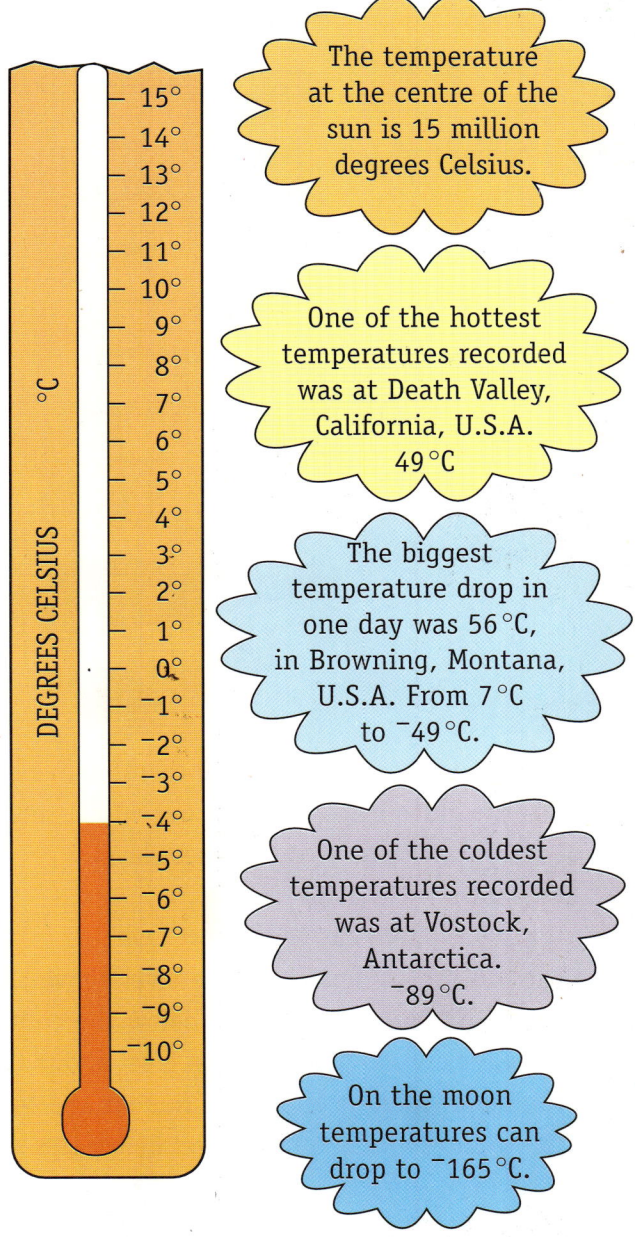

The temperature at the centre of the sun is 15 million degrees Celsius.

One of the hottest temperatures recorded was at Death Valley, California, U.S.A. 49 °C

The biggest temperature drop in one day was 56 °C, in Browning, Montana, U.S.A. From 7 °C to ⁻49 °C.

One of the coldest temperatures recorded was at Vostock, Antarctica. ⁻89 °C.

On the moon temperatures can drop to ⁻165 °C.

Exercise 2

Put these temperatures in order, coldest first.

1 5 °C, ⁻4 °C, ⁻1 °C, 3 °C, 8 °C

2 ⁻5 °C, 5 °C, 2 °C, ⁻8 °C, ⁻2 °C

3 7 °C, ⁻8 °C, 4 °C, ⁻9 °C, 0 °C

4 If a thermometer goes **down** by 10 degrees, what would you notice about the temperature?

5 What things might you notice if the temperature was ⁻15 °C?

Below Zero 29

Professor Fishbird, the inventor, lives on Rock Island. His base is hidden inside the island. Some of the rooms are **above** sea-level; other rooms are **below** sea-level.
A lift takes him from level to level.

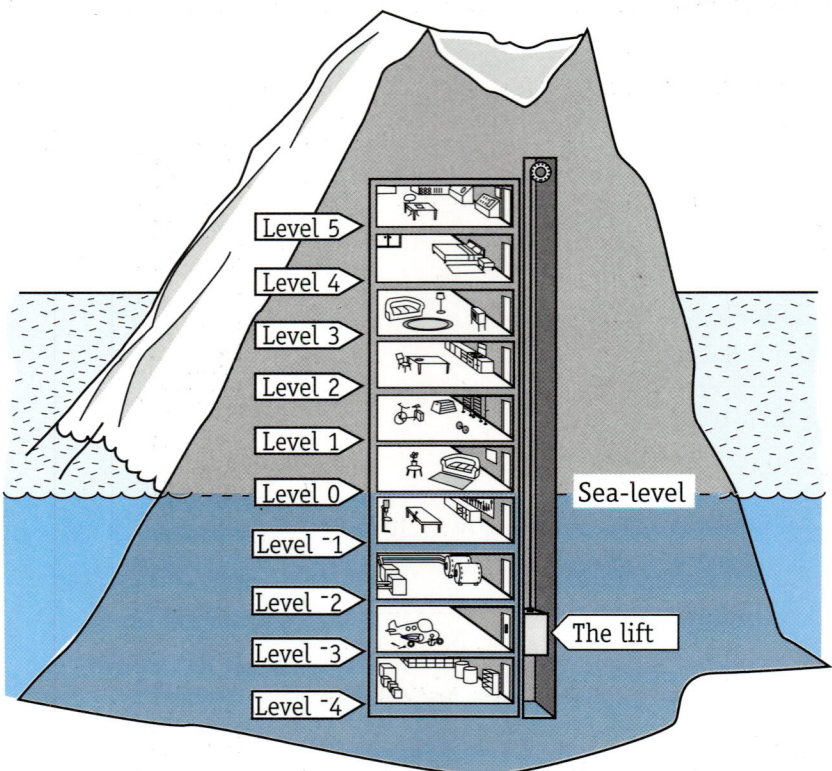

Exercise 3

Make a list of the levels of the Professor's base; Level 5 to Level ⁻4.
Use the clues below to work out which room is on which level.

1 The control room is the highest level.
2 The entrance is at Level 0.
3 The storeroom is at the lowest level.
4 The professor's gym is on the level above the entrance.
5 The bedroom is on the level below the control room.
6 The Aerosub hangar is on the level above the storeroom.
7 The boiler room is above the hangar and below the workshop.
8 The living room is on the level below the bedroom and on the level above the kitchen.

Level 5 is the control room
Level 4 is the
Level 3
Level 2

Exercise 4

1 The lift goes down 5 levels from Level 3. Which level are you on?
2 The lift goes up 3 levels from Level ⁻1. Which level are you on?
3 The lift goes down 7 levels from Level 5. Which level are you on?
4 The lift goes up 8 levels from Level ⁻3. Which level are you on?
5 The lift goes down 5 levels from Level 1. Which level are you on?

Exercise 5

Professor Fishbird takes his new invention, the Aerosub, for a ride.
The drawing below shows the journey of the Aerosub. The scale shows how many metres above or below sea-level (zero metres) the Aerosub is.
Answer the questions and match the measurement on each dial to one of the positions.

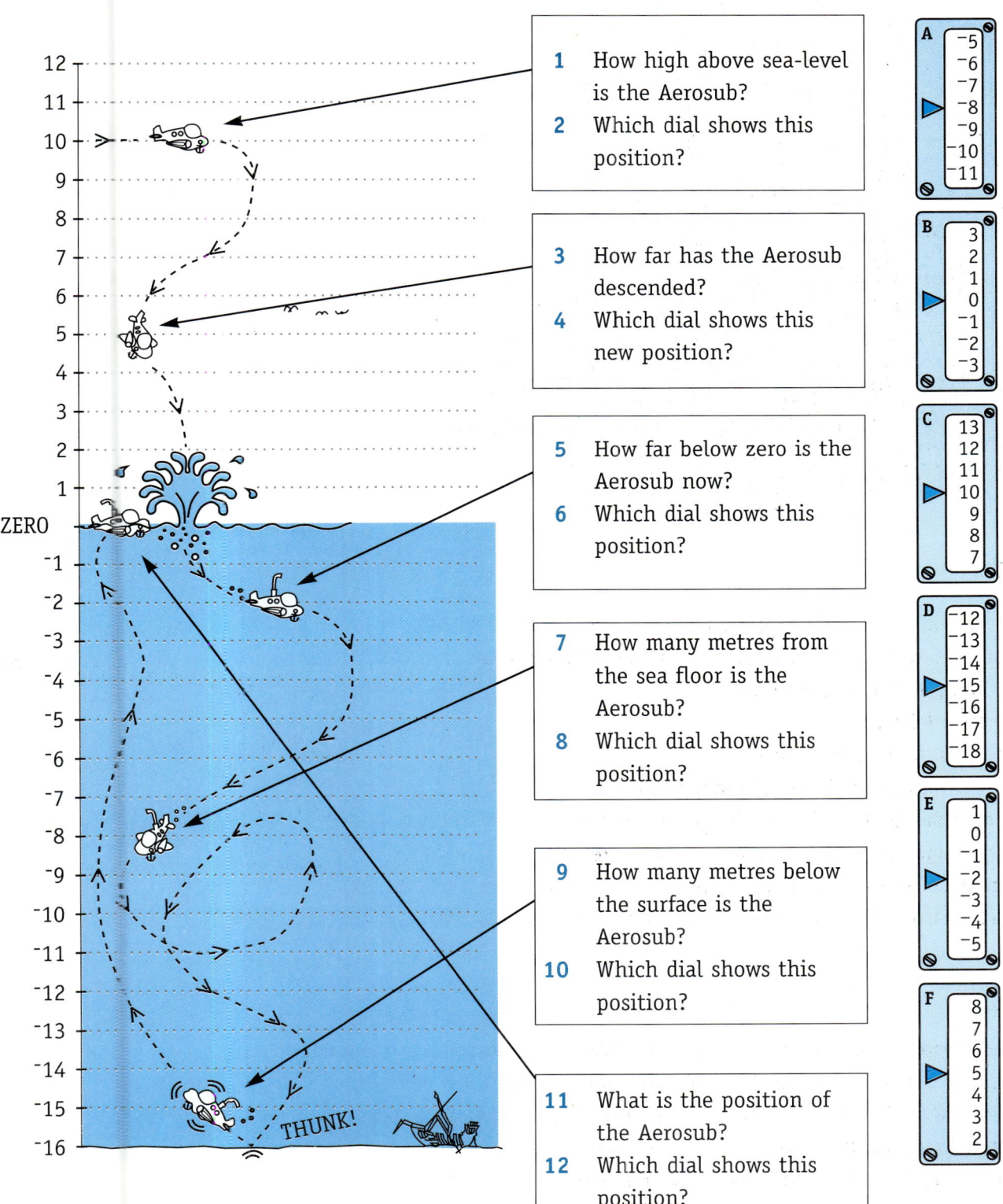

1 How high above sea-level is the Aerosub?
2 Which dial shows this position?

3 How far has the Aerosub descended?
4 Which dial shows this new position?

5 How far below zero is the Aerosub now?
6 Which dial shows this position?

7 How many metres from the sea floor is the Aerosub?
8 Which dial shows this position?

9 How many metres below the surface is the Aerosub?
10 Which dial shows this position?

11 What is the position of the Aerosub?
12 Which dial shows this position?

Below Zero   31

Exercise 6

Professor Fishbird decides to take another trip. First he dives into the sea.
The drawing below shows his journey. Use the drawing to help you to answer these questions.
Worksheet 18 will help you.

1 What will you find at ⁻4 metres?
2 What will you find at ⁻20 metres?
3 At its deepest the sea is ? metres deep.
4 At what depth is the fisherman's hook?
5 The wreck is ? metres below the surface.
6 The whale is ? metres below the surface.

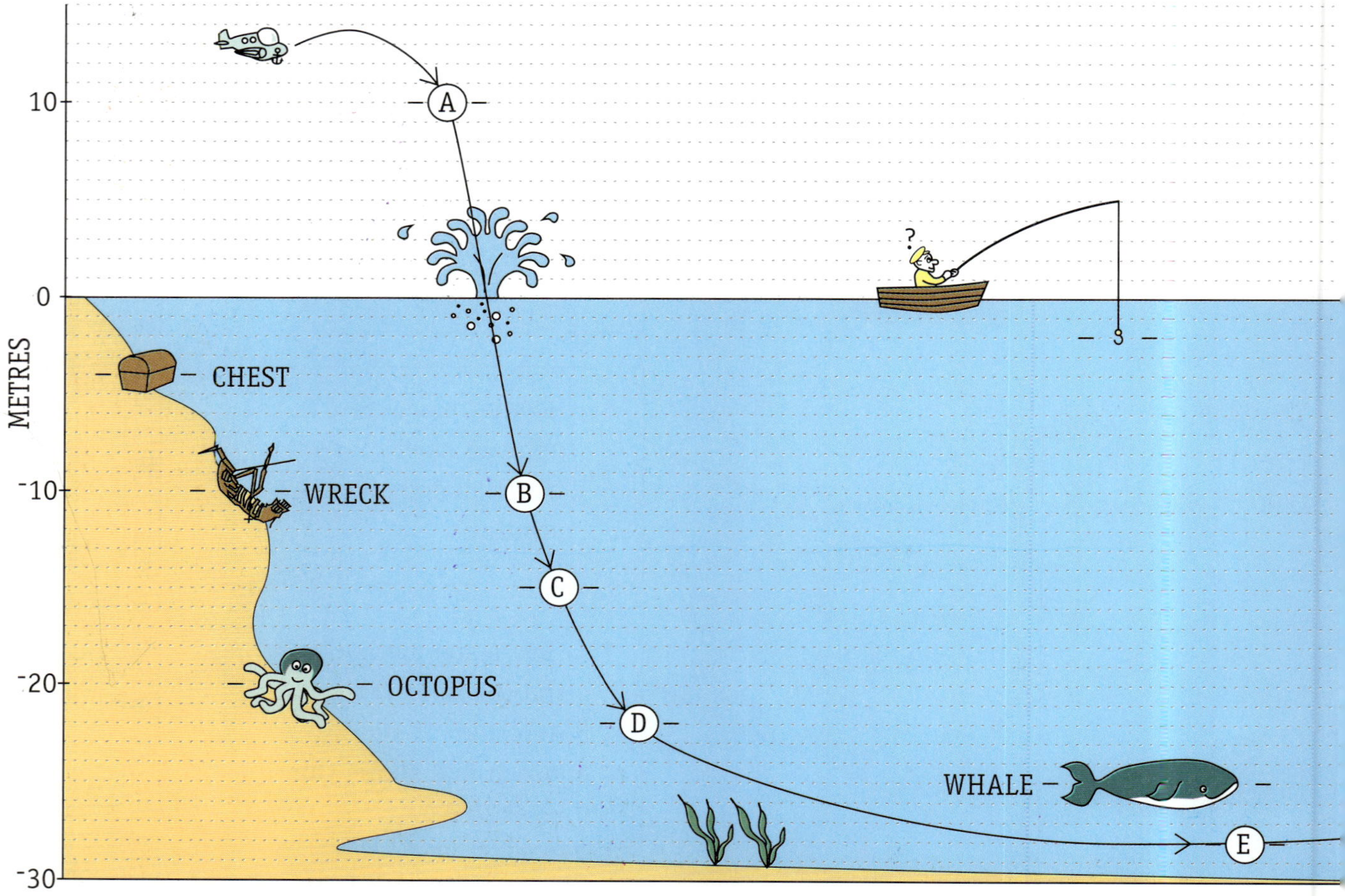

7 The octopus is resting ? metres below the wreck.
8 The whale is floating ? metres above the sea-bed.
9 How many metres below the chest is the wreck?
10 How many metres **above** sea-level is the Aerosub when it is at point **A**?
11 How many metres **below** sea-level is the Aerosub when it is at point **B**?
12 The Aerosub moves from point **B** to point **C**. How many metres has it **descended**?
13 How many metres **above** the sea-bed is the Aerosub when it is at point **D**?
14 If the Aerosub is at ⁻20 and it goes down **another** 8 metres what is its new depth?
15 If the Aerosub is at ⁻15 and it goes down to ⁻26 metres, how far has it just **descended**?

Chapter 4

Exercise 7

In the drawing below we see the Aerosub **ascending** (going up).

1. How many metres is it between sea-level and the top of the lighthouse?
2. How many metres below the surface of the water is the diver?

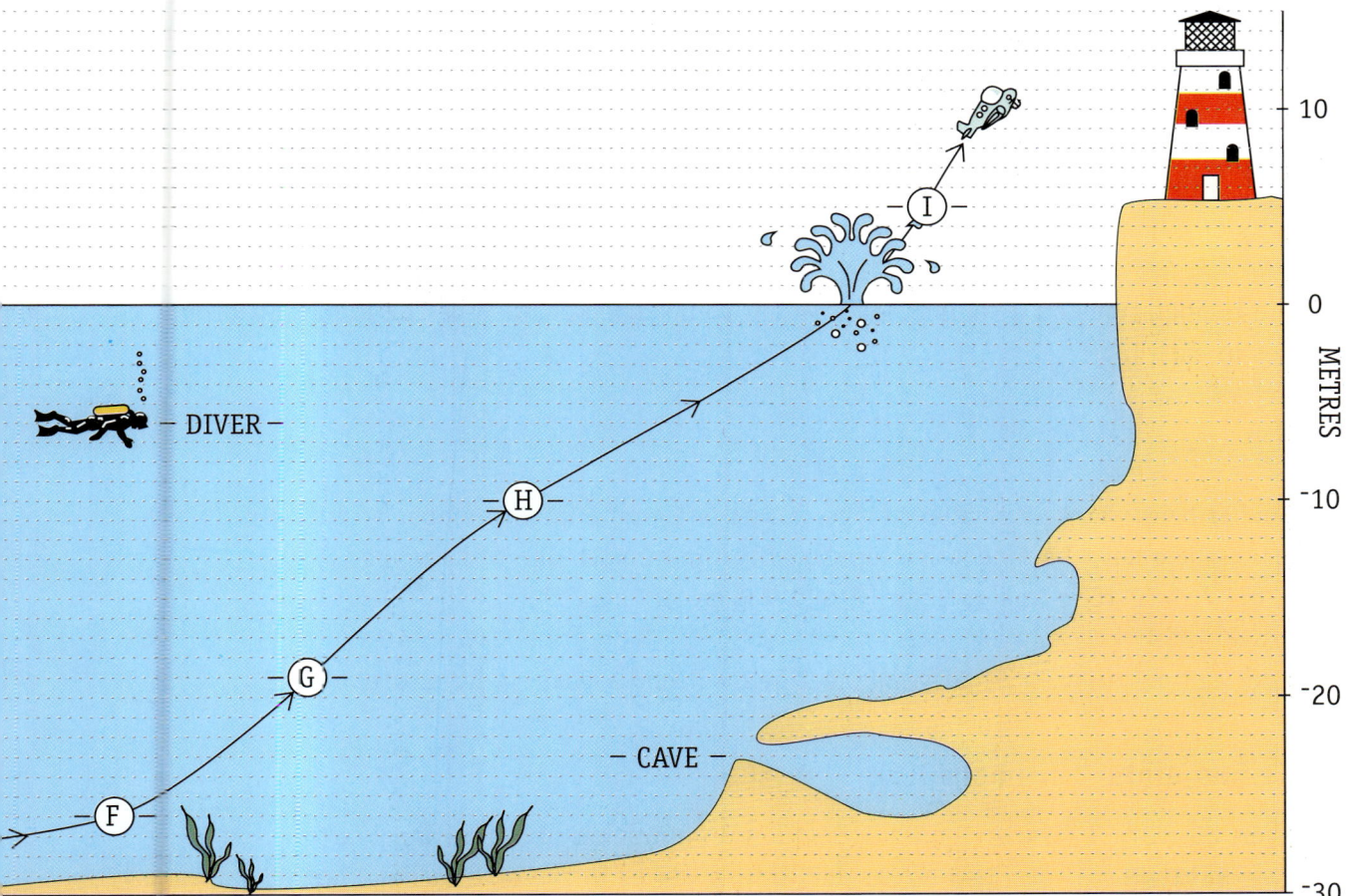

3. How many metres below sea-level is the mouth of the cave?
4. Can the diver **ascend** 8 metres?
5. What is the depth of the Aerosub when it is at point **F**?
6. How many metres does the Aerosub **ascend** between points **F** and **G**?
7. To reach the surface from point **G** the Aerosub will have to **ascend** ? metres.
8. At what depth is the Aerosub when it is 6 metres above point **G**?
9. Rising from point **G** to point **H** the Aerosub **ascends** ? metres.
10. How many metres difference is there between points **H** and **I**?

Below Zero

Number lines and negative numbers

When a thermometer is laid on its side it looks like a number line.

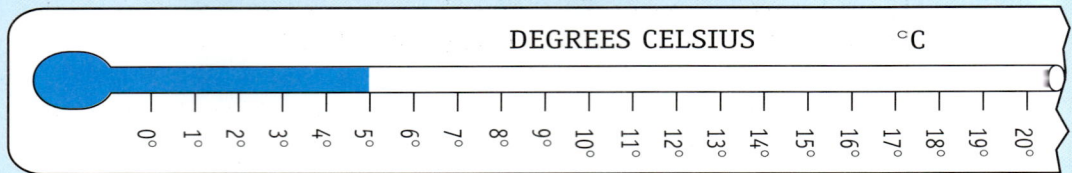

On a number line the numbers **increase** as you move from **left to right**. ⁻5 is smaller than ⁻1.

⁻10 ⁻9 ⁻8 ⁻7 ⁻6 ⁻5 ⁻4 ⁻3 ⁻2 ⁻1 0 1 2 3 4 5 6 7 8 9 10 11 12 13 14 15

Exercise 8

Copy the pairs of numbers. Circle the **larger** number in each pair. Use the thermometer to help you.

1. ⁻5, 1   2. ⁻2, 4   3. 7, ⁻9   4. 1, ⁻1   5. ⁻10, ⁻5   6. ⁻2, 0

7. If these were temperatures on a thermometer, would your circled answers be the higher or lower temperatures in each pair?

Exercise 9

For each number below, write a smaller number on its left, and a larger number on its right.
One of your numbers must be a negative number. Use the number line to help you.
Example: ⁻10, ⁻7, 3. (⁻10 is smaller than ⁻7 and 3 is larger than ⁻7).

1. ⁻5   2. ⁻9   3. 1   4. ⁻3   5. 4   6. 0

7. Which number can only have a negative number below it and a positive number above it?

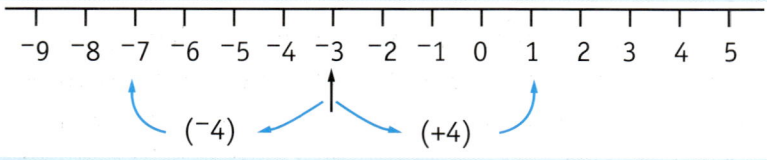

Moving along a number line

When we write ⁻3 we are giving a position on a number line. The black arrow is at ⁻3.
If we **subtract** 4 from ⁻3 we move the arrow **4** places to the **left** and the new position is ⁻**7**.
If we **add** 4 to ⁻3 we move the arrow **4** places to the **right** and the new position is at **1**.

Exercise 10

In each question below, say where the arrow will finish after moving either **left (−)** or **right (+)**.

1. Start at ⁻2 and add 3.
2. Start at ⁻5 and add 5.
3. Start at 2 and take away 3.
4. Start at ⁻1 and take away 4.
5. Start at ⁻5 and add 6.
6. Start at ⁻7 and take away 10.

$^-2 + 6 = 4$ This sum can be written as a 'statement':

'The temperature was $^-2\,°C$. It rose by 6°. The new temperature was $4\,°C$.' **or**, 'Imran got into the lift at Level $^-2$. He went up 6 levels and got out at Level 4.'

Exercise 11

Write a short statement for each of these additions or subtractions.

1   $^-1 + 2 = 1$
2   $^-2 - 3 = {^-5}$
3   $4 - 5 = {^-1}$

Exercise 12

Complete the statements below.
Rewrite the statements as additions or subtractions. Be careful to make sure that you remember to use the (⁻) negative sign in the correct place.

1   Holly got into the lift at Level 6. She went down 6 floors.
   (a) She got out at Level ?
   (b) 6 − ? = ?

2   The temperature started at $^-3\,°C$ and rose by 7 degrees.
   (a) The temperature rose to ?
   (b) $^-3 +$? = ?

3   Jake had £10 in his bank. He wrote a cheque for £12.
   (a) Jake owed the bank £ ?
   (b) 10 − 12 = ?

Key ideas

Our number counting system can go below, or less than, zero.
Numbers that are at positions less than zero are called **negative numbers.**
A number six places below zero is called 'negative 6'. It is written $^-6$.
$^-2$ is a greater number than $^-5$. (Look at the number line in this chapter.)
$^-5$ is a position five spaces below zero, but −5 means, 'take five away'.

Ascend is to move upwards.
Descend is to move downwards.

Below Zero   35

Chapter 5 Estimation

Step-up

1 Is the pointer closer to 8 or 9?

2  Is the pointer closer to 50 or 60?

3 Is the pointer closer to 400 or 500?

4 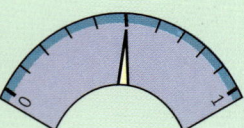 Is the pointer closer to 19 or 20?

5 Is the pointer closer to 1 or 0?

6 Round these numbers to the nearest ten.
   (a) 22   (b) 59   (c) 19   (d) 33   (e) 66   (f) 81   (g) 99   (h) 3

> **Remember:** 15 is exactly halfway between 10 and 20.
> When this happens we always 'round up' to the nearest ten.
> So 15 rounded to the nearest ten, is 20.

7 Round these numbers to the nearest ten.
   (a) 31   (b) 47   (c) 45   (d) 65   (e) 7   (f) 5   (g) 24   (h) 85

8 If you are rounding to the nearest hundred, what number makes the difference between **rounding up** and **rounding down**?

9 Round these to the nearest hundred.
   (a) 122   (b) 590   (c) 250   (d) 353   (e) 850   (f) 749   (g) 927   (h) 351

10 Estimate how many cubes each tray will hold. Choose your answers from the numbers below each tray.

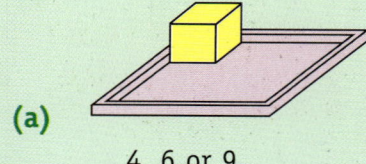
(a)
4, 6 or 9

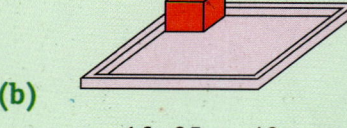
(b)
16, 35 or 48

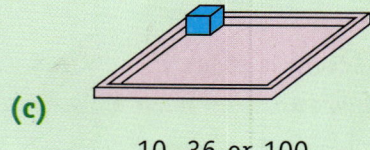
(c)
10, 36 or 100

36 Chapter 5

Estimates are more than 'wild' guesses.

When we estimate an answer to a problem, we use information or clues about the problem to give a rough or 'near' answer.

When exact or accurate answers are needed, estimates will not do.

*Can you tell me **exactly** how many people are in the world?*

*It is impossible to be **exact**, Miss.*

Yes, people are dying and being born all the time. The total keeps changing.

*But as an **estimate** it is about 7 billion, Miss.*

Exercise 1

Some of the situations below need exact answers, others could be solved with estimations. Say which situations are best estimated.

1. *How many people are here today, Dad?*
2. *Exactly 500 grams of cheese, please.*
3. *I need 1.75 metres of this lace, please.*
4. *I reckon there are about 200 cars here.*
5. *That will be £4.17, thank you.*
6. *Roughly how many stars are in the sky?*

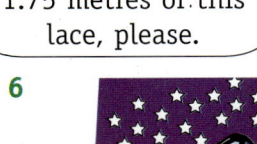

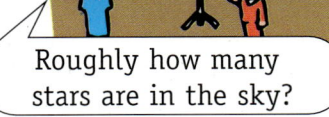

Exercise 2

Use estimation to give answers to the problems below.

1. Who looks the tallest?
2. Who looks the oldest?
3. Who looks the lightest?
4. Who looks the shortest?
5. Who looks the heaviest?
6. What clues did you use to make your estimations?

Daisy, Roger, Tim, Ben

Estimation 37

Exercise 3

Estimate the answers to the questions in the pictures below.

1. Are there about 10, 35, or 100 numbers on the Wheel of Fortune?

2. Roughly how many doughnuts can Khan get for £1.80? 3, 4, or 7?

3. Roughly how many squares are there on the Target Darts board? 12, 32 or 52?

4. The cake weighs about 2 kg, 20 kg, or 30 kg?

5. Alison has £5.40. About how many rides can she have on the Flying Boat? 5, 10, or 20?

6. About how many goes on the Hoop-La can Ruby have for £7.10?

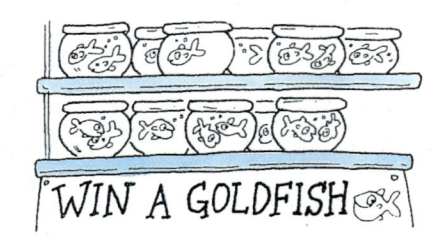

7. Estimate the number of goldfish on this stall.

8. Roughly how many people are there on the Ghost Train?

9. Choose any two of your answers and say how you made your estimations. What clues did you use?

> £2.85 is nearer to £3.00. We can say that £2.85 is **roughly** £3.00.
> £4.25 is nearer to £4.00. We can say that £4.25 is **roughly** £4.00.

Exercise 4

Give an estimation of each total.

1. £5.00 + £1.99 + £1.80 = ?
2. £0.99 + £1.10 + £5.20 = ?
3. £3.95 + £1.05 + £4.00 = ?
4. £6.90 + £2.20 + £25.00 = ?
5. £0.95 + £2.80 + £3.49 = ?
6. £9.99 + £4.20 + £2.69 = ?

Chapter 5

Liam buys three sweets:

17p + 21p + 9p = ?

Liam thinks the shopkeeper's total is wrong – it is more than his estimate.

That will be 92p please.

17p is about 20p
21p is about 20p
9p is about 10p
The total should be about 50p!

Exercise 5

Choose the best estimate to answer these problems.

1 9 + 11 + 9 is about ? (20, 30 or 40)
2 11 + 12 + 8 + 8 is about ? (20, 30 or 40)
3 22 + 19 + 18 is about ? (60, 70 or 80)
4 99 + 98 + 101 is about ? (100, 200 or 300)
5 20 + 18 + 21 + 17 is about ? (80, 90 or 100)
6 20 + 10 + 8 + 19 is about ? (40, 50 or 60)

Exercise 6

Fred weighs 75 kg. The villagers are about to put five rocks into the basket on the see-saw. If the rocks weigh more than 75 kg the see-saw will lift the wheels onto the track, and Fred will end up in The Stinking Swamp! As an estimate, the rocks weigh about 45 kg. Fred is safe.

Work with your partner. Agree a time limit. Start this exercise together and see who finishes first.

Quickly estimate the total weight of rocks in each group and name the people who end up in the swamp.

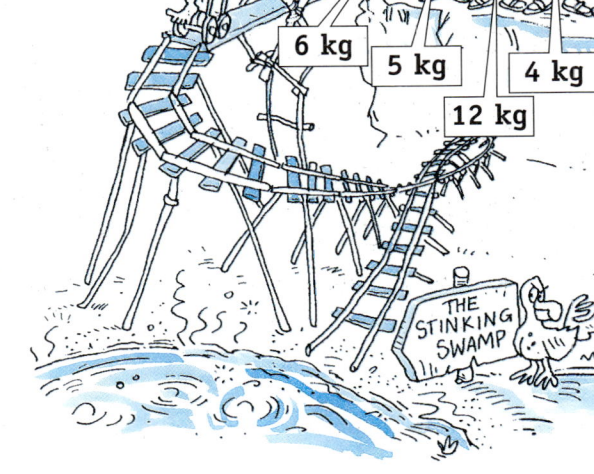

(a) JACK WEIGHS 138 kg — 10 kg, 11 kg, 12 kg, 30 kg, 106 kg
(b) KYLIE WEIGHS 54 kg — 8 kg, 12 kg, 5 kg, 4 kg, 7 kg
(c) LEELA WEIGHS 71 kg — 15 kg, 10 kg, 30 kg, 15 kg, 24 kg
(d) SANDY WEIGHS 80 kg — 15 kg, 20 kg, 19 kg, 20 kg, 15 kg
(e) MIKE WEIGHS 94 kg — 26 kg, 9 kg, 5 kg, 11 kg, 21 kg
(f) HOLLY WEIGHS 47 kg — 9 kg, 11 kg, 12 kg, 8 kg, 18 kg

Estimation of fractions and decimals

$\frac{1}{2}$ is shaded. 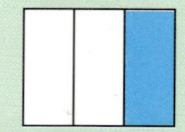 $\frac{1}{3}$ is shaded. 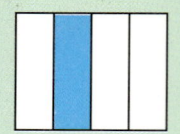 $\frac{1}{4}$ is shaded. 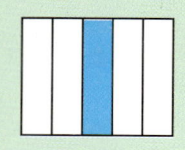 $\frac{1}{5}$ is shaded. 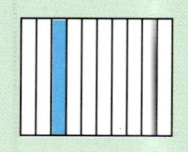 $\frac{1}{10}$ or 0.1, is shaded.

Exercise 7

Use the fractions above to make these estimations.

1 The glass is about ? full.

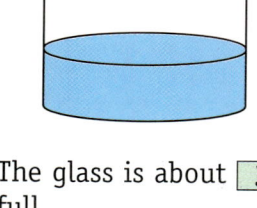

2 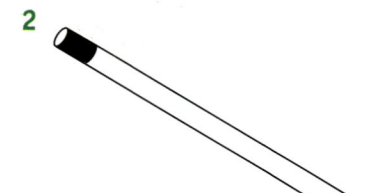 About ? of the stick is black.

3  Tim is about ? of the way up the rope.

4  About ? of the pizza is eaten.

5 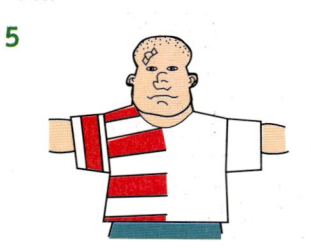 About ? of the T-shirt is striped.

6  About ? of the sweets are eaten.

7  Ann is about ? of the way up the stairs.

8 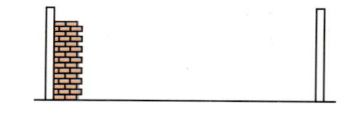 About ? of the wall is built.

Exercise 8

How much of each shape is shaded? Use decimals to make estimations.

0.1 0.2 0.3 0.4 0.5 0.6 0.7 0.8 0.9 1.0

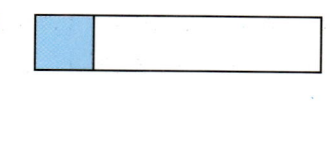

1 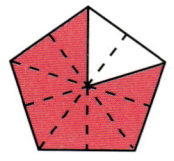   2 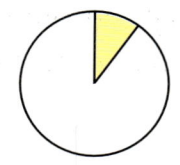   3   4

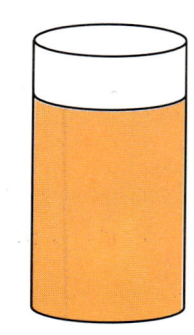

5 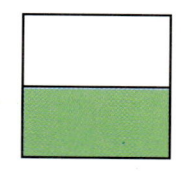   6

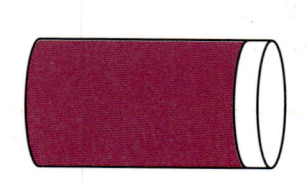

40   Chapter 5

When using a calculator it is possible to make mistakes.
It is very important to have a rough idea of the final answer before using the calculator.
If you then make a mistake you will recognise it.

Exercise 9

Here are a number of problems that are to be 'keyed' into a calculator.
Match each problem with an **estimated** answer.

1 299 − 304
2 21 + 31
3 199 × 2
4 1003 × 3
5 99 + 199 + 100
6 500 − 198
7 104 × 7
8 52 ÷ 10
9 Explain what you did to get your answer.

about **5**   about **3000**
about **300**   about **600**
about **700**   about **200**
about **50**   about **400**

Exercise 10

Below are some problems that are answered with a calculator.
Mistakes have been made when keying in the problem. Which display shows the right answer?

1 200 + 199 + 200 = ?   A 203.   B 21992.   C 599.

2 650 − 50 = ?   A 600.   B 700.   C 150.

3 1000 + 5000 + 2000 = ? A 80.   B 8000.   C 15200.

4 29 − 31 + 29 = ?   A 89.   B 8.9   C 293129.

5 102 − 99 = ?   A 101.   B 201.   C 3.

Key ideas

An estimate is **not** a 'wild' guess. An **estimate is a thoughtful and sensible guess**.
When estimating the answer to a calculation we often have to round to the nearest useful amount.

Remember to **round up** from five: 25 is rounded up to 30.
You **round down** from below five: 24 is rounded down to 20.

Estimation

Chapter 6 Area and Perimeter

Step-up

1 When the shelf is full, how many tins will it hold?

2 When both shelves are full, how many boxes will there be altogether?

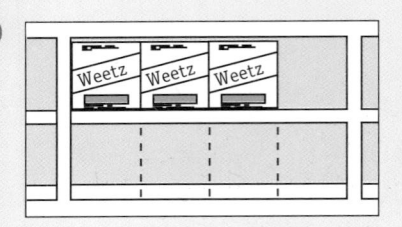

3 There is one box on the top shelf. How many boxes will there be when all three shelves are full?

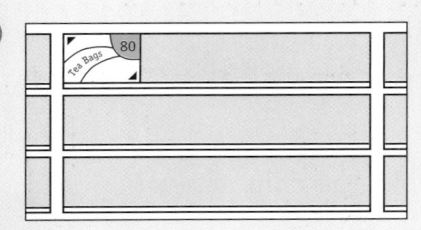

4 How many boxes will there be on these shelves when all four shelves are full?

5 How many square tiles are needed to cover each shape?.

(a)

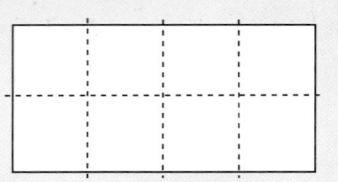

(b)

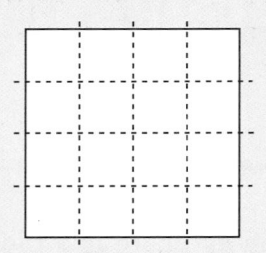

(c)

(d)

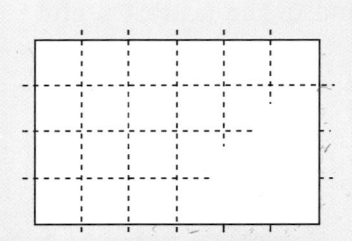

(e)

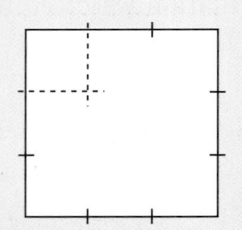

(f)

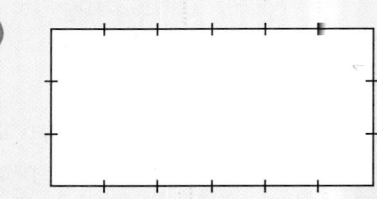

42   Chapter 6

6 Toby is laying square tiles in this garden.
Work out how many square tiles he uses for each area.
Write: 'Area A = ? squares.'

7 Did you find the answer by counting or by multiplying?

8 Do these multiplications in your head. Time yourself.

(a) $4 \times 5 = $?
(b) $6 \times 2 = $?
(c) $3 \times $? $= 12$
(d) ? $\times 7 = 21$
(e) $10 \times 5 = $?
(f) ? $\times 4 = 20$
(g) $10 \times 6 = $?
(h) $5 \times 6 = $?
(i) $8 \times 5 = $?
(j) $6 \times $? $= 24$
(k) $3 \times $? $= 30$
(l) ? $\times 4 = 16$

Area and Perimeter

1 square centimetre (1 cm²)

This is a square centimetre.
Its sides are all 1 cm long.

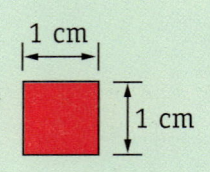

The unit used to measure area is the **square**.
The area of this rectangle is measured by finding how many square centimetres (cm²) would cover the shape.

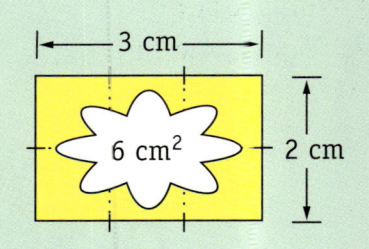

Exercise 1

Find the area of each shape. Give your answers in cm², like this: 'Area = ? cm².'
Draw at least two full-size diagrams in your book.

1. 3 cm × 3 cm
2. 5 cm × 3 cm
3. 4 cm × 4 cm
4. 6 cm × 2 cm
5. 6 cm × 5 cm
6. 5 cm × 4 cm

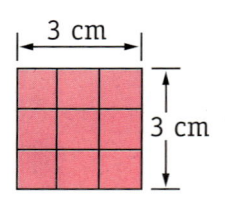

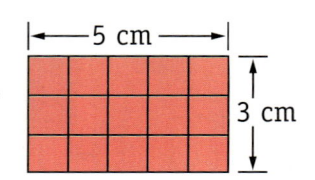

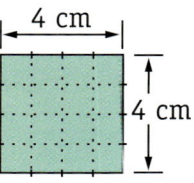

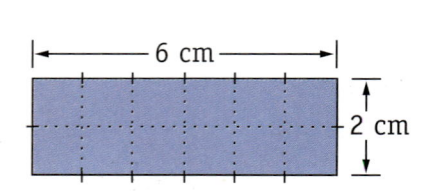

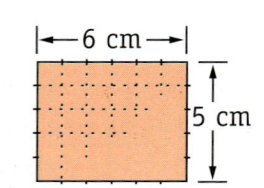

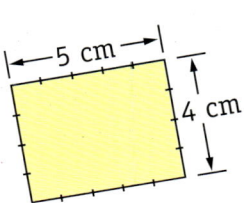

Area = length × width

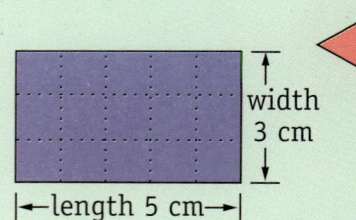

The area of this rectangle is 15 cm².
The **length** is 5 cm. The **width** is 3 cm.

There are **3 rows** of **5** squares.
3 **lots** of 5 makes 15 squares.

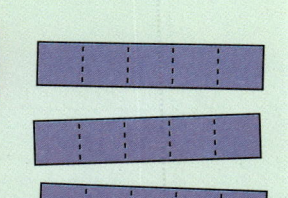

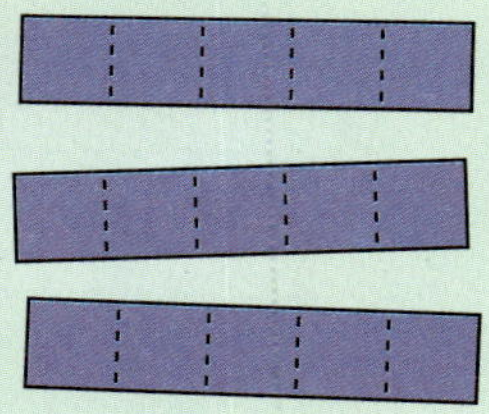

width 3 cm
length 5 cm

The **length × width** gives us the area of a square or rectangle in square centimetres.

Exercise 2

Calculate the area of each rectangle. The calculations are laid out to help you.

1. 5 cm × 2 cm

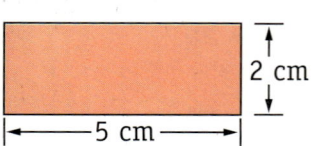

   Area = length × width
   = 5 cm × 2 cm
   = ? cm²

44 Chapter 6

2

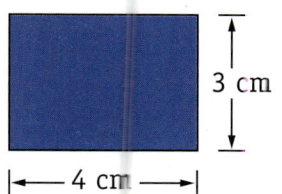

3 cm
4 cm

Area = length × width
= 4 cm × 3 cm
= ? cm²

3

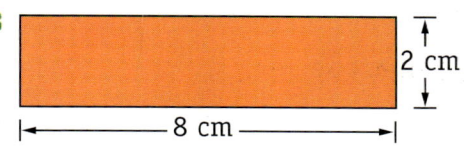

2 cm
8 cm

Area = length × width
= 8 cm × 2 cm
= ? cm²

The rectangle and the square both have an area of 4 cm².

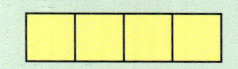

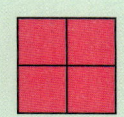

The rectangle has **1 row** of **4 cm²**.   The square has **2 rows** of **2 cm²**.

Exercise 3

Draw another rectangle or square which has the **same area** as each one of these.
They do not have to be drawn to full size. Write the length and width on each drawing.

1   6 cm / 2 cm

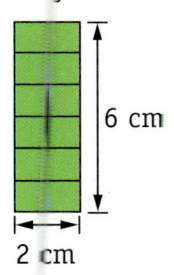

2   6 cm / 1 cm

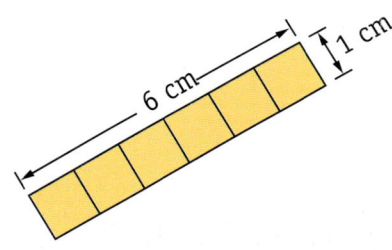

3   8 cm / 2 cm

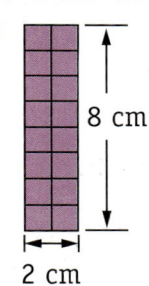

4   8 cm / 3 cm

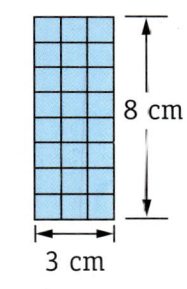

5   What is the total area of all four shapes in questions 1 to 4?

Exercise 4

Find the missing length or width of each rectangle. They are not drawn to full size.
Write: 'The length is ?,' or 'The width is ?.'

1   12 cm²   ?   length 4 cm

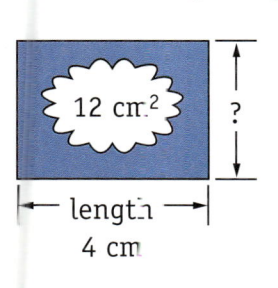

2   15 cm²   ?   width 3 cm

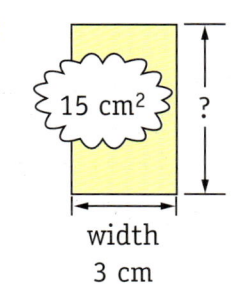

3   30 cm²   length 10 cm   ?

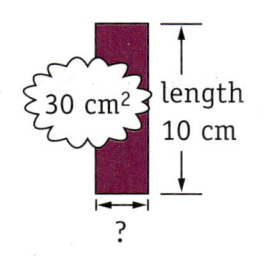

4   20 cm²   length 5 cm   ?

Area and Perimeter 45

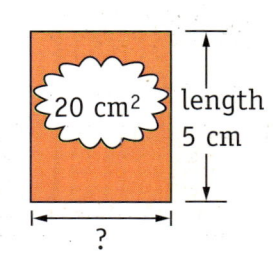

Larger areas

Square centimetres (cm²) are used to measure small areas like the cover of a book.

For larger areas we need a larger square – the **square metre** (m²).

There are 100 × 100 cm² in one square metre (m²).

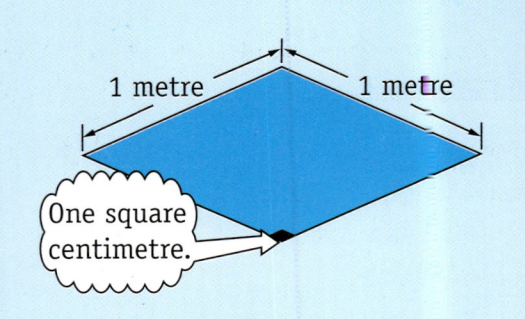

1 metre 1 metre
One square centimetre.

Exercise 5

Use **square metres** (m²) to answer these questions.

1 Find the paved area in each question.
   (a)   (b)    (c)

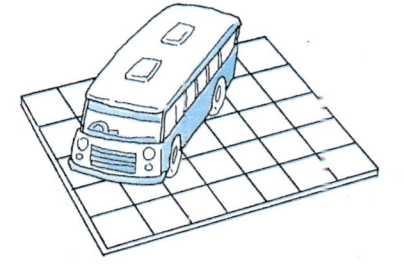

2 Some slabs are missing from this patio. All slabs are 1 m².
   (a) What is the area of the patio?   (b) What is the area still to be paved?

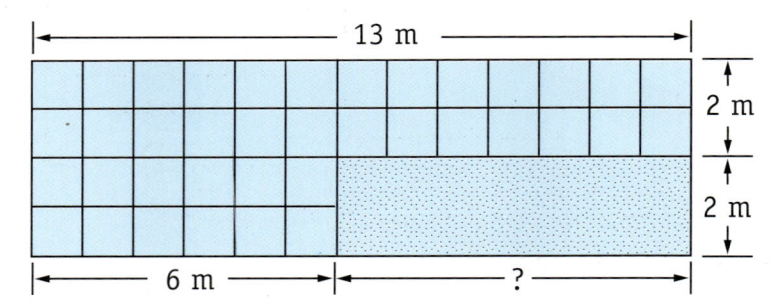

   13 m
   2 m
   2 m
   6 m   ?

3 Here is a pile of 1 m² paving slabs. Some slabs are white and some are grey. Count them carefully.
   (a) Draw a **square** using all of these slabs. Try to create a pattern using the white and grey slabs.
   (b) Draw a **rectangle** using all of these slabs. Try to create a pattern using the white and grey slabs.

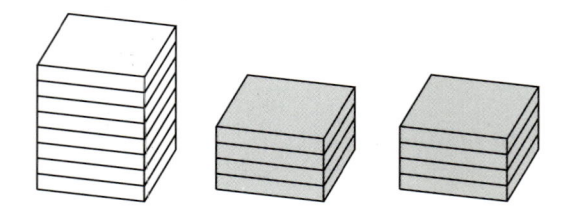

Your drawings do not need to be to scale, but you should show the measurements in metres.

Exercise 6

Calculate the area of each rectangle, using **area = length × width**.
You will have to choose whether to use **cm²** or **m²**.

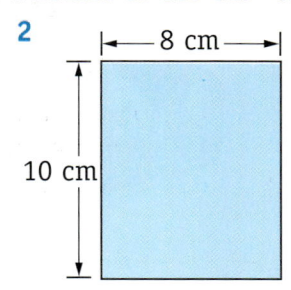

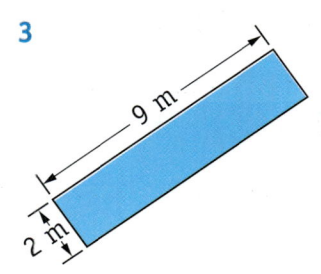

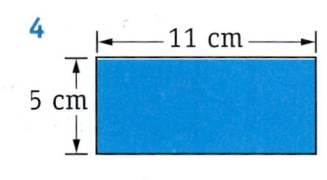

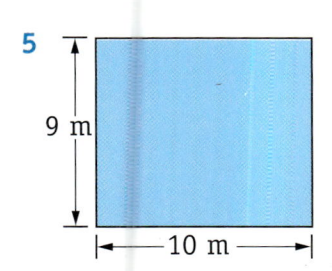

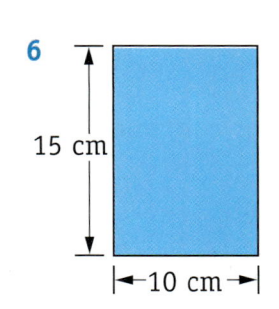

1. 5 m by 3 m
2. 8 cm by 10 cm
3. 9 m by 2 m
4. 11 cm by 5 cm
5. 9 m by 10 m
6. 15 cm by 10 cm
7. 12 m by 8 m
8. How did you decide whether to use cm² or m²?

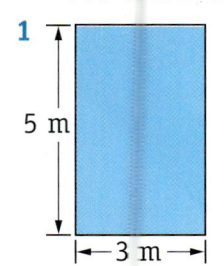

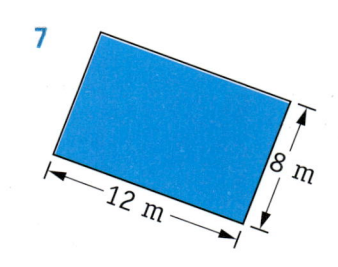

Exercise 7

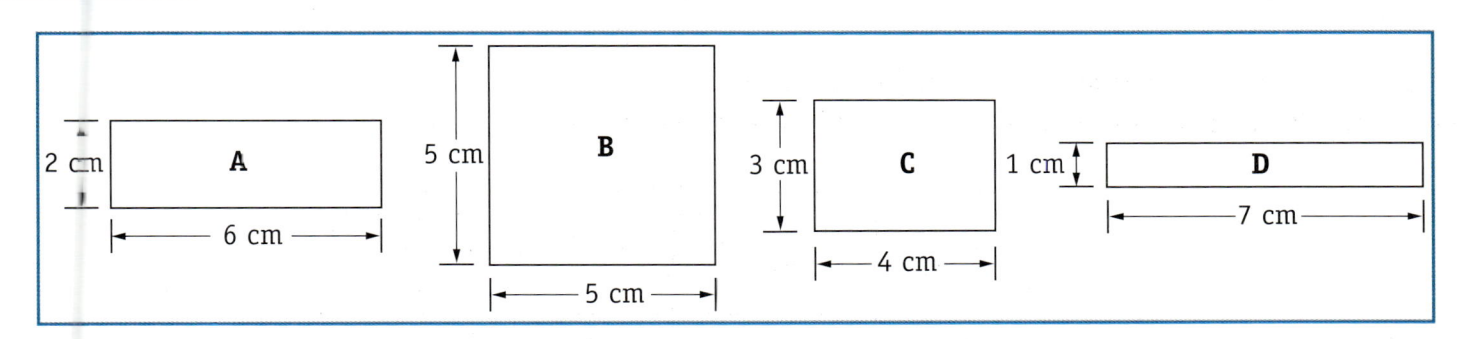

A: 2 cm by 6 cm
B: 5 cm by 5 cm
C: 3 cm by 4 cm
D: 1 cm by 7 cm

The shaded shapes are made up from the shapes in the box above.
Calculate the area of each shaded shape.

1. D, C, A
2. A, B, D
3. C, B, A

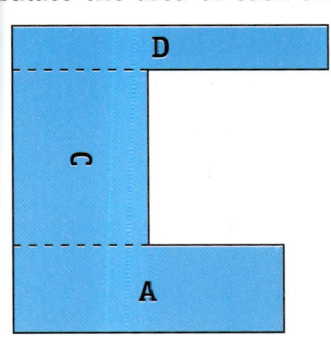

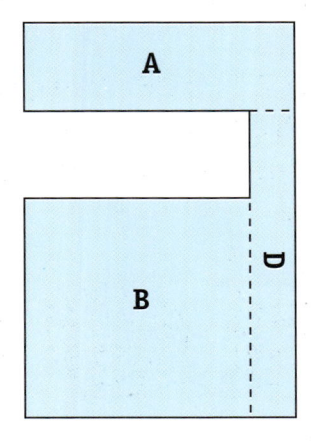

Area and Perimeter 47

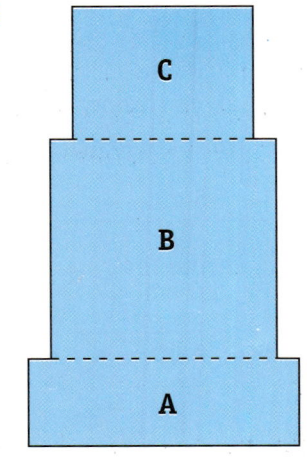

Perimeter

Here we see someone balancing along the top of a fence. When she has walked once around the top of the fence she has walked the **perimeter** of the fence.

The distance **once** around the edge of the fence is called the **perimeter**.

The **perimeter** of this fence is:
3 m + 4 m + 3 m + 4 m = 14 m.

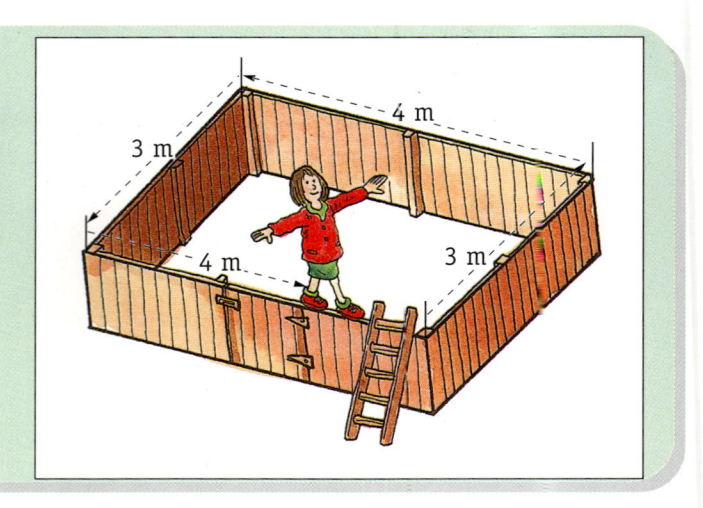

Exercise 8

Calculate the perimeter of each shape. Use either **metres** or **centimetres**.

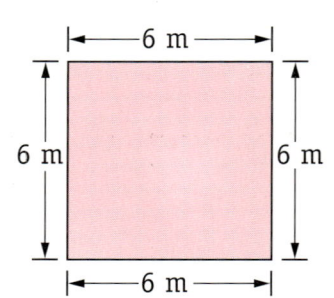

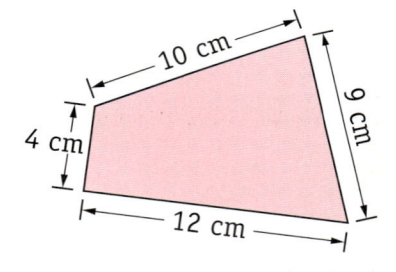

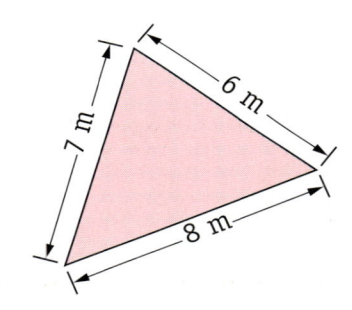

1. Rectangle: 8 cm × 5 cm
2. Square: 6 m × 6 m
3. Rectangle: 7 cm × 11 cm
4. Quadrilateral: 4 cm, 10 cm, 9 cm, 12 cm
5. Triangle: 7 m, 6 m, 8 m
6. L-shape: 8 m, 5 m, 4 m, 2 m, 12 m, 7 m

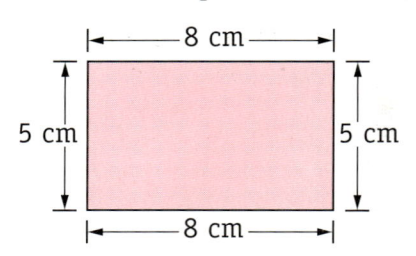

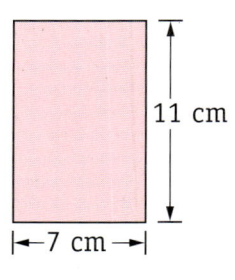

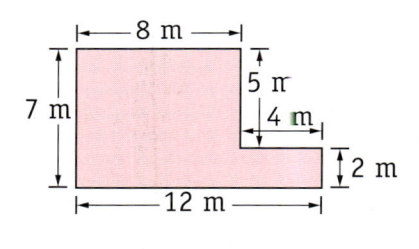

Exercise 9

Use what you know about perimeter to find the missing distances. These are marked with a letter **d**.

1. Rectangle 6 cm × 4 cm, Perimeter 20 cm, find d
2. Triangle with sides d, 9 cm, 9 cm, Perimeter 25 cm
3. Quadrilateral 11 cm, 7 cm, d, 10 cm, Perimeter 36 cm
4. Rectangle d × 4 cm with base 4 cm, Perimeter 16 cm

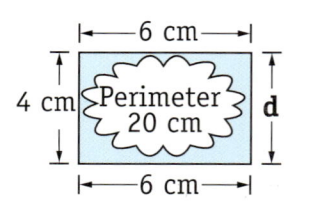

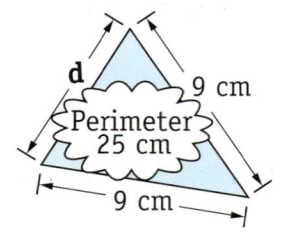

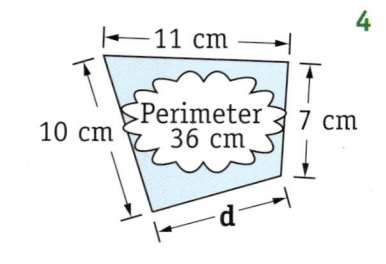

48   Chapter 6

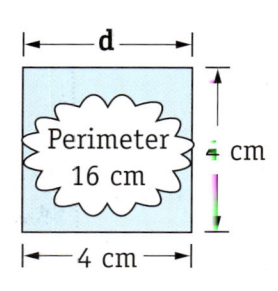

Try this!

You will need squared paper and tiles.
Use the tiles to make shapes like these below. Put them onto the squared paper.

Perimeter = 8 units.
Area = 3 squares.

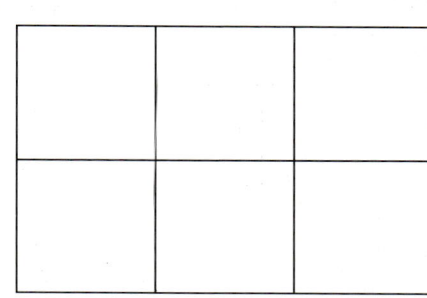

Perimeter = 10 units.
Area = 6 squares.

Make some shapes for yourself. Find the areas.

Can you make a shape that has the same number of squares for its area, as it has units of perimeter?

Key ideas

Area measures how much surface a shape has. It is measured in **squares**.

We use different-sized squares to measure large or small areas.

The way to calculate the area of a square or a rectangle is **A = l × w**
Multiply the number of rows by the number of squares in the row.

l = length   **w** = width

Perimeter is measured in centimetres or metres. It is the distance once around the edge of a shape.

Area and Perimeter 49

Chapter 7 Angles

Step-up

1 Which drawing shows the largest 'turn': **A**, **B** or **C**?

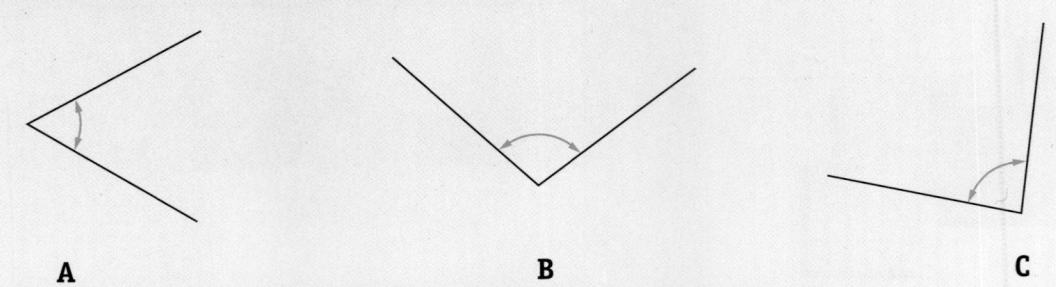

A   B   C

2 Put these angles in order of size, from the smallest to the largest. Use their initials to make your list.

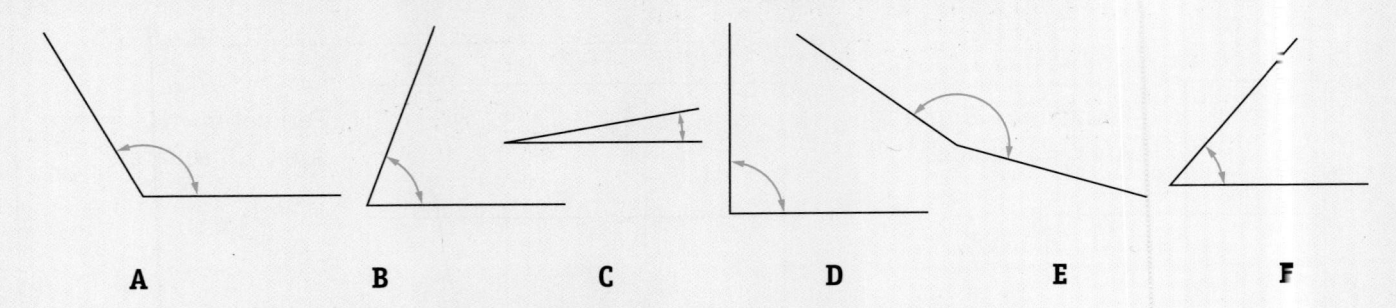

A   B   C   D   E   F

3 London's Tower Bridge raises and lowers its spans to let ships through.
They turn from horizontal (0°) towards the vertical, but they do not reach 90°.
Estimate the angles marked as the spans rise. Write: 'Angle **(a)** is about ...'
Choose from these angles: 30°, 60°, 45°, 10° or 80°.

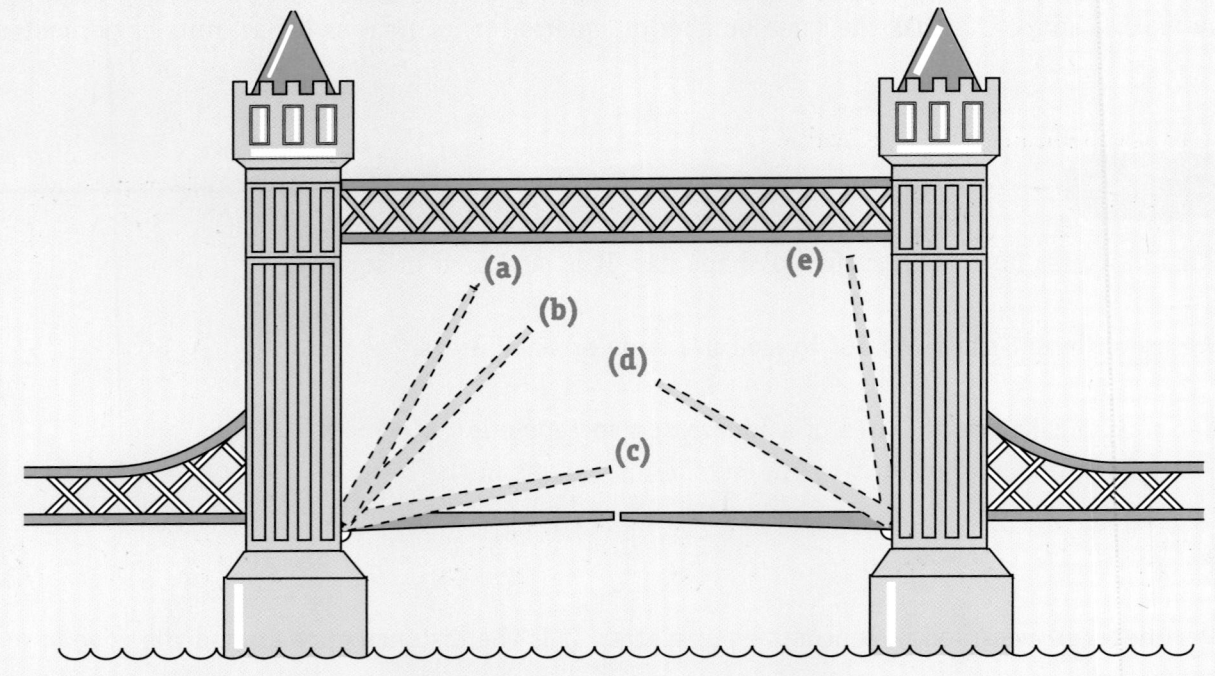

4 Which angle makes the sentence below true: 45°, 90°, 180°, 30° or 60°?
'A right angle is ? .'

5 Say whether each angle is: acute (less than 90°), right (90°) or obtuse (more than 90°, but less than 180°).

(a) (b) 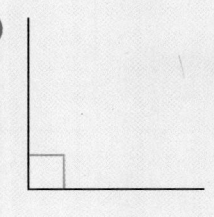 (c) 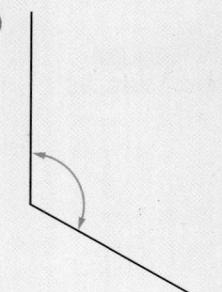 (d) 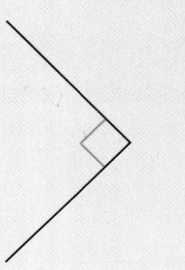 (e)

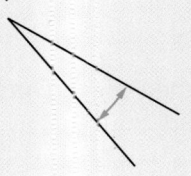

Reading scales

6 Give the readings on these scales to the nearest 10 units.
Write: 'Line (a) is nearer to ? than ? so we would read it as ?.'

(a) (b)

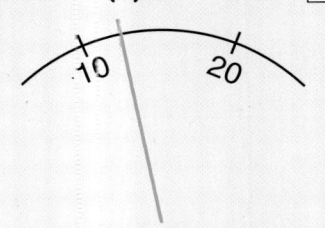

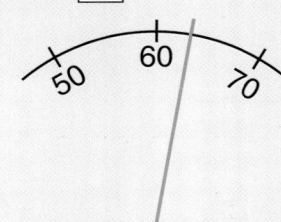

(c) 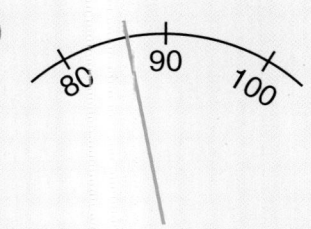 (d)

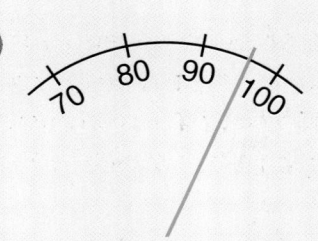

7 Give the **exact** readings on these scales.

(a) (b) 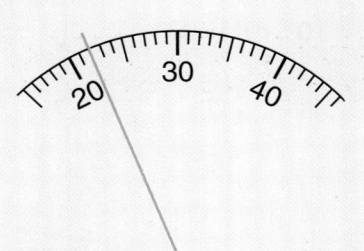 (c)

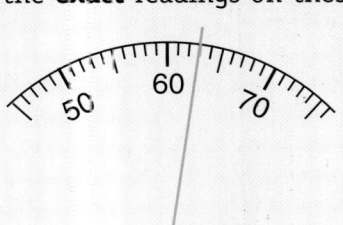

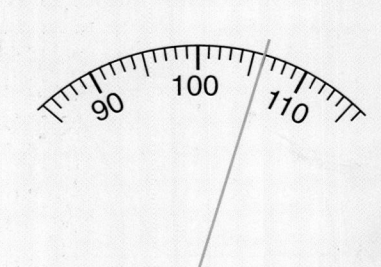

(d) 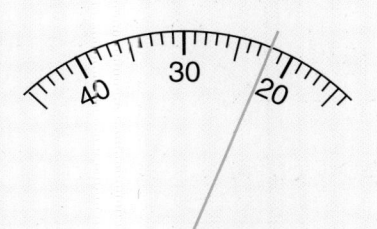 (e) 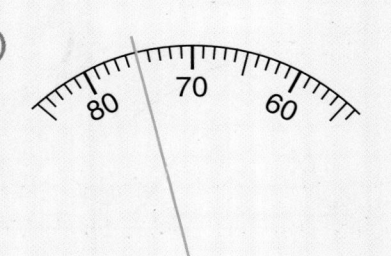 (f)

Angles 51

Estimating the size of angles

This angle is about 20°.
You can see that it has turned **less than** 90°.

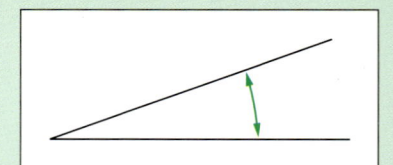

This angle is about 150°.
You can see that it has turned **more than** 90°.

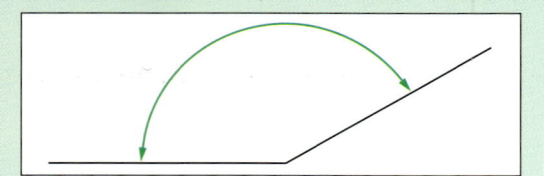

Exercise 1

Estimate the size of each angle by thinking about whether it is more or less than 90°.

1

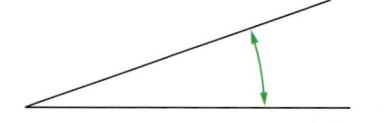

2

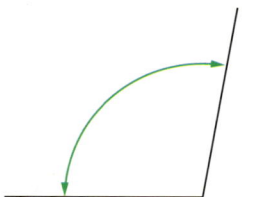

3

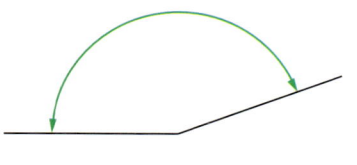

4

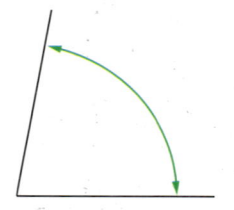

5

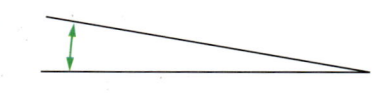

6

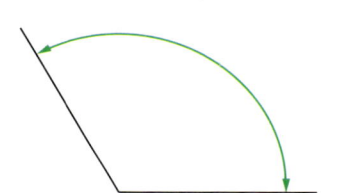

Exercise 2

A pair of measurements is given for each angle. Which one **cannot be correct**?

1 **120° or 60°**

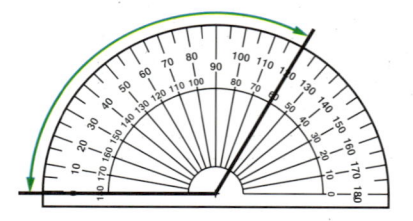

2 **10° or 170°**

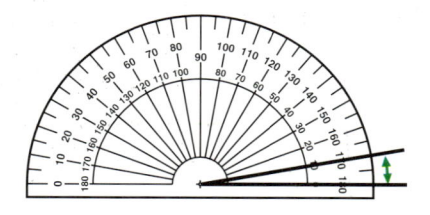

3 **45° or 135°**

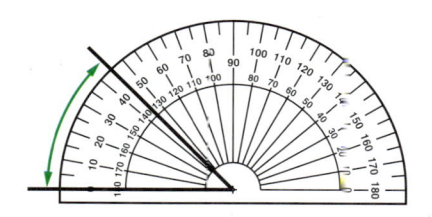

4 **30° or 150°**

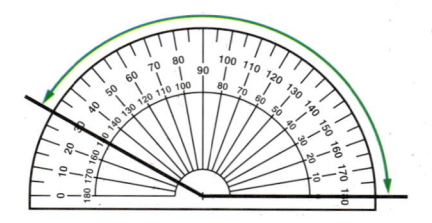

5 **55° or 125°**

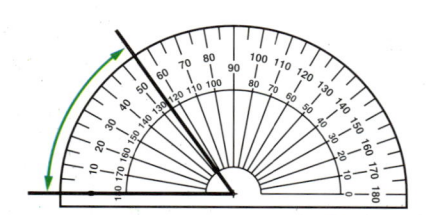

6 **70° or 110°**

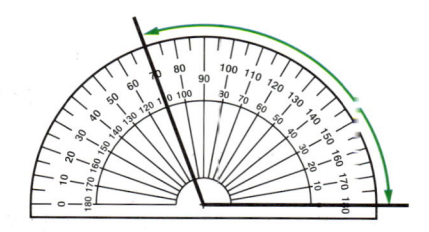

52 Chapter 7

Measuring angles

The unit used to measure the amount of turn in an angle is the **degree**.
When we write an angle we can use this symbol: °.
Therefore 20 degrees is written like this: **20°**.

To measure an angle we use an **angle measurer** or a **protractor**.

Step 1

This is the angle to be measured.

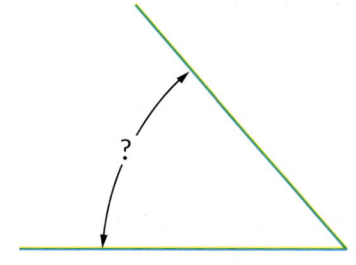

Step 2

We put the protractor in position.

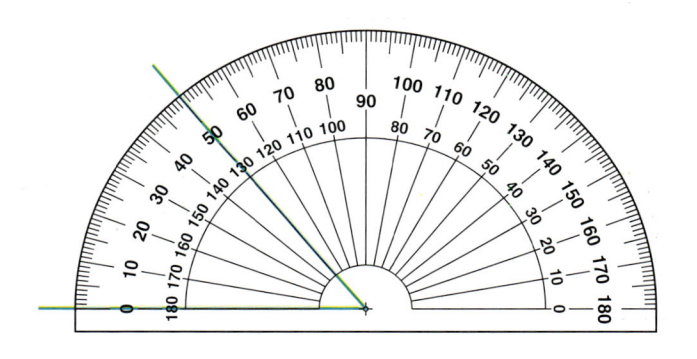

Step 3

Make sure the base-line of the protractor is lined up with one side of the angle.

Make sure the centre of the base-line is on the vertex (corner) of the angle.

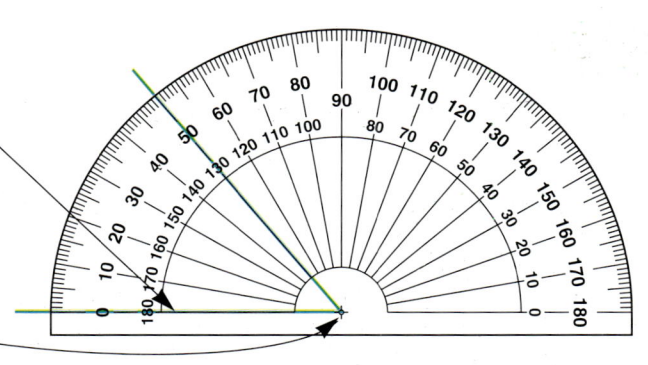

Step 4

We see two figures: 50° and 130°.

Carefully choose the **scale** that starts at zero (0°), and read round the scale to 50°.

The angle is 50°.

(If you look at the angle you can see that it is less than 90°; it cannot be 130°.)

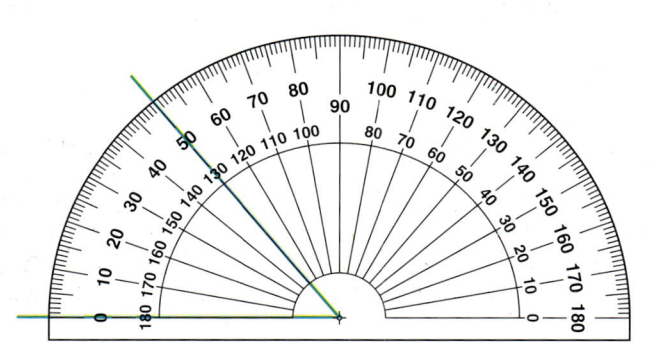

Angles

Exercise 3

Write down the size of each angle. Remember to use the symbol for degrees (°).

1.

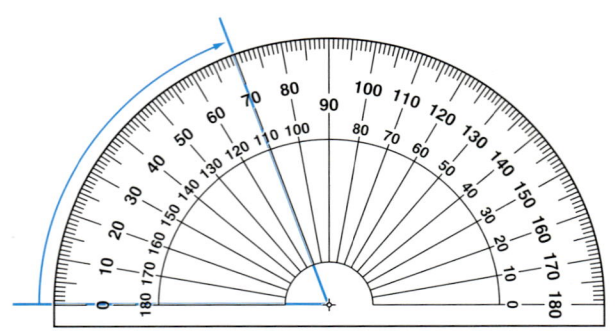

2.

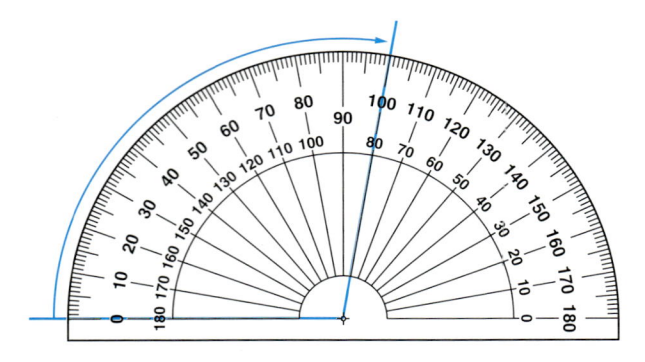

3.

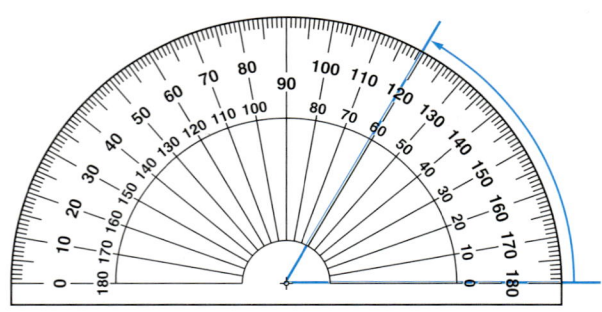

4.

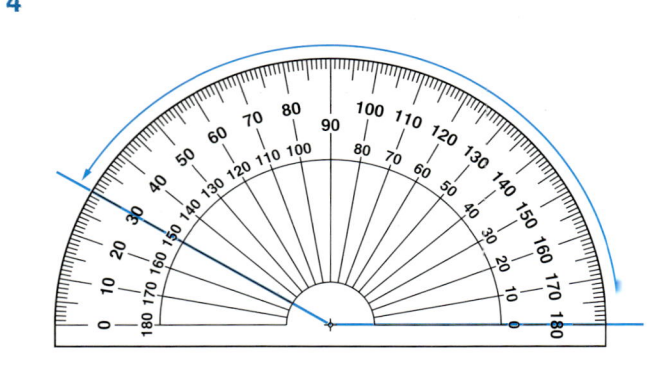

5.

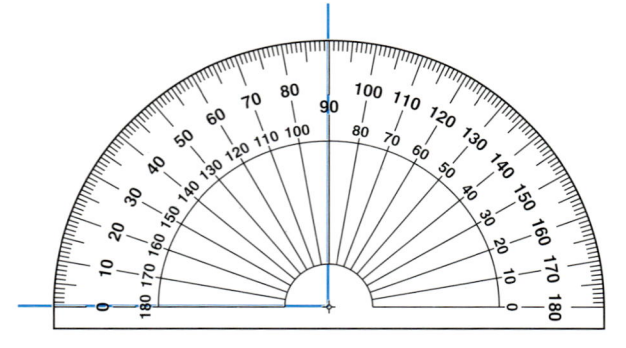

6.

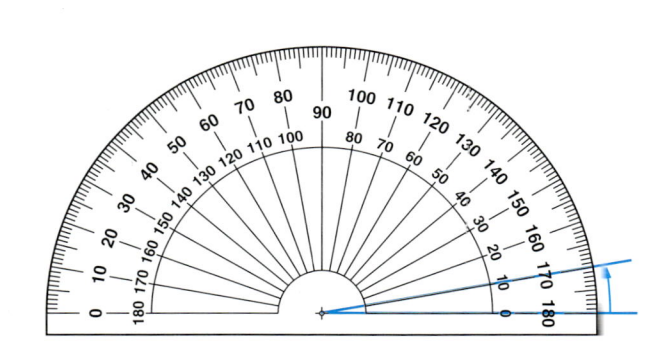

7.

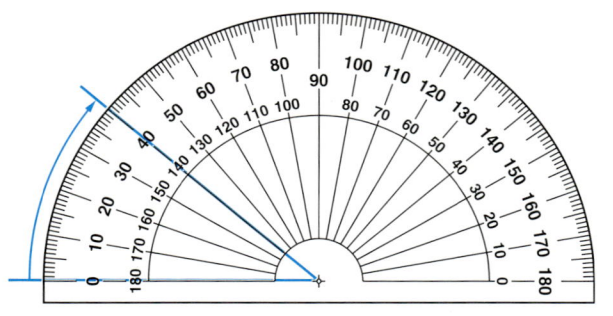

8.

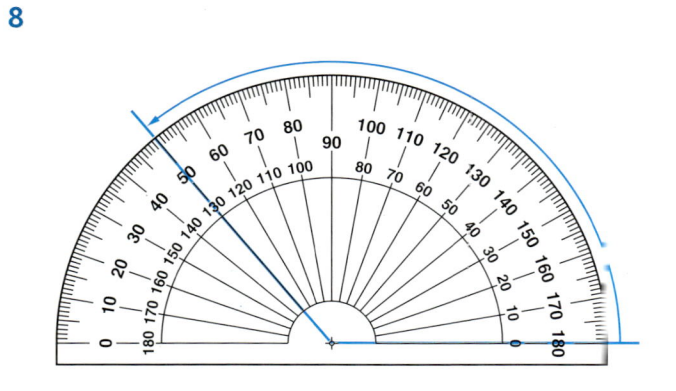

Exercise 4

Use a protractor or angle measurer to measure each angle.
Remember to use the symbol for degrees (°).

1

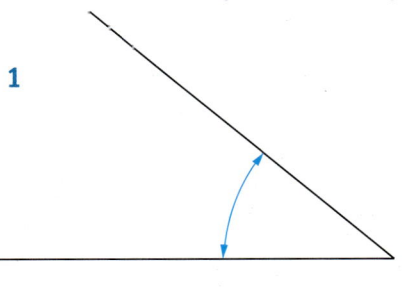

2

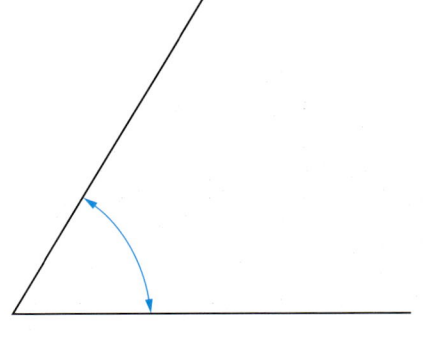

3

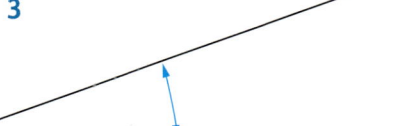

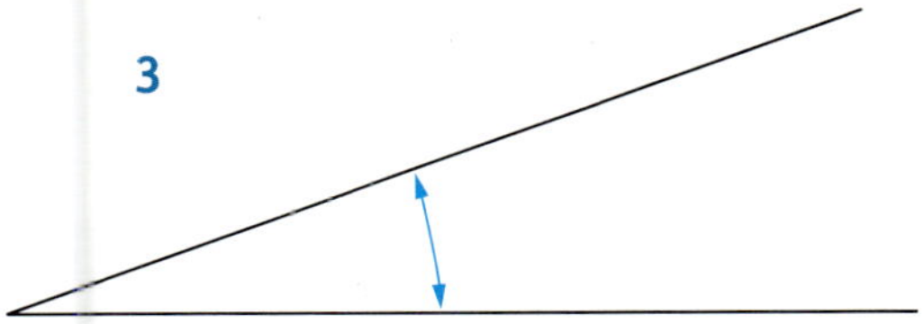

4

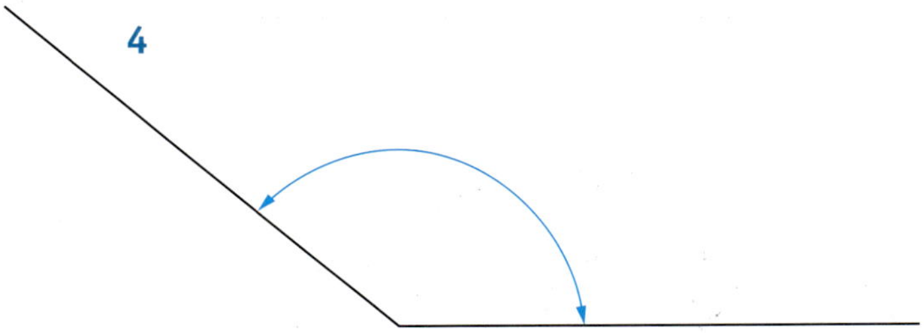

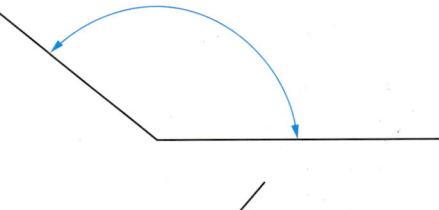

5

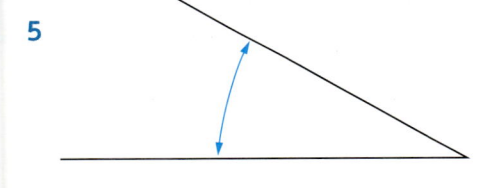

6

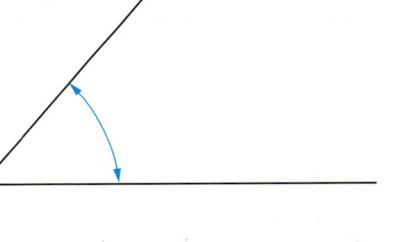

7

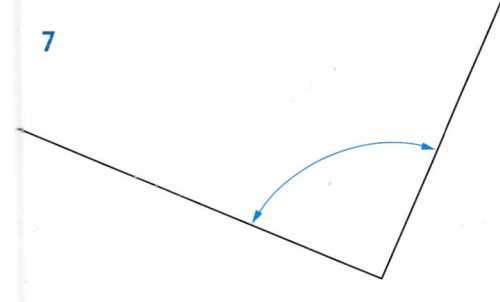

8

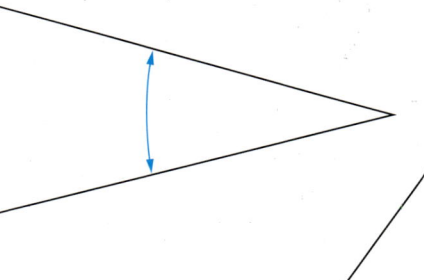

9

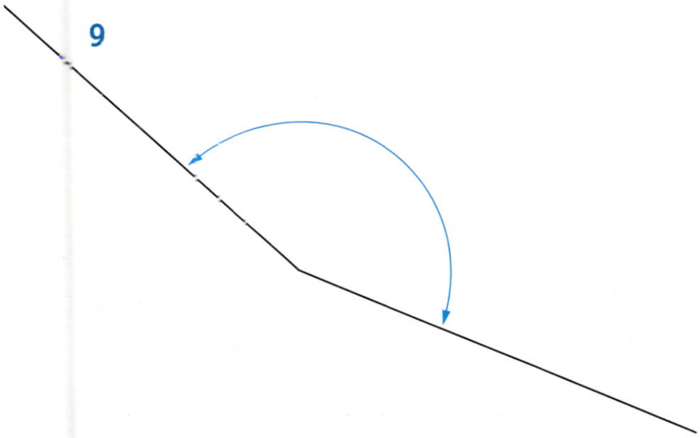

10

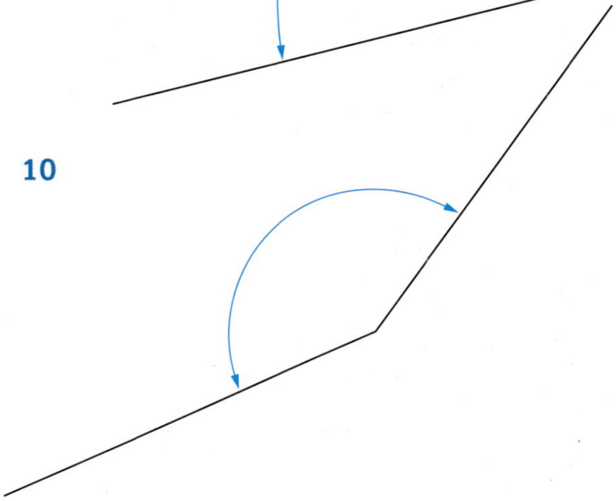

Angles 55

When an angle turns to 180° it becomes a straight line.

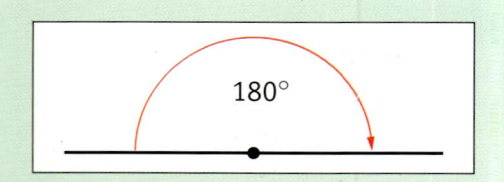

Exercise 5

How many degrees does each angle have to turn through before it reaches 180° (a straight line)?

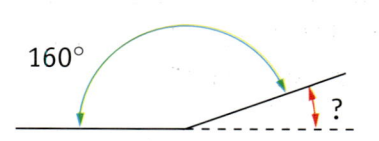

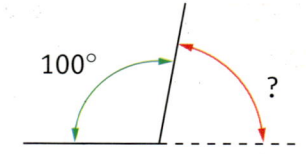

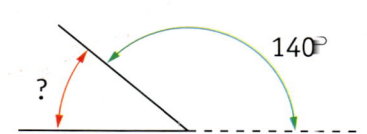

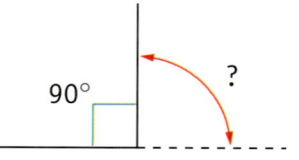

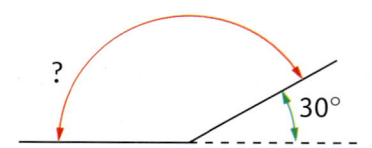

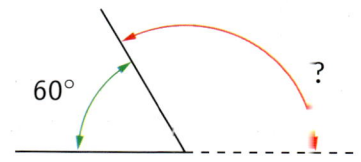

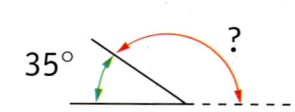

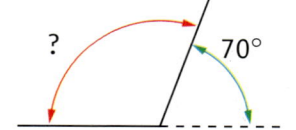

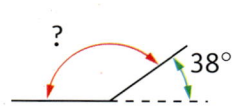

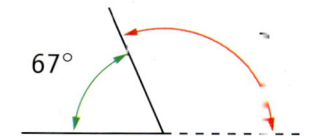

1. 160°
2. 100°
3. 140°
4. 90°
5. 30°
6. 60°
7. 35°
8. 70°
9. 38°
10. 67°

Exercise 6

Find the missing angle in each drawing. Remember that the angles have to add up to 180°.

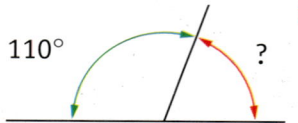

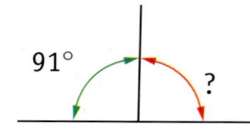

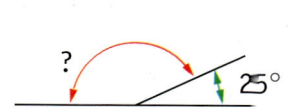

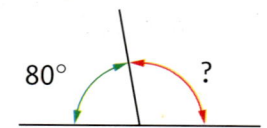

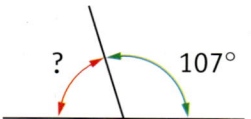

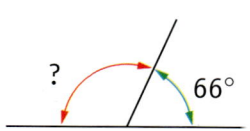

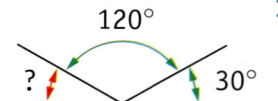

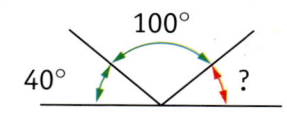

1. 110°
2. 130°
3. 91°
4. 25°
5. 80°
6. 20°
7. 107°
8. 66°
9. 120°, 30°
10. 100°, 40°

56   Chapter 7

A full turn – 360°

Tom is sitting on the roundabout. Each time the roundabout turns **one full turn** Tom turns through an angle of **360°**.

You can see that he turns through **four right angles**: 4 × 90° = 360°

Here, Tom has not made a full turn yet. He has only turned 260°. To complete a full turn he will have to turn another 100°.

Exercise 7

For each drawing, what angle must Tom turn through to complete a full turn? Remember that a full turn is 360°.

1. 110°
2. 200°
3. 310°
4. 80°
5. 160°
6. 230°

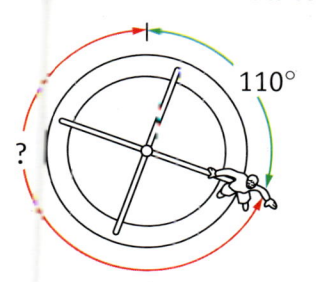

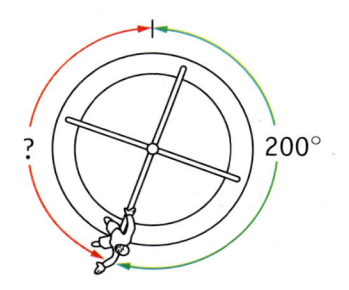

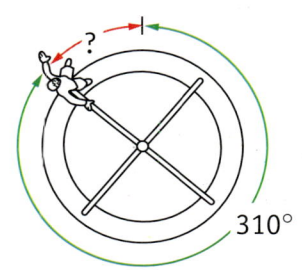

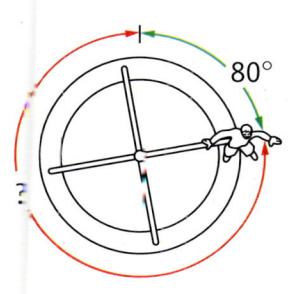

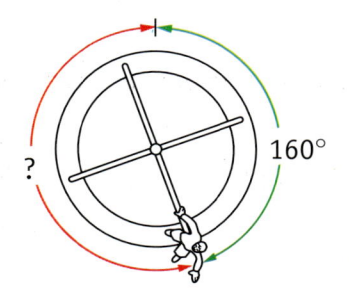

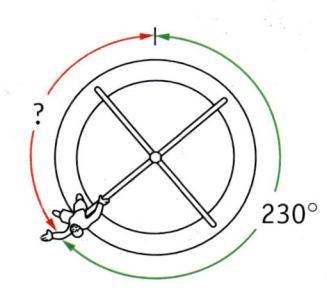

These problems are the same as the ones above, but Tom and the roundabout have been removed.

7. 145°
8. 251°
9. 54°

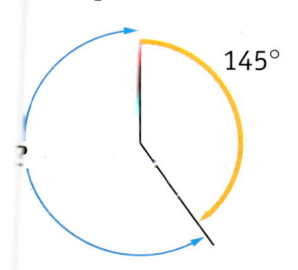

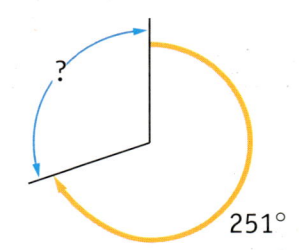

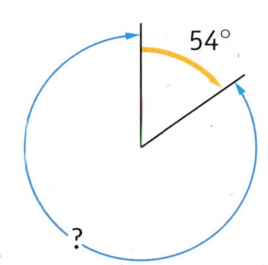

Angles that are more than 180° are called **reflex angles**.

Angles 57

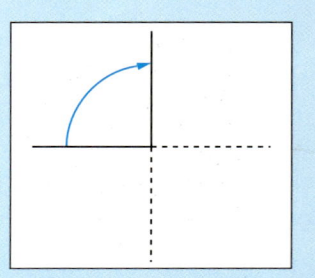

The angle shown here is 90° (one right angle).

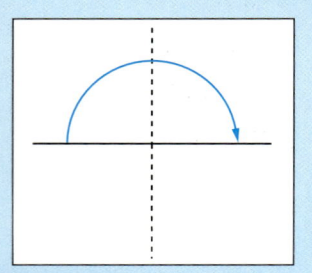

The angle shown here is 180° (two right angles).

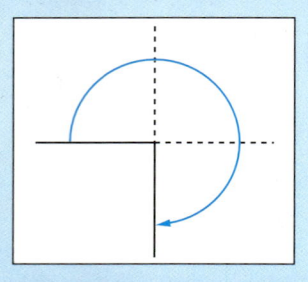

The angle shown here is 270° (three right angles).

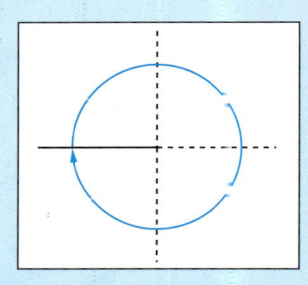

The angle shown here is 360° (four right angles).

Using these as guides we can **estimate** angles.

Exercise 8

(a) State how many right angles you can see in each angle.
(b) **Estimate** the size of each angle in degrees. The first one is done for you.

1

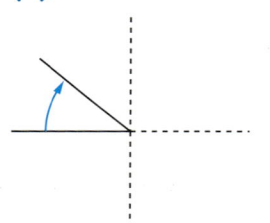

(a) No right angles
(b) About 40°

2

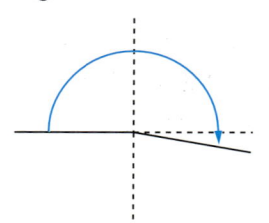

3

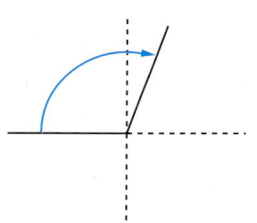

4

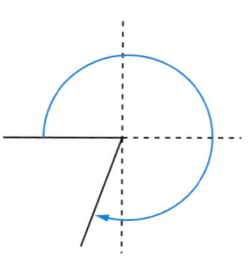

5

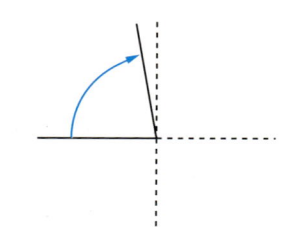

6

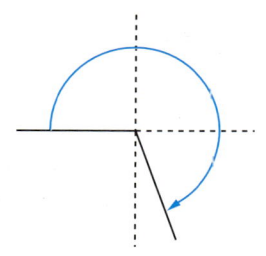

7

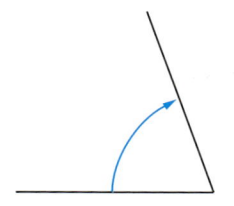

8

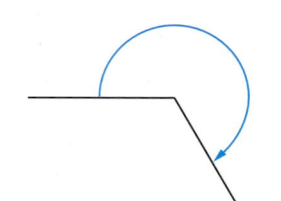

9

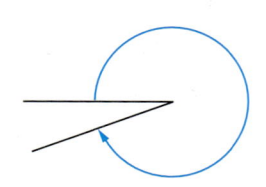

10

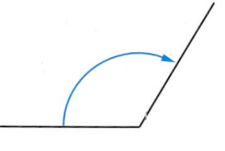

Getting it right!

Here are Leon's attempts at measuring different angles.

A   B 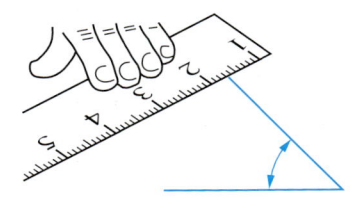   C

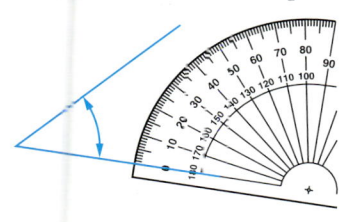

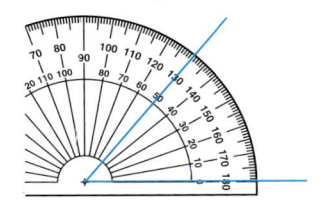

D    E 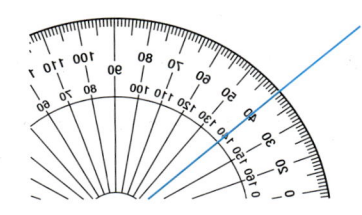   F 'I think it is 160°.'

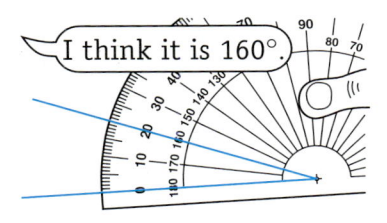

Exercise 9

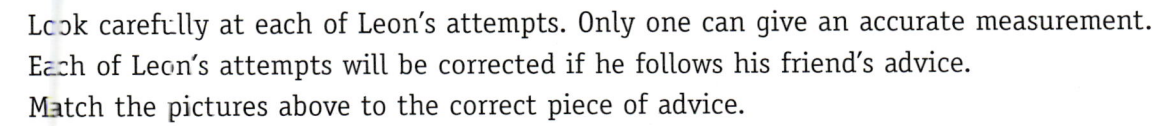

Look carefully at each of Leon's attempts. Only one can give an accurate measurement.
Each of Leon's attempts will be corrected if he follows his friend's advice.
Match the pictures above to the correct piece of advice.

1 'Use the other scale.'

2 'Put the protractor down on the angle.'

3 'Turn the protractor the right way round.'

4 'This one is right.'

5 'Put the centre of the protractor on the vertex of the angle.'

6 'Choose the right instrument.'

Key ideas

Angles tell us how many degrees something has **turned** through.
Angles are measured in **degrees**, and the sign is a small circle. So 30° means thirty degrees.
Protractors and **angle measurers** are used to measure angles.

Acute angles are less than 90°.
Obtuse angles are more than 90°, but less than 180°.
Reflex angles are more than 180°.

Right angles are exactly 90°.
Straight lines are 180°.
One **full turn** is exactly 360°.

The **vertex** is the point where two lines come together to make an angle.   ← The vertex

Angles   59

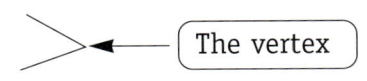

Chapter 8   Work Out 1   The Airport

A

This is a pilot's view of London Heathrow International Airport.

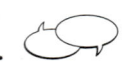

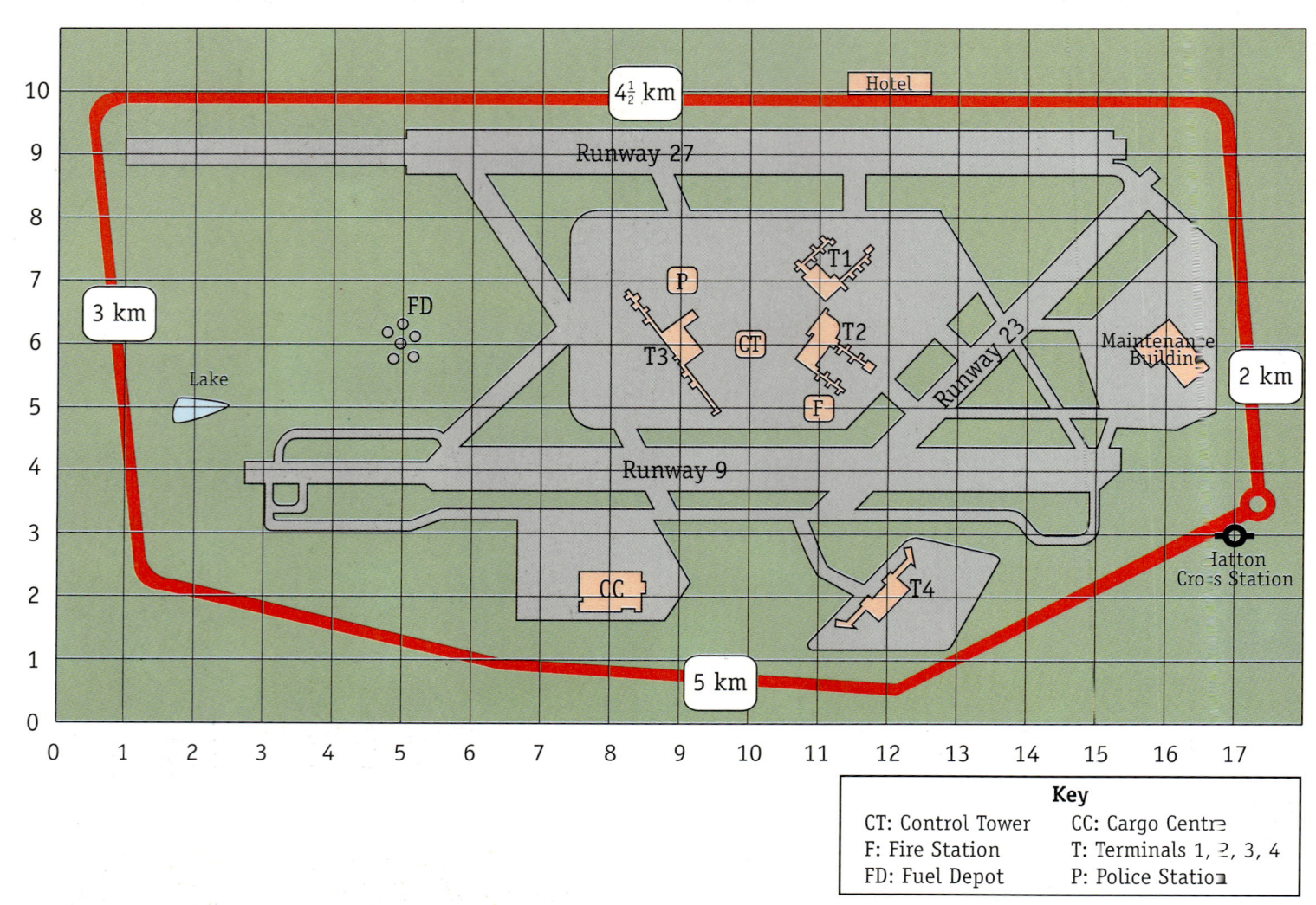

1 What will you find at these co-ordinates?
   (a) (16, 6)   (b) (2, 5)   (c) (17, 3)   (d) (9, 7)   (e) (12, 10)

2 Give the co-ordinates for these places.
   (a) Terminal 1   (b) Terminal 2   (c) Terminal 3   (d) Terminal 4
   (e) Control Tower (f) Fire Station   (g) Cargo Centre   (h) Fuel Depot
   (i) Where runways 23 and 9 cross.   (j) The end of runway 27 (left-hand side).

3 The road that goes all around the airport is called Perimeter Road. On the map it is coloured red. How long is Perimeter Road?

4 Is runway 27 **parallel** with runway 9? Use a ruler to confirm your answer.

B

Ruth is piloting the 6.30 pm flight to Palma. She arrives at Terminal 2, two hours before take off.
As she walks through the terminal she hears travel announcements. Answer the questions about time.

> The 5 o'clock service to Leeds is delayed by 45 minutes.

1. What time will it take off?

> Flight SK405 from Paris will land in 20 minutes.

2. What time will it land?

> Flight MT883 will take off in 25 minutes.

3. What time will it take off?

> Flight EP804 from Oslo will land in 35 minutes.

4. What time will it land?

> The flight from Moscow that was due to land at 6.15 pm has been delayed by 30 minutes.

5. What time will it land?

> The 5 o'clock flight to Malta will take off $1\frac{1}{2}$ hours late.

6. What time will it take off?

C

Before the pre-flight check, Ruth and her first officer have to check the cargo and fuel.

1. What is the total weight of cargo in the hold?

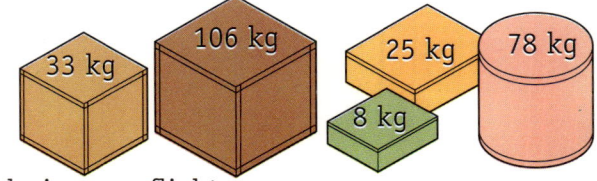

   (33 kg, 106 kg, 25 kg, 8 kg, 78 kg)

2. Here are three fuel tank readings taken at different times during one flight.
   - Say when each reading was taken: at the beginning, in the middle, or at the end of the flight.
   - If the fuel tank holds 21 000 litres, say how much fuel would be needed to fill the tank at each stage of the journey.

   (a) 18500 LITRES   (b) 10000 LITRES   (c) 15000 LITRES

3. The aircraft can carry 18 First Class passengers, 27 Club Class passengers and 82 Economy Class passengers. How many passengers can it carry in total?

4. For this flight there are 5 First Class passengers, 18 Club Class passengers and 51 Economy Class passengers.
   (a) How many passengers are there on board?   (b) How many empty seats will there be?

Work Out 1 61

D

This diagram shows how the temperature changes as aircraft climb higher.
Use the diagram to answer these questions.

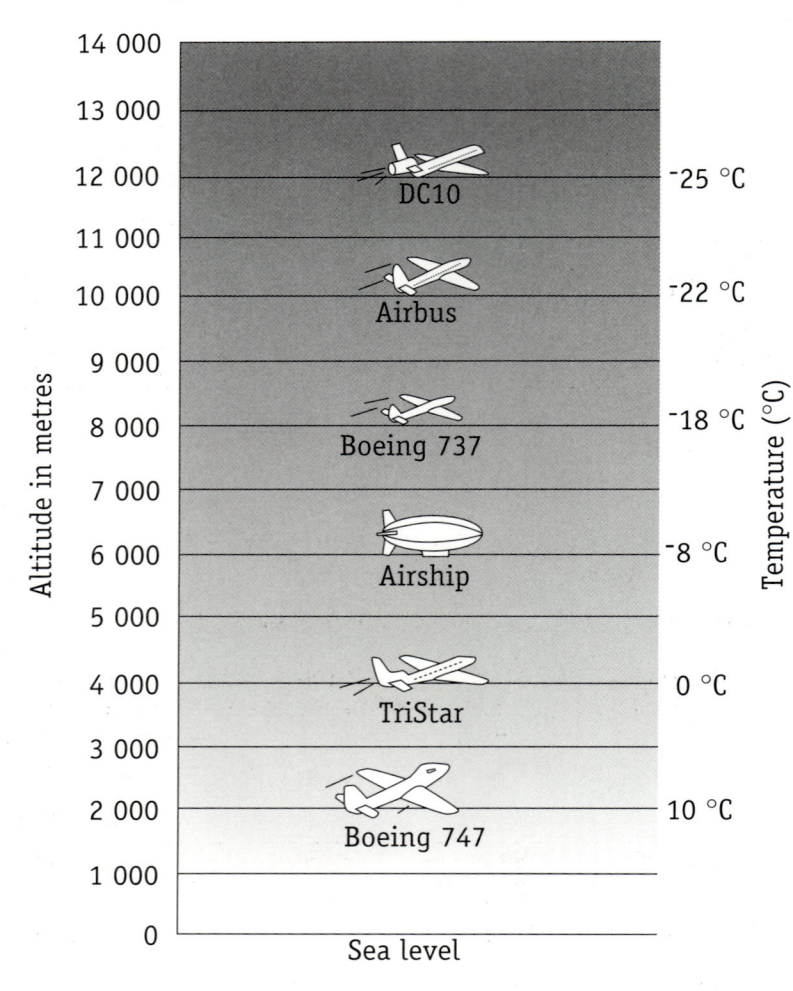

1. What happens to the temperature as the aircraft climb higher?
2. At what altitudes, or heights, are these aircraft?
   - (a) Boeing 747
   - (b) Airship
   - (c) Airbus
   - (d) Boeing 737
3. How many metres must the Boeing 747 climb to be at the same height as the Airbus?
4. As the DC10 loses 6000 m of altitude, how much will the temperature rise?
5. When the Boeing 747 climbs to 8000 m, the temperature drops. By how many degrees will the temperature fall?
6. The temperature at sea level (0 m) has not been recorded. Use the diagram to estimate the temperature at sea level.
7. Estimate the temperatures at:
   - (a) 5000 m
   - (b) 11 000 m
   - (c) 1000 m
   - (d) 3500 m

E

Use a protractor or an angle measurer to find the angles of **ascent** and **descent** for each aircraft.
Write: '1 BU141 is descending at 20°.'

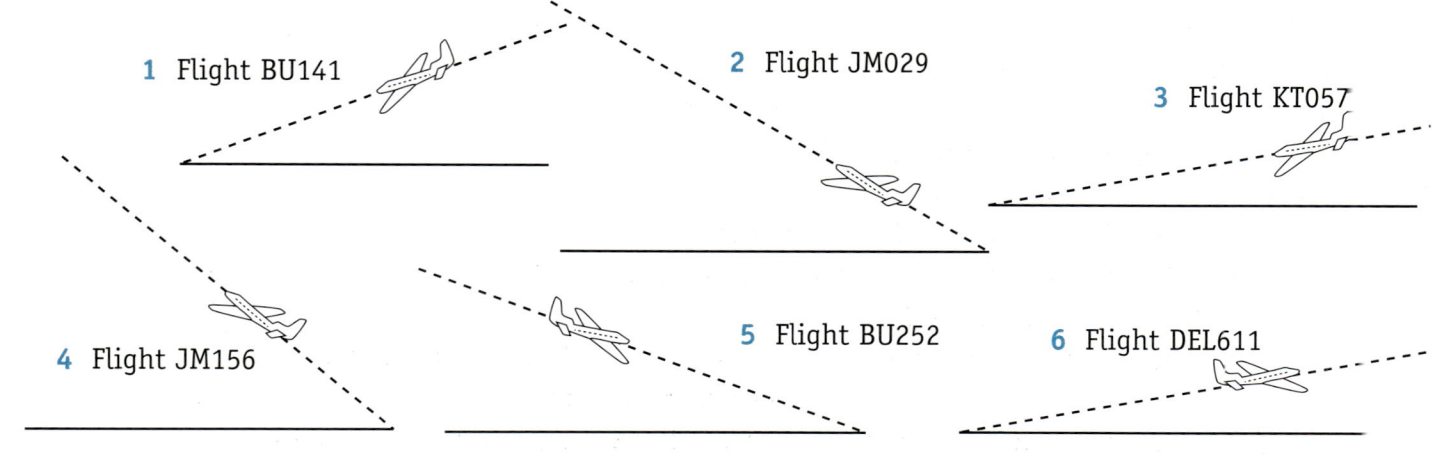

1. Flight BU141
2. Flight JM029
3. Flight KT057
4. Flight JM156
5. Flight BU252
6. Flight DEL611

F

The building on the left-hand side of the drawing is 10 metres high.
Using this as a guide, estimate the measurements shown on the drawing.

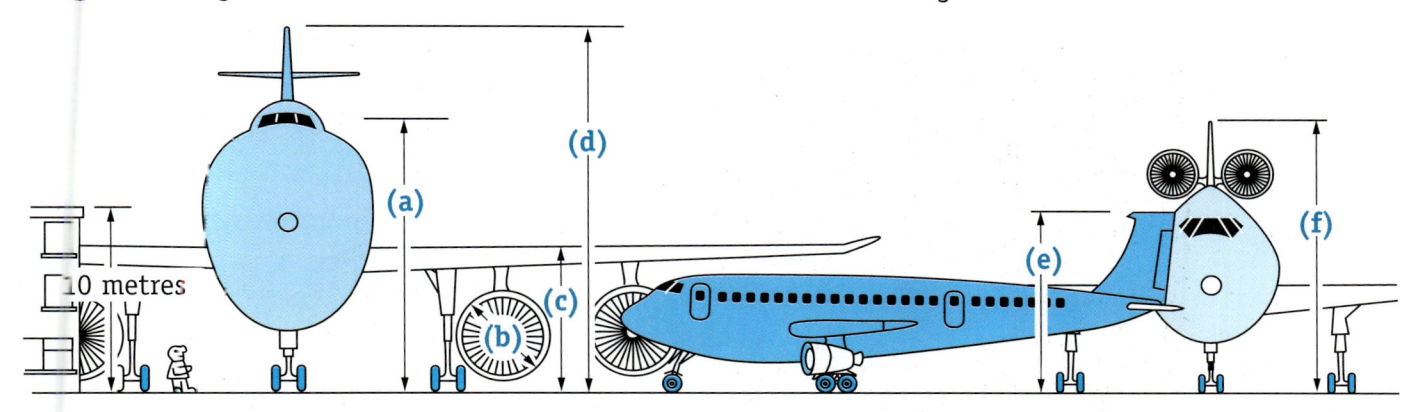

G

There are many different aircraft. The chart below shows some data about five famous aircraft.

Aircraft	Length metres	Wingspan metres	Weight kilograms	Speed kilometres per hour	Number of passengers	Range (max. distance travelled without refuelling) kilometres
Lockheed TriStar	50.1	47.4	224 980	895	256	9653
Boeing 747	70.5	59.6	365 150	969	550	10 040
Boeing 737	29.5	28.8	53 050	927	125	4448
BAe Airbus	53.6	44.8	157 500	911	263	5930
McDonnell Douglas DC10	55.5	50.5	259 450	908	250	7413

1. Which aircraft:
   (a) carries the fewest passengers?
   (b) has a top speed of 911 kilometres per hour?
   (c) can carry 550 passengers?
   (d) have wingspans greater than 45 metres?
   (e) is the slowest?
   (f) is the heaviest?
2. What is the top speed of the McDonnell Douglas DC10?
3. How many passengers can the Lockheed TriStar carry?
4. What is the wingspan of the Boeing 737?
5. What is the range of the BAe Airbus?
6. The distance from London to New York is 5600 km.
   List the aircraft that could complete the journey without refuelling.
7. Is the smallest aircraft the fastest?
8. Look at **all of the data** in the chart. (a) Which two aircraft are most similar?
   (b) How did you decide?
9. Write the names of the aircraft in order of weight, from the lightest to the heaviest.

Work Out 1

H

Ruth's aeroplane is moving down runway 9 at Heathrow airport.

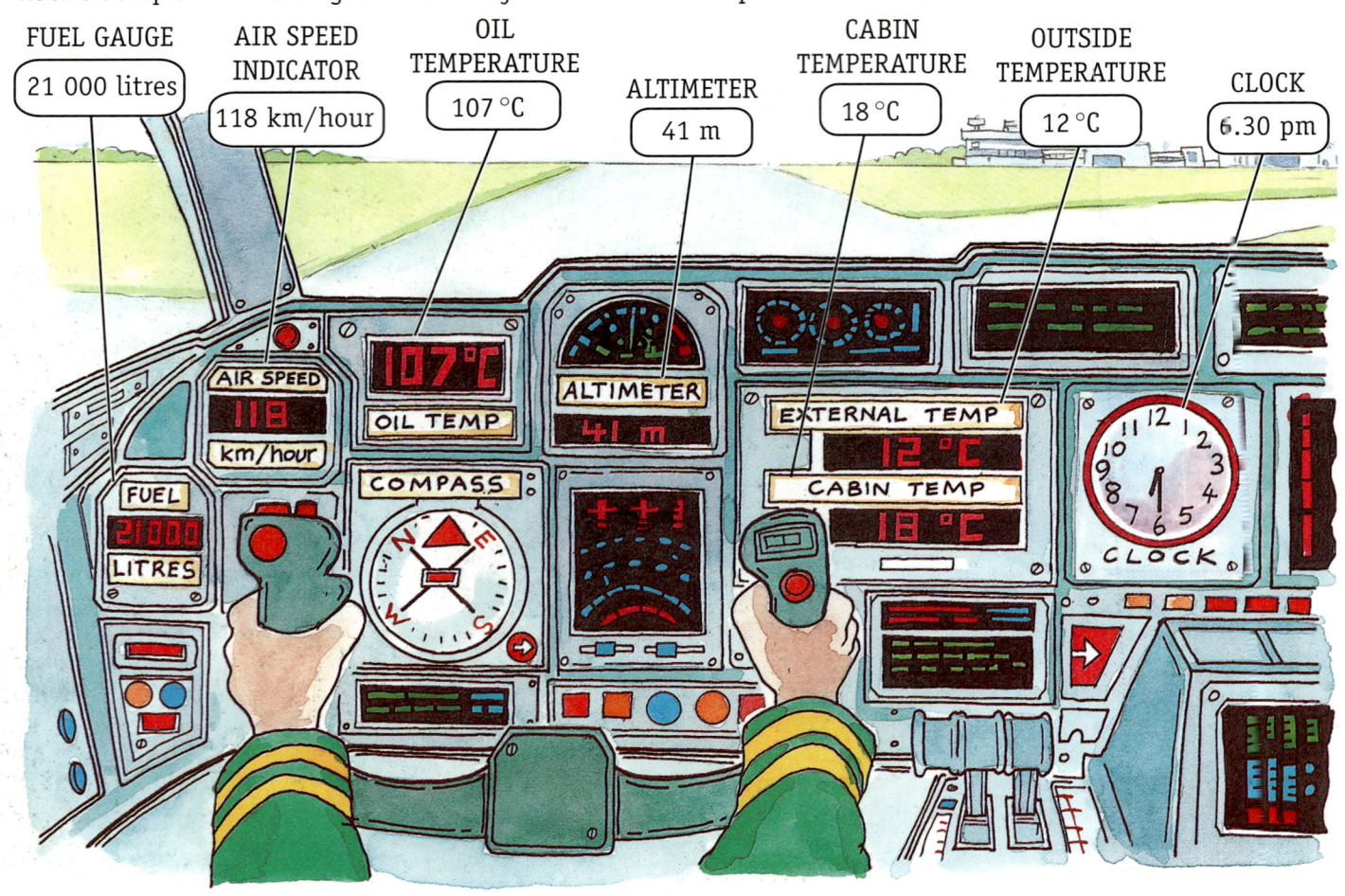

FUEL GAUGE: 21 000 litres
AIR SPEED INDICATOR: 118 km/hour
OIL TEMPERATURE: 107 °C
ALTIMETER: 41 m
CABIN TEMPERATURE: 18 °C
OUTSIDE TEMPERATURE: 12 °C
CLOCK: 6.30 pm

The instrument panel:

Time:	the clock
Speed:	air speed indicator
How much fuel left:	fuel gauge
Direction:	compass
Height above sea level:	altimeter
Oil temperature:	
Cabin temperature:	temperature gauges
External (outside) temperature:	

1. What time is it?
2. What altitude is shown on the altimeter?
3. At what speed is the aircraft travelling?
4. What is the outside temperature?
5. What is the oil temperature?
6. How many litres of fuel are in the aircraft?

Chapter 8

I

Sometime later we see Ruth approaching Majorca, preparing to land at Palma airport.

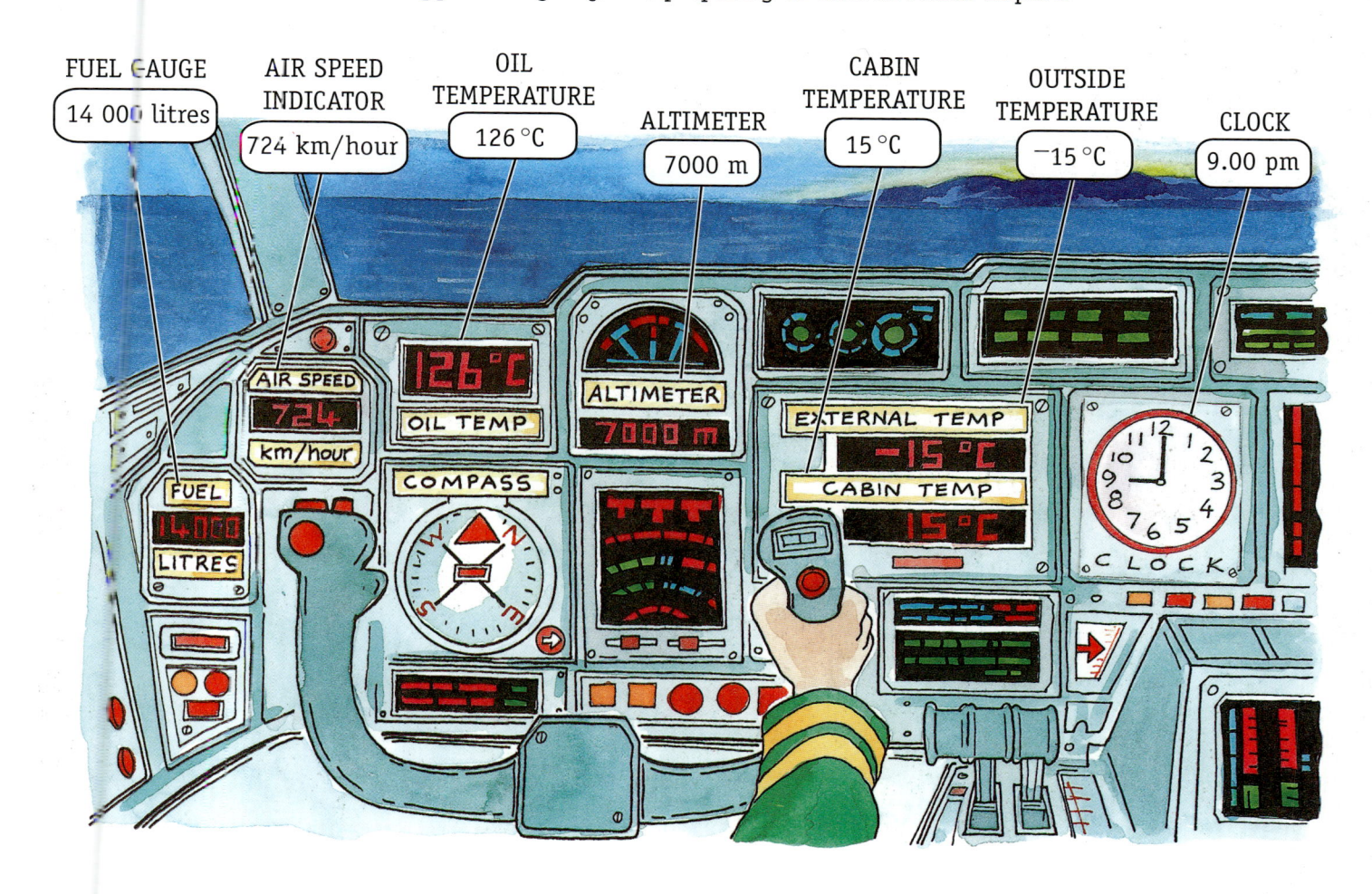

FUEL GAUGE: 14 000 litres
AIR SPEED INDICATOR: 724 km/hour
OIL TEMPERATURE: 126 °C
ALTIMETER: 7000 m
CABIN TEMPERATURE: 15 °C
OUTSIDE TEMPERATURE: −15 °C
CLOCK: 9.00 pm

You will need to use both drawings to answer some of these questions.

1. (a) How long has the flight taken so far?
   (b) At how many metres above sea level is the aircraft flying?
   (c) If the ground controller tells Ruth to **descend** by 2000 metres, what will the new altitude be?

2. (a) How many litres of fuel are left?
   (b) How many litres of fuel have been used since take off?

3. (a) Has the cabin temperature gone up or down?
   (b) By how many degrees has the temperature changed?

4. (a) What is the oil temperature?
   (b) How many degrees hotter has the oil become since take off?

5. (a) What is the speed of the aircraft?
   (b) By how much has the aircraft's speed increased since take off?

6. (a) What is the outside temperature?
   (b) By how many degrees has the temperature fallen since take off?

Work Out 1   65

Chapter 9 Multiplication and Division

Step-up 1 Multiplication

This triangle has been enlarged to make it ten times larger. The sketches are not drawn to scale.

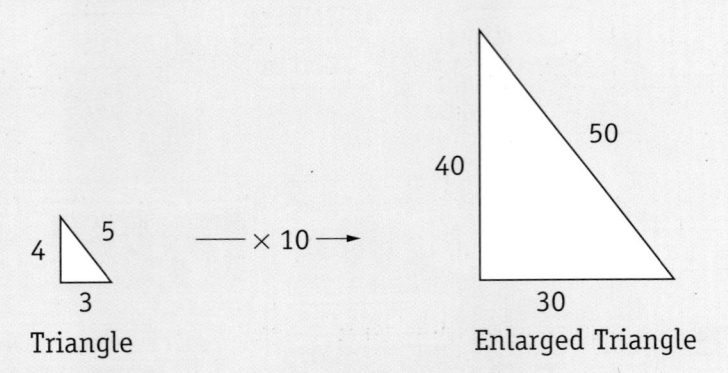

Triangle (sides 3, 4, 5) — × 10 → Enlarged Triangle (sides 30, 40, 50)

1 (a) Make neat sketches of the triangles below, as if their measurements had been enlarged ten times bigger.

(b) Write the new dimensions onto the shapes.

A: 10 cm, 9 cm, 8 cm

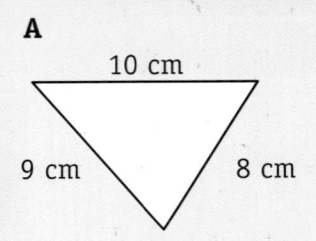

B: 12 cm, 7 cm, 8 cm

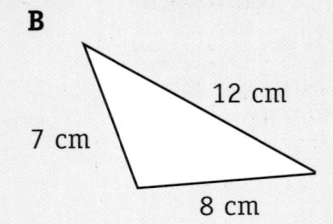

C: 13 cm, 5 cm, 12 cm

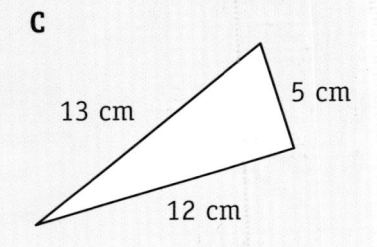

This 'machine' multiplies numbers by 10. The input is 5, the output is 50 (5 × 10 = 50).

5 → × 10 → 50

2 Find the missing outputs to these machines that multiply by 10.

(a) 8 → × 10 → ?   (b) 6 → × 10 → ?   (c) 10 → × 10 → ?

(d) 15 → × 10 → ?   (e) 11 → × 10 → ?   (f) 9 → × 10 → ?

3 Multiply these numbers by ten. Re-draw each abacus to show your answer.

(a) H T U
14 × 10 = ?

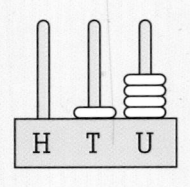

(b) Th H T U
302 × 10 = ?

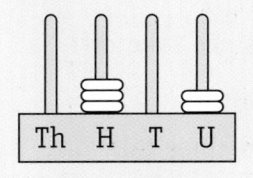

(c) Th H T U
236 × 10 = ?

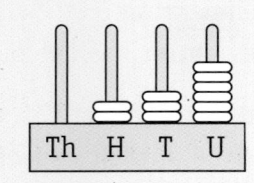

Multiplying by 100

To multiply a number by 100 we move it **two places** to the **left**.

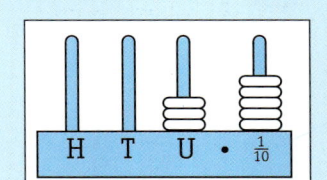

$$3.5 \times 100 = 350$$

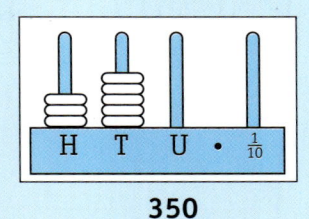

3.5 → × 100 → 350

Exercise 1

Multiply by 100. Re-draw each abacus to show your answer.

1 2.1 × 100 = ?

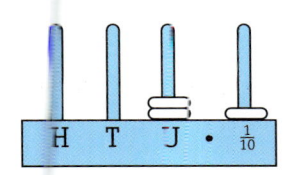

2 1.2 × 100 = ?

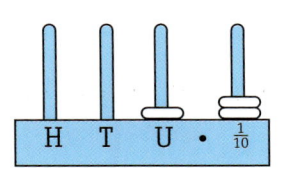

3 4.3 × 100 = ?

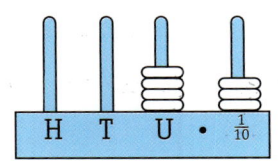

4 0.5 × 100 = ?

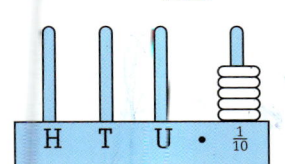

5 6.0 × 100 = ?

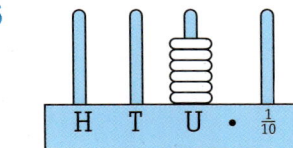

6 0.1 × 100 = ?

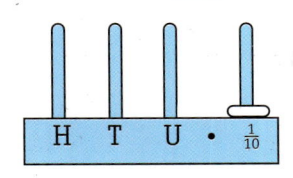

Exercise 2

Multiply these numbers by one hundred.

1   4 × 100 = ?
2   7 × 100 = ?
3   2.1 × 100 = ?
4   3.2 × 100 = ?
5   6 × 100 = ?
6   4.8 × 100 = ?
7   100 × 9.0 = ?
8   6.4 × 100 = ?
9   1.1 × 100 = ?
10 5 × 100 = ?
11 0.8 × 100 = ?
12 0.7 × 100 = ?

Exercise 3

Decide whether these numbers have been multiplied by ten or one hundred.

1   3 × ? = 300
2   3.4 × ? = 340
3   0.6 × ? = 60
4   ? × 5.6 = 56
5   ? × 0.1 = 10
6   18 × ? = 180
7   3.2 × ? = 320
8   ? × 0.42 = 4.2
9   13.5 × ? = 135
10 What do you think the '?' stands for in this number machine?

1.6 → ×? → 1600

Multiplication 67

Step-up Division

When we divide by 10 we move the numbers **one place** to the **right**.

Your answer can be written like this: 23.0 or 23.

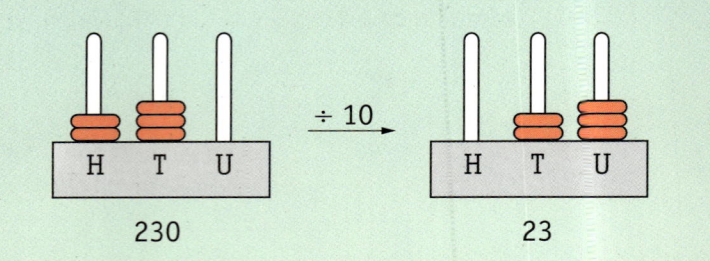

230 ÷ 10 = 23

Divide these numbers by ten.

1. 40 ÷ 10 = ?
2. 70 ÷ 10 = ?
3. 20 ÷ 10 = ?
4. 80 ÷ 10 = ?
5. 100 ÷ 10 = ?
6. 120 ÷ 10 = ?
7. 200 ÷ 10 = ?
8. 350 ÷ 10 = ?

All of the numbers above are whole tens, they all end with '0'. When the number is not a whole ten and does not end with a '0', we have to use **decimals**.

23 ÷ 10 = 2.3 (two units and 3 tenths)

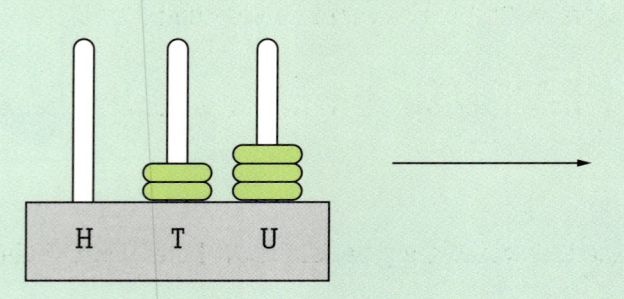

We have to use a decimal spike.

Draw simple abacuses to show these divisions.

9. 11 ÷ 10 = ?
10. 34 ÷ 10 = ?
11. 50 ÷ 10 = ?
12. 16 ÷ 10 = ?
13. 137 ÷ 10 = ?
14. 302 ÷ 10 = ?

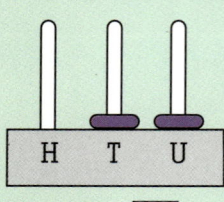

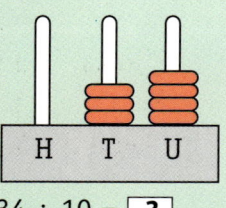

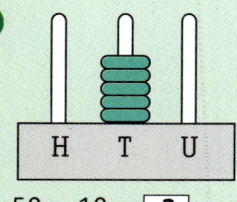

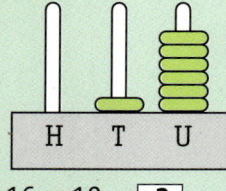

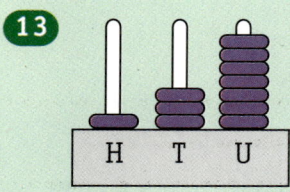

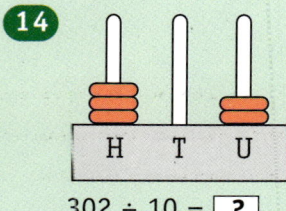

Chapter 9

Exercise 4

Answer these division questions. Remember to show the decimal points clearly.

1. 23 ÷ 10 = ?
2. 15 ÷ 10 = ?
3. 33 ÷ 10 = ?
4. 44 ÷ 10 = ?
5. 75 ÷ 10 = ?
6. 78 ÷ 10 = ?
7. 91 ÷ 10 = ?
8. 67 ÷ 10 = ?
9. 164 ÷ 10 = ?
10. 100 ÷ 10 = ?
11. 250 ÷ 10 = ?
12. 505 ÷ 10 = ?

Professor Small has invented this shrinking machine. Whatever goes into the machine is shrunk ten times smaller and ten times lighter.

Leon falls into the machine. He used to be 150 cm tall and he weighed 50 kg. Now he is 15 cm tall and only weighs 5.0 kg.

Exercise 5

If these people went through the machine, how tall would they be, and how heavy would they be when they came out?

1. **Martin:** Before After
   Height 154 cm ?
   Weight 75 kg ?

2. **Janet:** Before After
   Height 160 cm ?
   Weight 51 kg ?

3. **Khalid:** Before After
   Height 210 cm ?
   Weight 68 kg ?

4. **Ajeeta:** Before After
   Height 206 cm ?
   Weight 82 kg ?

Exercise 6

Redraw these lines making them **10 times** smaller.

1. ─────────────────────────────
2. ──────────────────────
3. ────────────────────────
4. ──────────────
5. ────────

Multiplying and dividing money by tens and hundreds

Jasmin pays 13p (£0.13) per minute for her weekend calls.

Hi, Rodney you cool dude.

I'll be there in two minutes.

If she calls Rodney for 10 minutes the cost will be:

£0.13 × 10 = £1.3

This is written as £1.30 because we say 'One pound thirty'. When we are dealing with decimal amounts that are not money, they can be written as 1.3 and we would say 'One point three'.

Exercise 7

1. Rewrite these amounts as pounds like this: 15p = £0.15.
   (a) 18p (b) 51p (c) 21p (d) 97p (e) 48p (f) 1p (g) 39p (h) 49p

2. These are the charges of six different phone companies for **one minute** calls. Jasmin can only afford to spend £4.50 for her **ten-minute** call. Which of these companies could she afford to use?
   A 'TimeCall' ....19p a minute. B 'Airwaves' ....78p a minute. C 'Wisetime' ....22p a minute.
   D 'Flexline' ....30p a minute. E 'M Calls' ....48p a minute. F 'Talktime' ....49p a minute.

3. Here are the costs of six different calls made by Jasmin's friends.
   Each call was **ten minutes** long. How much did each call cost for **one minute**?
   (a) Tom   £3.80   (b) Jan   £7.20
   (c) Imran £2.10   (d) Dipika £5.50
   (e) Jacob £1.30   (f) Mick   £0.90

Exercise 8

Use multiplication and division by 10 and 100 to work out these problems.

1. Anton buys 10 CDs. Each one costs £6.99. How much does he have to pay altogether?
2. If the total bill for another 10 CDs is £159.00, what is the cost of each disc?
3. The cost of each tile on this patio is 75p. How much will it cost to tile the whole patio?

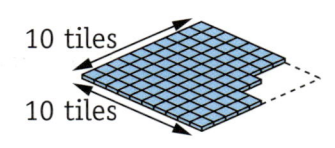

   10 tiles
   10 tiles

4. One hundred eye-liner pencils cost £35.00.
   How much would you pay for one pencil?

Chapter 9

Exercise 9

1. Make two lists that show two groups of weights:
   Those that are lighter than the box on the scales. Those that are heavier than the box on the scales.
   Write: 'Lighter groups are... Heavier groups are...'

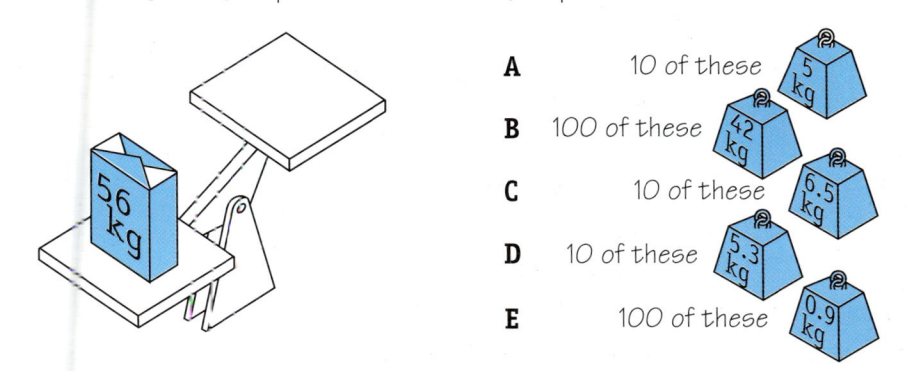

   A 10 of these 5 kg
   B 100 of these 4.2 kg
   C 10 of these 6.5 kg
   D 10 of these 5.3 kg
   E 100 of these 0.9 kg

   (Box on scales: 5.6 kg)

2. Which group would be the closest to making the scales balance?
3. If a group of ten equal weights balances, what would each one weigh?

Key ideas

After the units is the decimal point, although we do not always need to write it.
To multiply a number by ten we move the digit(s) **one place to the left**.
E.g. 25 × 10 ⟶

h	t	u
	2	5
2	5	0

× 10
There is nothing in the units place so we put in a 0.

When we divide units by ten we use a decimal point to separate the units from the tenths ($\frac{1}{10}$).
E.g. 36 ÷ 10 ⟶

h	t	u	•	$\frac{1}{10}$
	3	6		
		3	•	6

÷ 10

When we multiply by 100 we move the number's digit(s) **two places to the left**.
E.g. 4.5 × 100 ⟶

h	t	u	•	$\frac{1}{10}$
		4	•	5
4	5	0		

× 100
Each digit has moved 2 places to the left.
Check them.

When we divide a number by 100, we move its digits **two places to the right**.
E.g. 570 ÷ 100 = 5.70 ⟶

h	t	u	•	$\frac{1}{10}$
5	7	0		
		5	•	70

÷ 100
All digits have moved two places to the right.

Division

Chapter 10 Solid Shape

Step-up

1 Here are some flat shapes. Copy each shape carefully and label it.

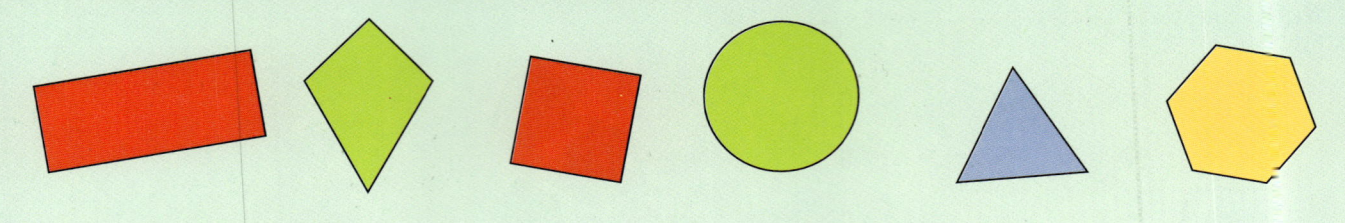

| circle | square | hexagon | triangle | rectangle | kite |

2 Draw two columns. Using the letters, sort the shapes below into two groups.
Give a title to each column and explain what the difference is between the two groups.

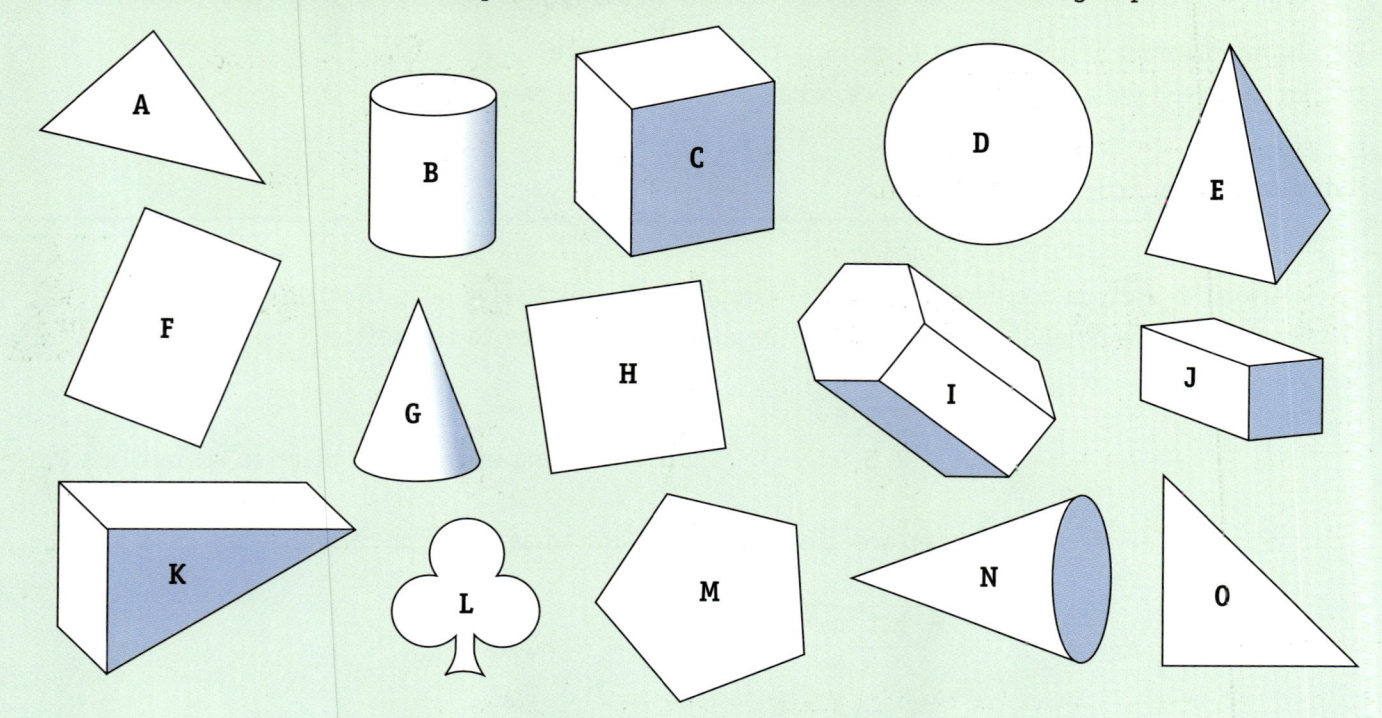

3 Give the area of each shape in square centimetres. Remember to use the rule **Area = length × width.**

(a) 4 cm × 2 cm

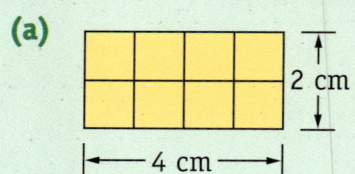

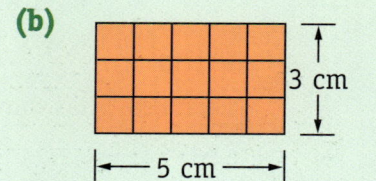

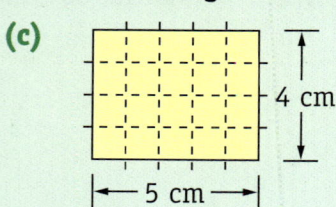

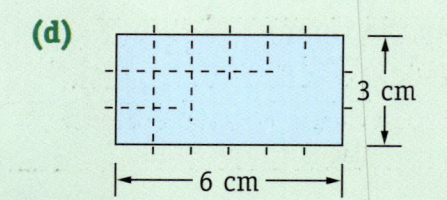

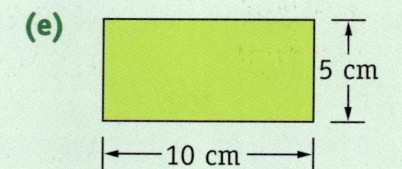

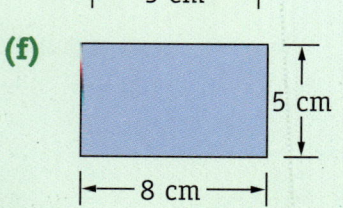

(b) 5 cm × 3 cm

(c) 5 cm × 4 cm

(d) 6 cm × 3 cm

(e) 10 cm × 5 cm

(f) 8 cm × 5 cm

72 Chapter 10

2D and 3D

Flat shape

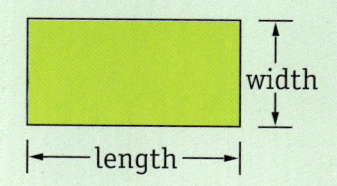

width
length

A **2D** shape has **two dimensions**: **length** and **width**.

Solid shape

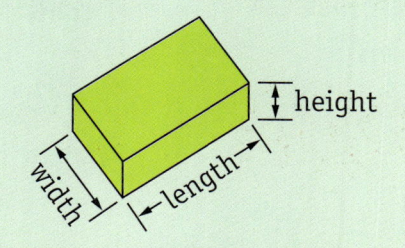

height
width
length

A **3D** shape has **three dimensions**: **length**, **width** and **height**.

Exercise 1

When a bright light is shone onto this **cube** it casts a shadow on the wall.
The shadow is a **square**.
Match each 3D shape with its 2D shadow.

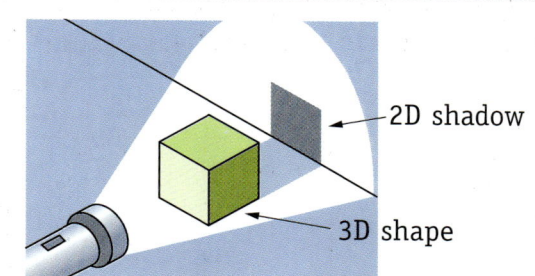

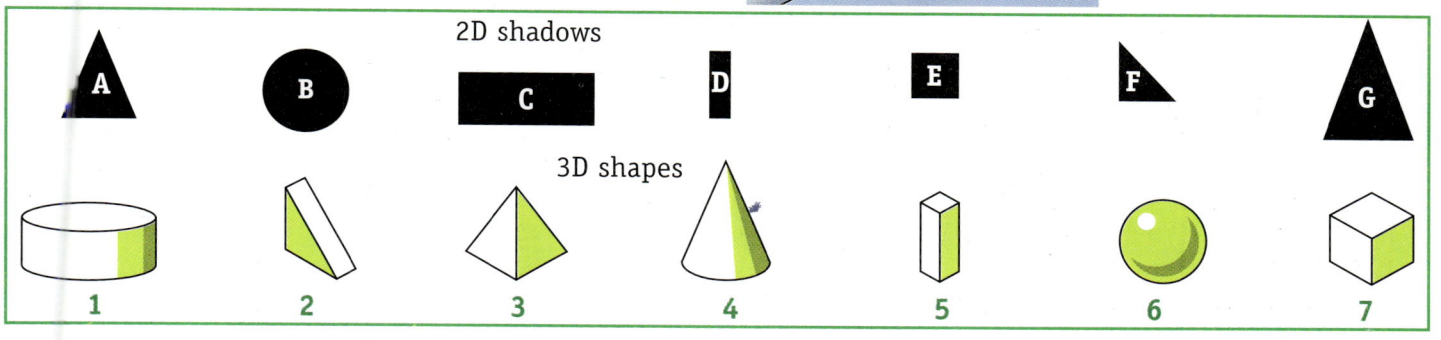

2D shadow
3D shape

2D shadows

A   B   C   D   E   F   G

3D shapes

1   2   3   4   5   6   7

Exercise 2

Match Alia's descriptions to the shapes. Write: 'Cylinder. This shape has …'

Cylinder

Sphere

Cube

Cone

Cuboid

Pyramid

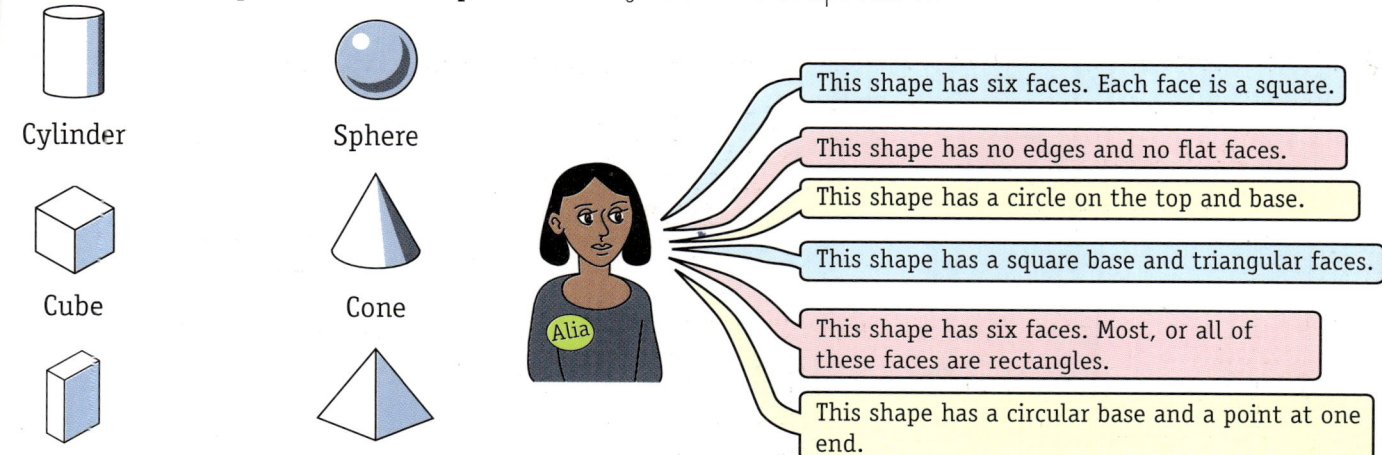

Alia:
- This shape has six faces. Each face is a square.
- This shape has no edges and no flat faces.
- This shape has a circle on the top and base.
- This shape has a square base and triangular faces.
- This shape has six faces. Most, or all of these faces are rectangles.
- This shape has a circular base and a point at one end.

Solid Shape

Exercise 3

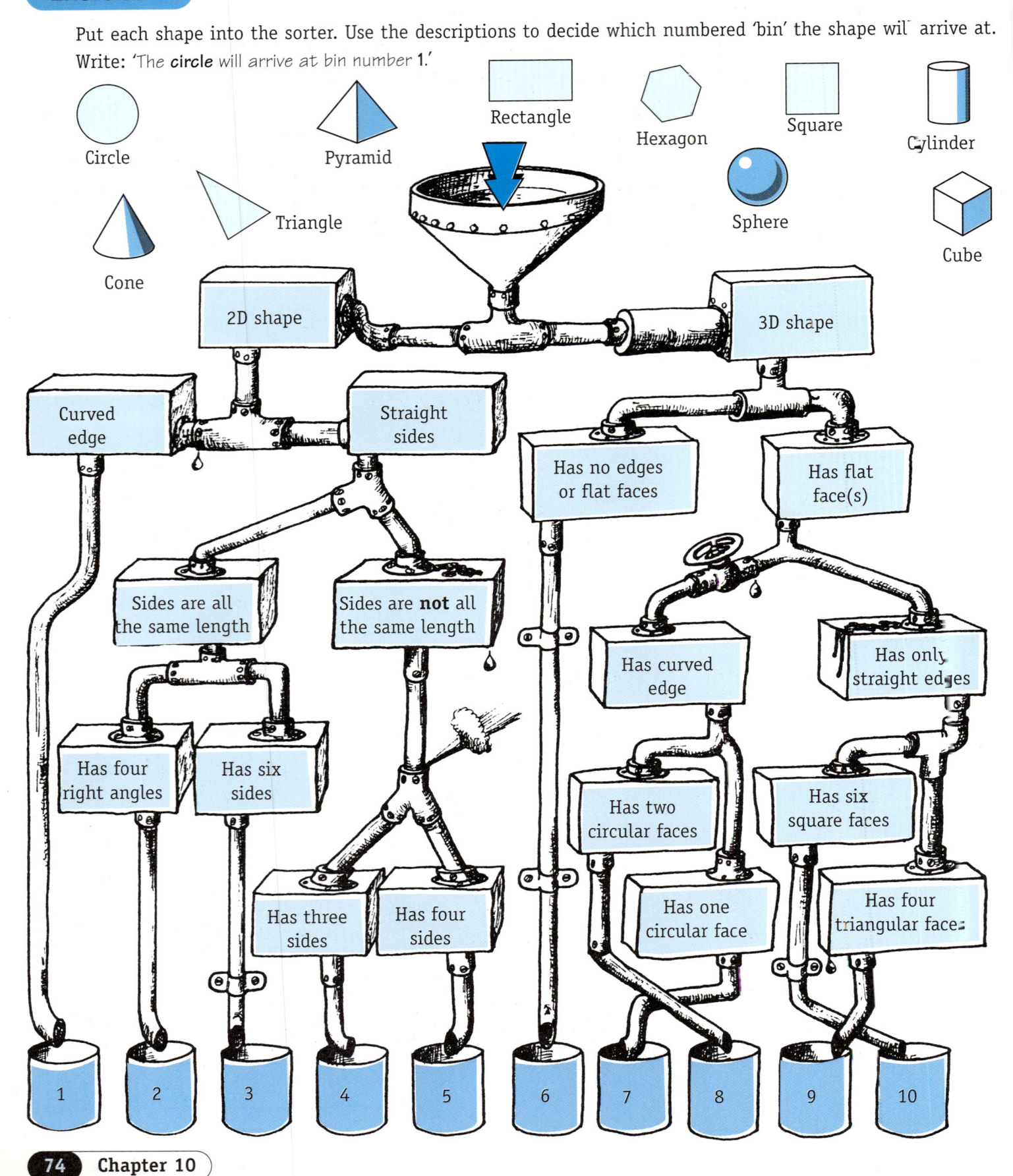

Put each shape into the sorter. Use the descriptions to decide which numbered 'bin' the shape will arrive at. Write: 'The **circle** will arrive at bin number **1**.'

Shapes: Circle, Pyramid, Rectangle, Hexagon, Square, Cylinder, Cone, Triangle, Sphere, Cube

Sorter flow:

- 2D shape
  - Curved edge → bin 1
  - Straight sides
    - Sides are all the same length
      - Has four right angles → bin 2
      - Has six sides → bin 3
    - Sides are **not** all the same length
      - Has three sides → bin 4
      - Has four sides → bin 5
- 3D shape
  - Has no edges or flat faces → bin 6
  - Has flat face(s)
    - Has curved edge
      - Has two circular faces → bin 7
      - Has one circular face → bin 8
    - Has only straight edges
      - Has six square faces → bin 9
      - Has four triangular faces → bin 10

Bins: 1, 2, 3, 4, 5, 6, 7, 8, 9, 10

74 Chapter 10

Volume is the amount of space taken up by a solid object.

For small solid shapes the unit of measurement is the **centimetre cube** (cm^3).

For larger shapes the unit of measurement is the **metre cube** (m^3).

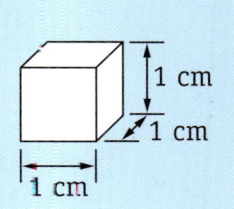

This is a centimetre cube. We can use 1 cm cubes to calculate the volume of solid shapes.

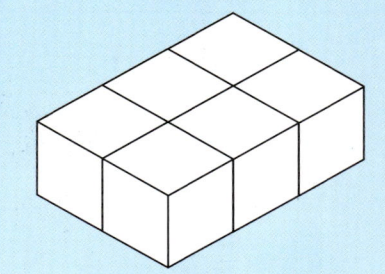

This solid shape has a volume of **6 centimetre cubes** which is written as **6 cm^3**. Count them to check.

Exercise 4

Find the volume of each solid shape by counting the centimetre cubes.
Give your answers in **cm^3** (centimetre cubes).

1

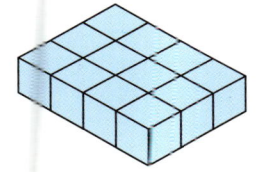

2

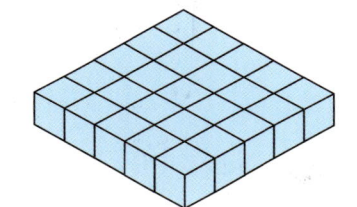

3

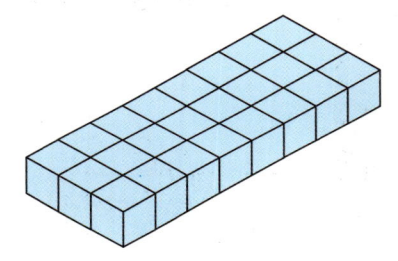

Exercise 5

Here are groups of centimetre cubes. Each group is put together to make a solid shape.
Match each group with the shape that it makes.

1

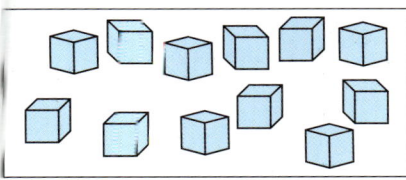

2

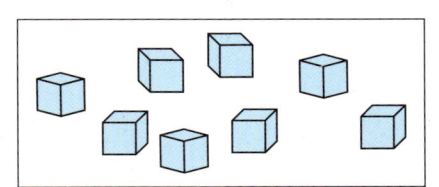

3

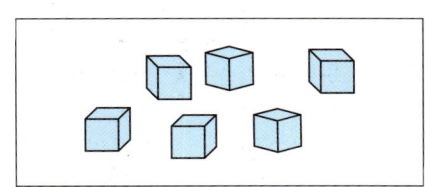

4

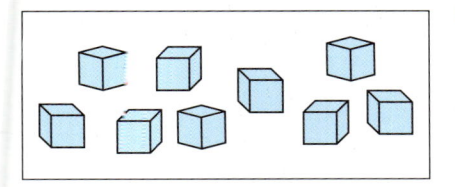

5

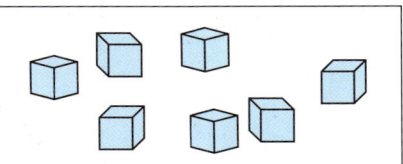

6

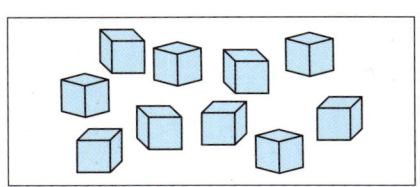

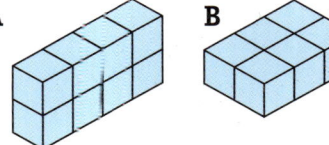

A   B   C 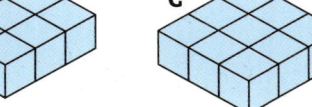   D 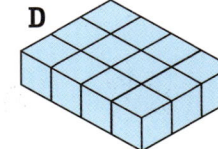   E 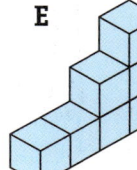   F

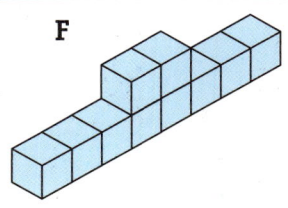

Solid Shape 75

Exercise 6

These solid shapes are made with 1 centimetre cubes. Match each shape with its volume.

| 7 cm³ | 11 cm³ | 18 cm³ | 5 cm³ | 14 cm³ | 24 cm³ | 16 cm³ | 20 cm³ |

1

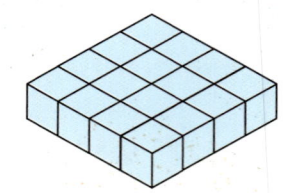

2

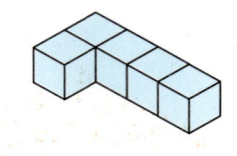

3

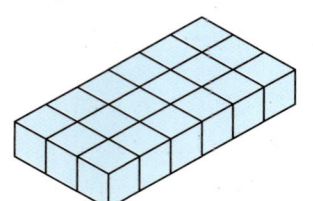

4

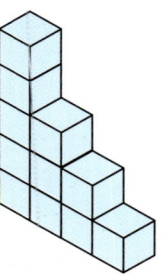

5

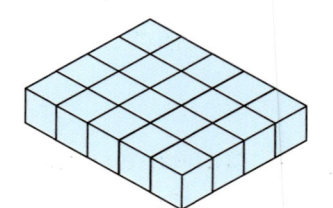

6

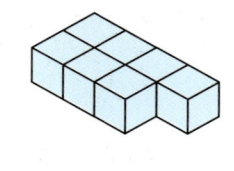

7

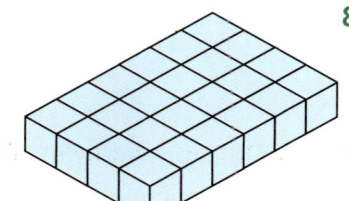

8

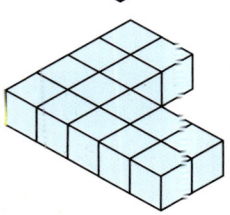

Exercise 7

1 These solid shapes are made with 1 centimetre cubes. Give the volume of each shape.

(a)

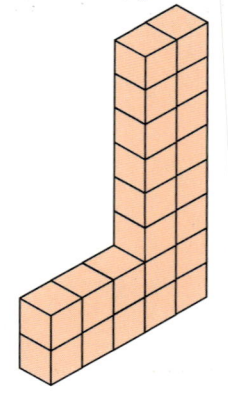

(b)

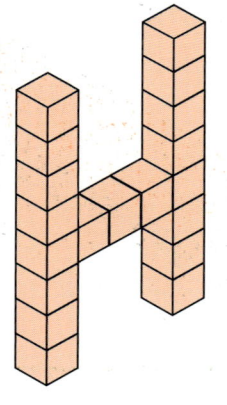

(c)

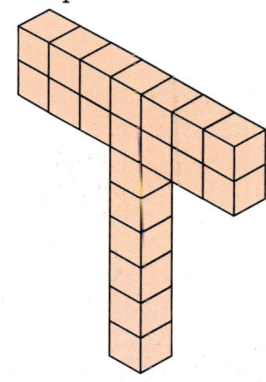

(d)

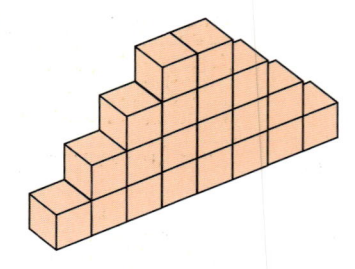

(e)

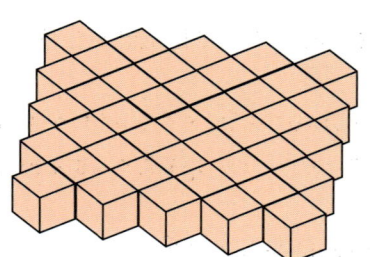

2 Which shape has the biggest volume?
3 Which shape has the smallest volume?
4 How many centimetre cubes were used in total to make all five shapes?

Chapter 10

Exercise 8

Each solid shape is made up of three layers of 1 centimetre cubes.

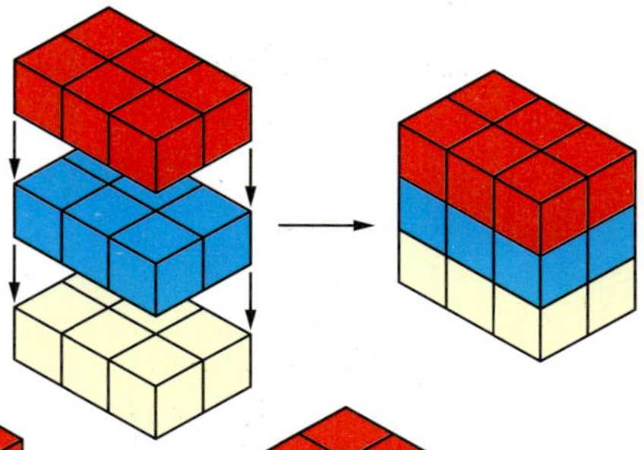

1. (a) What is the volume of the red layer?
   (b) What is the volume of the blue layer?
   (c) What is the volume of the yellow layer?
   (d) What is the volume of the shape when all the layers are put together?

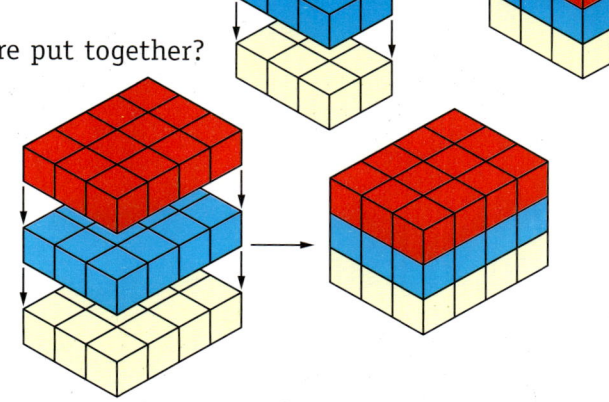

2. (a) What is the volume of the red layer?
   (b) What is the volume of the blue layer?
   (c) What is the volume of the yellow layer?
   (d) What is the volume of the shape when all the layers are put together?

Exercise 9

These solid shapes have more than one layer. Work out the volume of each shape in centimetre cubes.

1. 2 cm, 2 cm, 4 cm
2. 4 cm, 2 cm, 3 cm
3. 3 cm, 3 cm, 4 cm
4. 3 cm, 5 cm, 2 cm
5. 3 cm, 2 cm, 10 cm

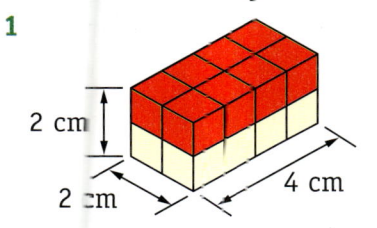

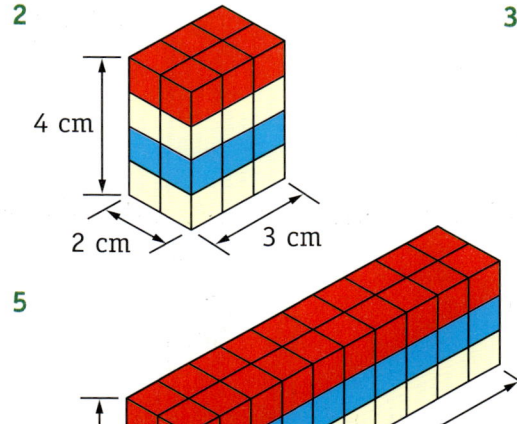

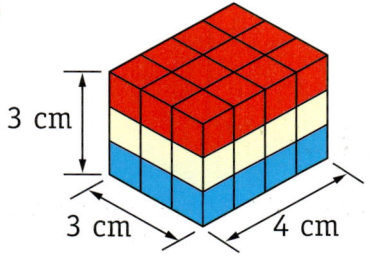

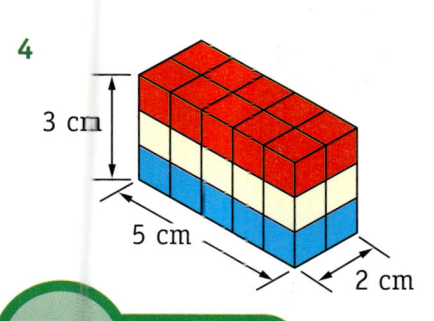

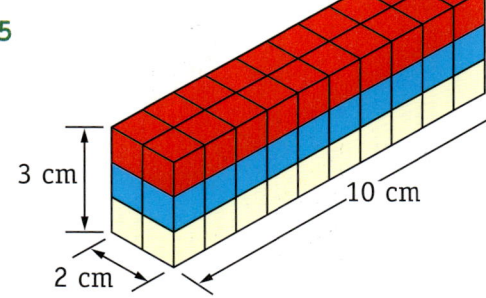

Key ideas

2D shapes have **two dimensions** – **length** and **width**.

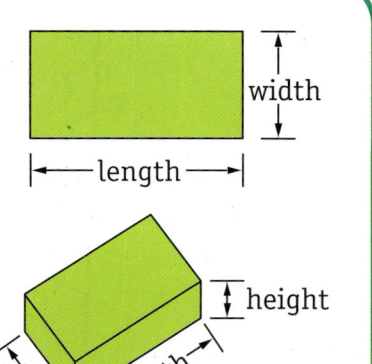

3D shapes have **three dimensions** – **length**, **width** and **height**.
3D shapes have volume. **Volume** is the space occupied by a solid shape.

The unit used to measure volume is the cube.
Small solid shapes are measured in **centimetre cubes** (cm^3).
Large solid shapes are measured in **metre cubes** (m^3).

Solid Shape 77

Chapter 11 Fractions

Step-up 1

1 (a) If you were making a spinner for a board game, which of the spinners below would be the most fair?

(b) Give a reason for your choice. 'I chose spinner [?] because...'

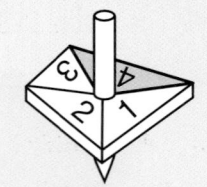

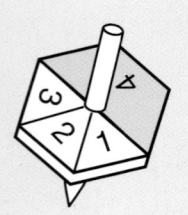

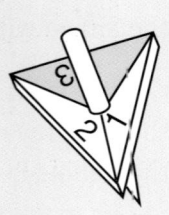

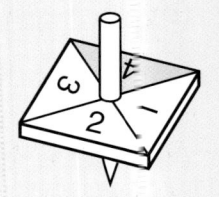

A   B   C   D

2 The drawings below show shapes that have been divided by shading, into these fractions: $\frac{1}{2}, \frac{1}{4}, \frac{1}{3}, \frac{1}{5}, \frac{1}{10}$
Copy this table. Match each drawing with the fraction that describes how much of the shape has been shaded.

Fraction	Drawing
$\frac{1}{2}$	A
$\frac{1}{4}$	
$\frac{1}{3}$	
$\frac{1}{5}$	
$\frac{1}{10}$	

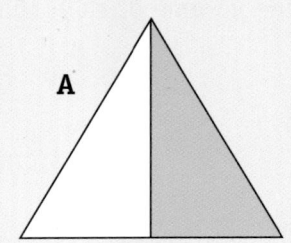

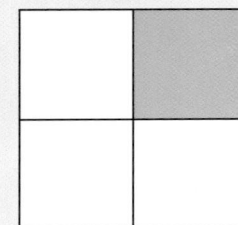

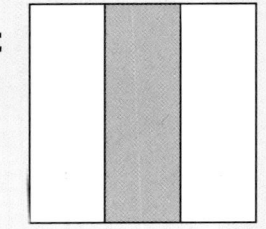

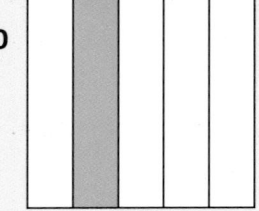

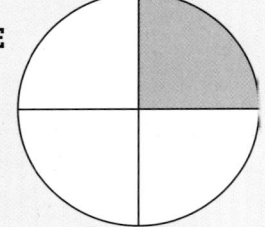

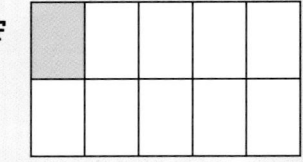

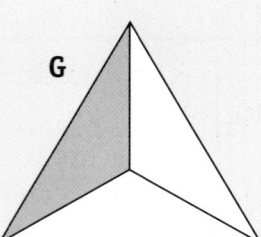

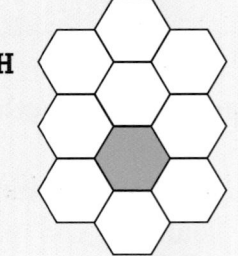

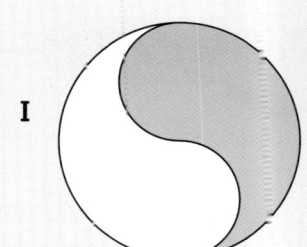

A   B   C
D   E   F
G   H   I

3 How many parts will there be if you divide a shape into:
(a) Thirds ($\frac{1}{3}$s) (b) Fifths ($\frac{1}{5}$s) (c) Halves ($\frac{1}{2}$s) (d) Ninths ($\frac{1}{9}$s)
(e) Sevenths ($\frac{1}{7}$s) (f) Sixths ($\frac{1}{6}$s) (g) Eighths ($\frac{1}{8}$s) (h) Tenths ($\frac{1}{10}$s)

Step-up 2

1 What fraction of each window has been broken?
Are more than half or less than half of the panes broken in each window?
(a) (b) (c) (d) (e)

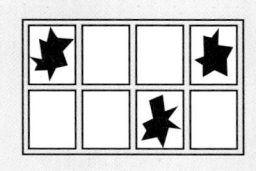

2 Here are 10 beach huts. What fraction has been blown over?

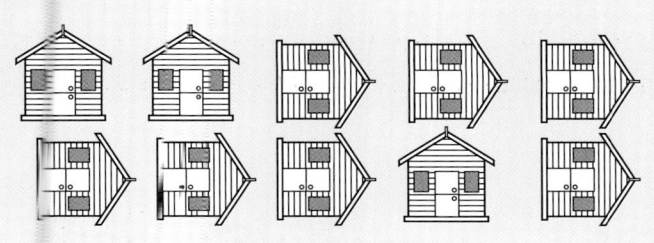

3 Some petals have been blown off this flower. What fraction of the petals has been blown away?

Before   After

4 Complete these division problems.
(a) 6 ÷ 2 = ?
(b) 8 ÷ 2 = ?
(c) 6 ÷ 3 = ?
(d) 10 ÷ 5 = ?
(e) 12 ÷ 2 = ?
(f) 8 ÷ 4 = ?
(g) 9 ÷ 3 = ?
(h) 12 ÷ 6 = ?
(i) 14 ÷ 2 = ?
(j) 15 ÷ 5 = ?
(k) 16 ÷ 4 = ?
(l) 15 ÷ 3 = ?

Remember: To find $\frac{1}{2}$ of a number we **divide** the number by 2.
$\frac{1}{2}$ of 10 = 10 ÷ 2 = 5
One half of 10 is 5.

5 Copy and complete these statements.
(a) To find $\frac{1}{3}$ of a number divide by ?
(b) To find $\frac{1}{10}$ of a number divide by ?
(c) To find $\frac{1}{4}$ of a number divide by ?
(d) To find $\frac{1}{5}$ of a number divide by ?

6 Copy these problems and fill in the missing figures. The first is done for you.
(a) $\frac{1}{4}$ of 8 = 8 ÷ 4 = 2
(b) $\frac{1}{2}$ of 6 = 6 ÷ 2 = ?
(c) $\frac{1}{3}$ of 9 = 9 ÷ 3 = ?
(d) $\frac{1}{10}$ of 20 = 20 ÷ 10 = ?
(e) $\frac{1}{5}$ of 15 = 15 ÷ 5 = ?
(f) $\frac{1}{3}$ of 15 = 15 ÷ 3 = ?
(g) $\frac{1}{2}$ of 12 = 12 ÷ ? = ?
(h) $\frac{1}{4}$ of 12 = 12 ÷ ? = ?
(i) $\frac{1}{5}$ of 10 = ? ÷ ? = ?
(j) $\frac{1}{2}$ of 10 = ? ÷ ? = ?
(k) $\frac{1}{2}$ of 18 = ? ÷ ? = ?
(l) $\frac{1}{3}$ of 18 = ? ÷ ? = ?

Fractions

Denominators and numerators

The **denominator** is the **bottom number**. It tells us how many equal parts something has been divided into.

$$\frac{3}{5}$$

The **numerator** is the **top number**. It tells us how many parts of the fraction we are working with.

This loaf of bread has been divided into 5 equal slices – as a fraction, the **bottom number** is 5.
3 of the slices are put onto a plate – the **top number** of the fraction (**numerator**) is 3.
$\frac{3}{5}$ of the loaf is on the plate.

Exercise 1

1 (a) This loaf is cut into 4 equal parts. What fraction is each slice? What is the bottom number?
   (b) 3 slices are eaten. What fraction has been eaten? What is the top number here?
   (c) One slice is left. What fraction is left? What is the top number?

2 (a) This loaf is cut into 8 equal parts. What fraction is each slice? What is the bottom number?
   (b) 3 slices are fed to the ducks. What fraction has been eaten? What is the top number here?
   (c) 5 slices are left. What fraction is left? What is the top number?

Exercise 2

Write out these fractions as words. Work with a partner.

1 $\frac{2}{3}$ 2 $\frac{3}{10}$ 3 $\frac{4}{5}$ 4 $\frac{2}{5}$

5 $\frac{3}{4}$ 6 $\frac{5}{6}$ 7 $\frac{7}{10}$ 8 $\frac{3}{5}$

| four-fifths | two-fifths | three-tenths | seven-tenths |
| two-thirds | three-fifths | five-sixths | three-quarters |

Exercise 3

Write out these fractions. Write the **bottom number** in red, and the **top number** in blue.
The first is done for you.

1 three-tenths   2 one-half   3 four-fifths
4 five-eighths   5 nine-tenths   6 one-eighth

one-tenth = $\frac{1}{10}$

80 Chapter 11

Remember

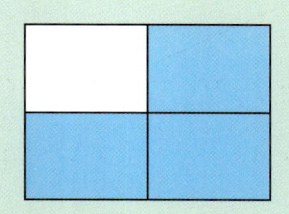

The **top number** tells us that 3 of the 4 parts are shaded. → $\dfrac{3}{4}$

The **bottom number** tells us that the shape is divided into 4 equal parts.

Exercise 4

What fraction of each drawing has been shaded?

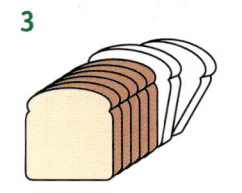

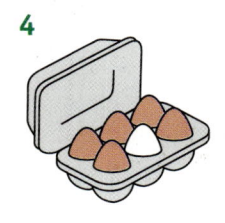

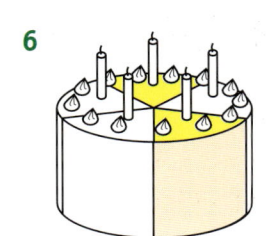

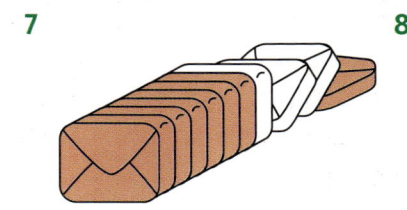

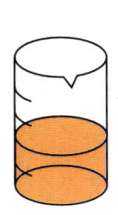

1   2   3   4

5   6   7   8

Exercise 5

Draw fractions into your book and shade them to match these descriptions. Like this:

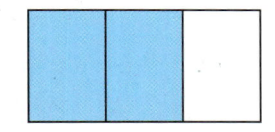

1 This fraction has a top number 2 and bottom number 3.
   3 parts with 2 parts shaded
2 This fraction has a top number 3, and bottom number 5. (Hint, use a rectangle 5 cm by 1 cm.)
3 This fraction has a bottom number 6 and five parts are shaded. (Hint, draw a rectangle 3 cm by 2 cm.)
4 This fraction has a top number of 5 and a bottom number of 8. (Hint, draw a rectangle 4 cm by 2 cm.)

Exercise 6

How many squares will you need to colour if you shade:
(a) $\frac{1}{4}$ of this rectangle.   (b) $\frac{3}{4}$ of the rectangle.

Fractions 81

Comparing fractions

Andy divides £12 into quarters ($\frac{1}{4}$s) and then into thirds ($\frac{1}{3}$s).

$\frac{1}{4}$ of £12 is £3 $\frac{1}{3}$ of £12 is £4

$\frac{1}{3}$ is a bigger amount than $\frac{1}{4}$ (if you are finding fractions of the same amount).

Exercise 7

Use the drawings to say which fraction is the larger.

1. Which is the larger amount, $\frac{1}{4}$ of £8 or $\frac{1}{2}$ of £8?

2. Which is the smaller, $\frac{1}{3}$ of £15 or $\frac{1}{5}$ of £15?

3. Which is larger, $\frac{1}{8}$ of £16 or $\frac{1}{4}$ of £16?

4. Which is the larger, $\frac{1}{5}$ of 10 kg or $\frac{1}{2}$ of 10 kg?

5. Which is the smaller, $\frac{1}{6}$ of 12 sweets or $\frac{1}{3}$ of 12 sweets?

6. Which is larger, $\frac{1}{2}$ of 18 kg or $\frac{1}{3}$ of 18 kg?

7. $\frac{2}{3}$ of this shape has been shaded. How many sixths ($\frac{1}{6}$s) are the same as $\frac{2}{3}$?

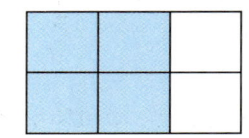

The collection of four £1 coins can be divided into ½s. It can also be divided into ¼s.

½ of £4 = £2   2/4 of £4 = £2

One-half (½) is the same as two quarters (2/4). These are equivalent fractions.

Exercise 8

In each drawing below, ½ of the coins have been shaded grey.
Use each drawing to find fractions that are the same as a ½, like ½ = 2/4.

1 6 coins

2 10 coins

3 12 coins

4 20 coins

5 8 coins

6 14 coins

7 What is wrong with this: 'I'm not very hungry so you have more of the pizza than me, I'll just have half'.

8 Rachel wants to share her drink equally with Anna. She says that Anna can have 3/6 of the drink. Anna says that Rachel is not being fair. Who is right? Explain your answer.

Key ideas

The **'bottom number' (denominator)** tells you how many equal parts there are in the fraction. The bottom number is 3. The shape is divided into 3 equal parts.

The **'top number' (numerator)** is the counter. It tells you how many divided parts you are working with.
The top number is 2 → 2/3. It tells you that 2 out of the 3 parts are shaded.

The same amount can be written as different fractions.
You can see that ½ is the same as 2/4 (a half is the same as two quarters).

Fractions   83

Chapter 12 Time

Step-up

1 For each clock choose the correct written time and the correct time in figures.
Write: 'Clock (a) – half past eleven, 11.30.'

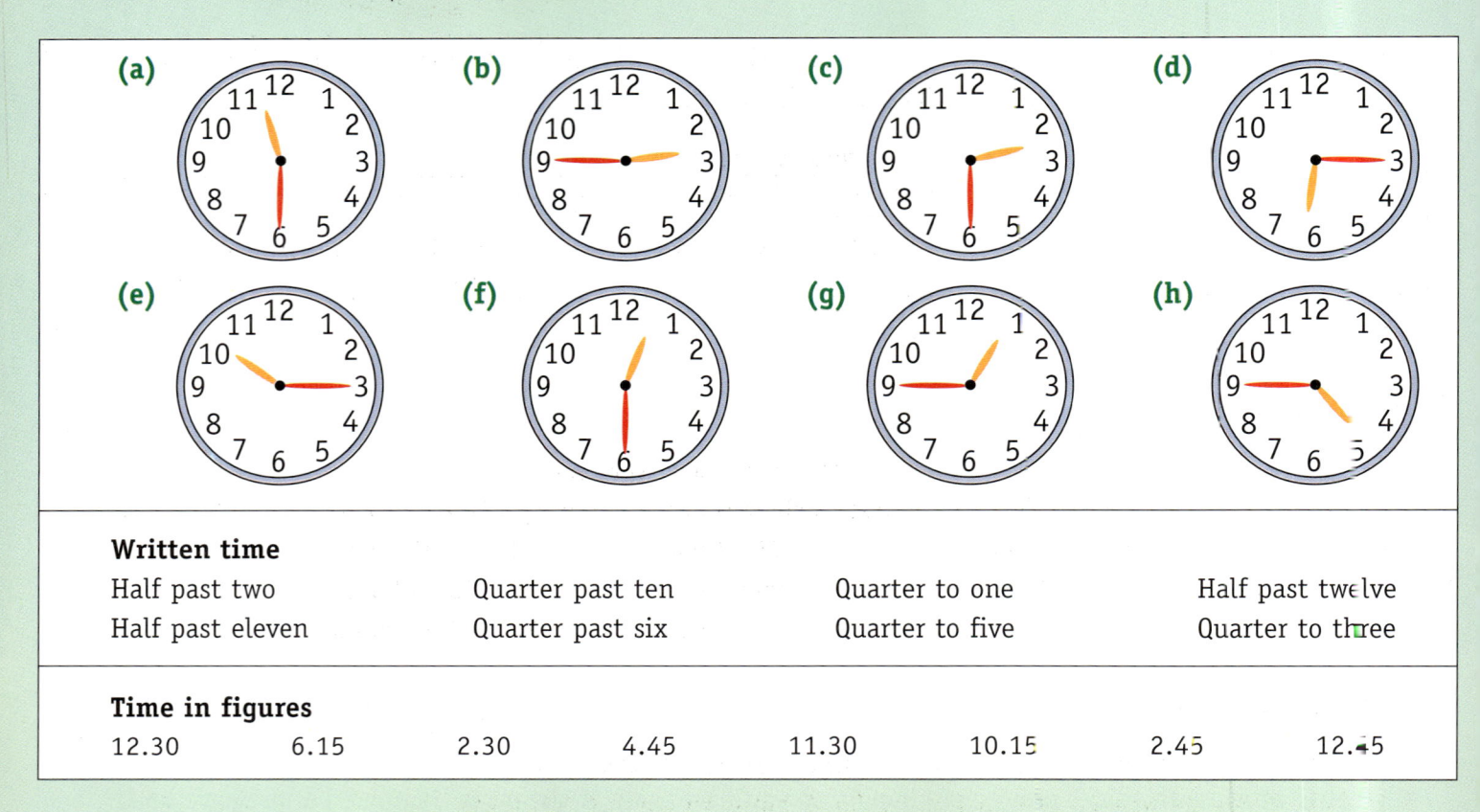

(a) (b) (c) (d) (e) (f) (g) (h)

Written time
Half past two   Quarter past ten   Quarter to one   Half past twelve
Half past eleven   Quarter past six   Quarter to five   Quarter to three

Time in figures
12.30   6.15   2.30   4.45   11.30   10.15   2.45   12.45

2 Remember: the hours from midnight, through the morning to midday are called **am**;
the hours from midday, through the evening to midnight are called **pm**.

Draw two columns and put these events under am or pm.

am	pm
	Sunset

(a) Sunset   (b) Bedtime   (c) Breakfast
(d) The evening news (e) Sunrise   (f) End of school
(g) Shops open   (h) Afternoon tea   (i) School starts
(j) Alarm clock rings (k) Shops shut (l) Street lights go on

3 What is the difference in time shown on each pair of clocks?
(a)   (b)

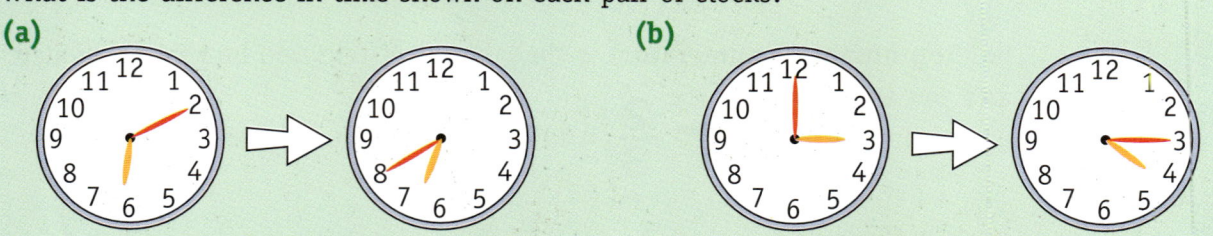

Chapter 12

The 24-hour clock

Joe is going on a train journey. His train leaves at 11.30. But is it 11.30 in the morning or 11.30 at night?

To avoid confusion, times are often given in 24-hour clock time. There are 24 hours in a day, so the hours are counted off from 0 to 24. The time line below shows this.

24-hour times

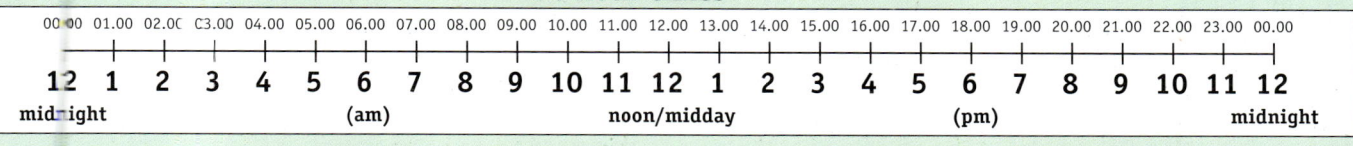

| 00.00 01.00 02.00 03.00 04.00 05.00 06.00 07.00 08.00 09.00 10.00 11.00 12.00 13.00 14.00 15.00 16.00 17.00 18.00 19.00 20.00 21.00 22.00 23.00 00.00 |
| 12   1   2   3   4   5   6   7   8   9   10 11 12   1   2   3   4   5   6   7   8   9   10 11 12 |
| midnight   (am)   noon/midday   (pm)   midnight |

Exercise 1

Use the time line to convert these **24-hour** times to **am** or **pm** times.

The word 'hours' is written after the figures to show that we are using 24-hour times.

1 07.00 hours   2 14.00 hours   3 03.00 hours   4 15.00 hours
5 18.00 hours   6 21.00 hours   7 09.00 hours   8 16.00 hours
9 02.00 hours   10 23.00 hours   11 04.00 hours   12 20.00 hours

Exercise 2

Use the time line to convert these **am** and **pm** times to **24-hour** times.

24-hour times are written as four figures. So, **6 am** is written **06.00 hours**.

1 2 am   2 2 pm   3 5 am   4 5 pm   5 10 am   6 10 pm
7 8 am   8 8 pm   9 9 pm   10 3 am   11 11 pm   12 4 pm

Exercise 3

The 24-hour times show when Joe is doing these things. Re-write the times as **am** or **pm** times.
Write: 'Combing hair – 7.15 am.'

Combing hair –
07.15 hours

Packing case –
09.25 hours

Phones Grannie –
12.20 hours

Has lunch –
13.30 hours

Goes to bank –
15.25 hours

Bus ride –
18.45 hours

Buys train ticket –
21.50 hours

Waiting for train –
23.20 hours

Time 85

24-hour times are also spoken in a certain way.

07.00 is spoken as 'O-seven hundred hours.'

13.00 would be 'Thirteen hundred hours.'

16.45 would be 'Sixteen forty-five.'

Exercise 4

1. Write these spoken times as figures.
   - (a) 'O-five hundred hours.'
   - (b) 'Sixteen hundred hours.'
   - (c) 'Twenty-one hundred hours.'
   - (d) 'O-nine hundred hours.'
   - (e) 'Twenty-three hundred hours.'
   - (f) 'Eleven hundred hours.'

2. These spoken times involve hours and minutes. Write them as figures.
   'O-six twenty-five' is written 06.25. 'Fifteen forty-five' is written 15.45.
   - (a) 'Eleven fifteen.'
   - (b) 'O-eight twenty.'
   - (c) 'Twelve O-five.'
   - (d) 'Twenty-three twenty-five.'
   - (e) 'O-five thirty-five.'
   - (f) 'Sixteen O-five.'

24-hour times

00.00	01.00	02.00	03.00	04.00	05.00	06.00	07.00	08.00	09.00	10.00	11.00	12.00	13.00	14.00	15.00	16.00	17.00	18.00	19.00	20.00	21.00	22.00	23.00	00.00
12	1	2	3	4	5	6	7	8	9	10	11	12	1	2	3	4	5	6	7	8	9	10	11	12
midnight					(am)							noon/midday						(pm)						midnight

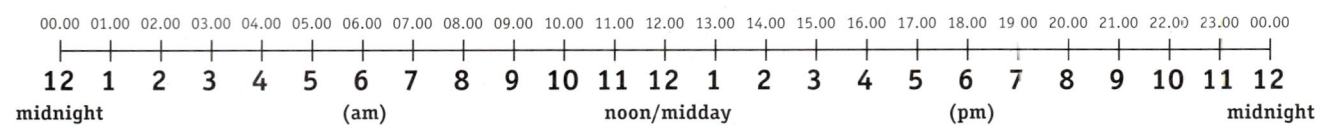

Exercise 5

Use the spoken information to answer the questions. The clock shows the time the train arrives.

1. Where is this train from?

2. Where is this train from?

3. Where is this train from?

4. Where is this train from?

5. Where is this train from?

The Stafford train will arrive at eleven thirty.

The Widnes train will arrive at seventeen ten.

The Glasgow train will arrive at nineteen forty-five.

The Preston train will arrive at twenty-one hundred hours.

The Chester train will arrive at twenty-three fifteen.

Joe is travelling from Newcastle to Dublin.
He arrives at Newcastle Central station to catch the Holyhead train.
He has been told that the train will leave at 11.30.
Joe thought that the train would leave at 11.30 at night.
He was wrong! The train will leave at 11.30 in the morning!
Here is the map of the journey.

Only twelve hours to wait and it's a nice night.

Exercise 6

Answer these questions about the map.

1. Which is the first station after Newcastle?
2. Which station comes between Chester and York?
3. Which station comes before Llandudno?
4. Between which two towns does the ferry travel?

24-hour times

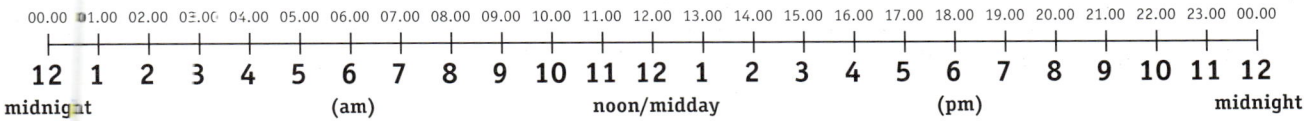

```
00.00 01.00 02.00 03.00 04.00 05.00 06.00 07.00 08.00 09.00 10.00 11.00 12.00 13.00 14.00 15.00 16.00 17.00 18.00 19.00 20.00 21.00 22.00 23.00 00.00
 12   1    2    3    4    5    6    7    8    9   10   11   12    1    2    3    4    5    6    7    8    9   10   11   12
midnight         (am)                          noon/midday                    (pm)                              midnight
```

Here is the timetable of Joe's train journey highlighted in **green**.

Newcastle	08.32	10.05	**11.30**	18.00
York	09.25	11.00	**12.30**	18.55
Manchester	10.40	12.09	**14.06**	19.02
Chester	11.45	13.05	**15.15**	20.00
Llandudno	12.48	14.08	**16.20**	—
Llanfairpwll.	—	14.40	**17.00**	—
Holyhead	13.50	15.00	**17.25**	22.10

Exercise 7

1. Use the timetable to answer these questions about Joe's train journey.
   (a) How long does the train take to travel from Newcastle to York?
   (b) At what time will the train arrive in Chester?
   (c) At what time will the train arrive in Holyhead?

2. You can use the timetable **and** the map to answer these questions.
   (a) At which station will the train be at 4.20 pm?
   (b) The train will be between which two stations at 12 noon?
   (c) The train will be between which two stations at 2.30 pm?
   (d) Where will the train be at 5 pm? (This village has the longest name in Britain! See page 88 for the full spelling.)

Time

25 minutes before arriving at Holyhead, Joe looks out of the window and sees the name of the station.

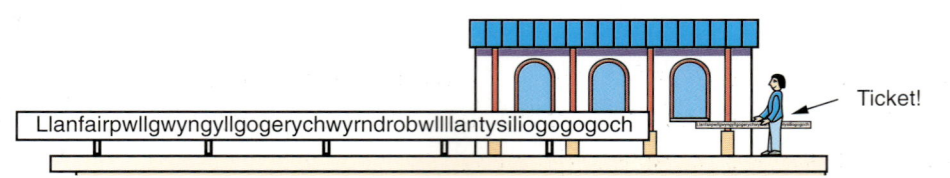

Llanfairpwllgwyngyllgogerychwyrndrobwllllantysiliogogogoch

Ticket!

At Holyhead Joe goes to the ferry terminal. Here are the times of the ferry.
Joe buys a ticket for the 18.30 ferry (it has been highlighted in green).

Holyhead	04.20	09.50	12.10	16.00	18.30
	↓	↓	↓	↓	↓
Dublin	08.30	13.20	15.45	19.30	22.00

Goodness, is that Professor Fishbird?

Exercise 8

1. Re-write the ferry timetable using am and pm times.
2. How long does the 18.30 ferry take to reach Dublin?
3. At what time does the 4 pm ferry from Holyhead arrive in Dublin?

Exercise 9

Match each am/pm time on the left with a clock display, a 24-hour time and a spoken time.
Write: '1 3.20 am → Clock F → 03.20 hours → 0-three twenty.'

	am/pm time	Clock display		24-hour time	Spoken time
1	3.20 am	A	B	14.00 hours	'O-eight hundred hours.'
2	2.00 pm			06.15 hours	'Seventeen twenty-five.'
3	7.45 pm	C	D	22.30 hours	'Twenty-two thirty.'
4	11.05 am			08.00 hours	'Eleven 0-five.'
5	5.25 pm	E	F	17.25 hours	'Fourteen hundred hours.'
6	6.15 am			19.45 hours	'O-three twenty.'
7	10.30 pm	G	H	11.05 hours	'Nineteen forty-five.'
8	8.00 am			03.20 hours	'Six fifteen.'

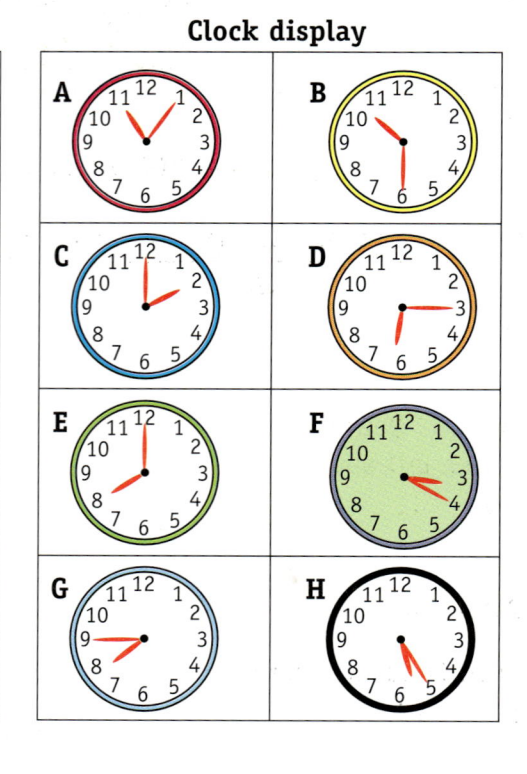

BC and AD

In this country we count the years of the calendar from the birth of Jesus Christ.
The years before Christ's birth have the letters **BC** (before Christ) added to them.
So **650 BC** is **six hundred and fifty** years **before** Christ's birth.

The letters **AD** (anno Domini) are added to a date to show that it is after the birth of Christ.
So **1066 AD** is a date **one thousand and sixty-six** years **after** the birth of Christ.
(**BC** is also known as **BCE** – Before Common Era, whilst **AD** can be called **CE** – Common Era.)

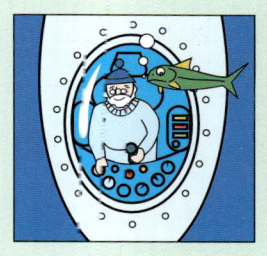

Professor Fishbird's favourite subject is history.
He builds a time machine to travel back in time and see events in the past.
In his first test run he takes a short jump in time to the year 2000 AD.
He arrives in the year 2000 AD and decides to make a bigger jump.
He wants to go back 1500 years to the year 500 AD. He sets the dials.

Professor Fishbird presses the start button and in a flash he arrives in the year 500 AD. However, he does not like what he sees and decides to go back further in time.

The journey so far...

Exercise 10

Calculate these problems in time. Use the time line to help you.

1. From the year 500 AD the next jump is 300 years back in time.
   (a) What year is he now in? (b) Is it AD or BC?

2. From this date, he jumps back 400 years.
   (a) What year is he now in? (b) Is it AD or BC?

3. The professor wants to jump to the moment at which Christ was born.
   (a) Does he have to jump backwards or forwards in time?
   (b) How many years does he have to jump?

4. He now wants to jump back further in time. Will the date be BC or AD?

Exercise 11

The professor plans to explore the Seven Wonders of the World.
He will start in 2600 BC when he can see the Great Pyramid of Khufu being built.

Here are the Seven Wonders of the World and the dates that the professor visited them.

- Mausoleum of Halicarnassus — 353 BC
- Colossus of Rhodes — 280 BC
- Hanging Gardens of Babylon — 600 BC
- Statue of Zeus — 450 BC
- Great Pyramid of Khufu — 2600 BC
- Pharos of Alexandria — 280 BC
- Temple of Artemis — 356 BC

1 The time line shows at which point in time the professor stopped to visit the Seven Wonders of the World.
Each letter on the time line stands for one of the Seven Wonders and when it was built.
Write the letter, the name of the 'Wonder' and the year that it was built, like this:
'A, Great Pyramid of Khufu, 2600 BC.'

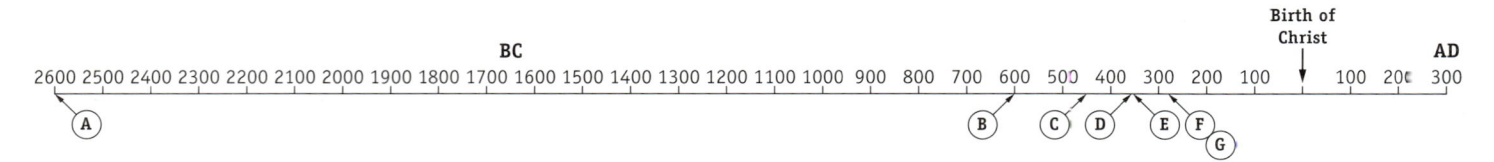

(Time line: A at 2600 BC; B at ~600 BC; C at ~450 BC; D at ~400 BC; E at ~350 BC; F at ~300 BC; G at ~280 BC; Birth of Christ marked, then AD 100, 200, 300.)

2 Which of the Seven Wonders was built in 356 BC?
3 Which two 'Wonders' were built in 280 BC?
4 Which is older, 250 BC or 100 BC?
5 Which is older, 530 BC or 900 BC?
6 Which is older, the Great Pyramid of Khufu or the Statue of Zeus?
7 Which date is closer to the modern day: 525 BC, 750 BC or 120 BC?
8 Which date is closer to the modern day: 2800 BC, 600 BC or 1300 BC?
9 How many years after the Great Pyramid of Khufu were the Hanging Gardens of Babylon built?
10 How many of the Seven Wonders were built between 500 BC and 300 BC?
11 How many of the Seven Wonders were built before 400 BC?
12 How many years has the professor travelled from 2600 BC to 280 BC?

Exercise 12

1. Julius Caesar lived from 100 BC to 44 BC.

   Use the time line to work out how long he lived.

2. Caesar Augustus ruled from 27 BC to 14 AD.

   Use the time line to work out how long he ruled (take care).

3. The Great Wall of China is 1900 km long. Work began in 221 BC and the wall was finished in 204 BC.

   Use the time line to work out how long it took to build the wall.

4. Ramses II ruled Egypt from about 1280 BC to 1220 BC.

   Use the time line to work out how long he ruled.

5. Professor Fishbird is returning home. His journey begins in 800 BC.
   He will complete the journey back to the modern day in four jumps.
   Calculate the length in time of each jump.

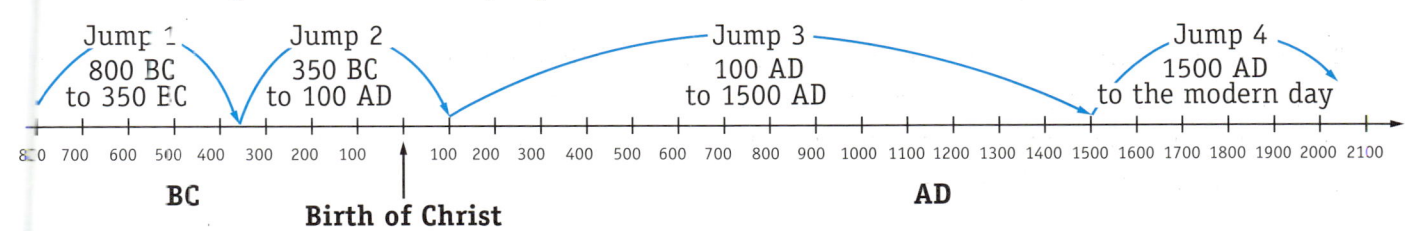

   Jump 1: 800 BC to 350 BC
   Jump 2: 350 BC to 100 AD
   Jump 3: 100 AD to 1500 AD
   Jump 4: 1500 AD to the modern day

Key ideas

am These are the hours from midnight, through the morning to midday.
pm These are the hours from midday, through the evening to midnight.

24-hour time counts the hours from 0 to 24.

BC Dates and events before the birth of Christ have the letters BC (before Christ).
So, 100 BC is the year one hundred years before the birth of Christ.
AD Dates and events after the birth of Christ have the letters AD (anno Domini).
(**BC** is also known as **BCE** – Before Common Era, whilst **AD** can be called **CE** – Common Era.)

Time 91

Chapter 13 Data Handling
Step-up

Liz is collecting coins showing the heads of these four British monarchs.

King George IV   King William IV   Queen Victoria   King Edward VII

1 She sorts the coins below into four groups by making a **tally chart** and finding the frequency of each coin.
Use Worksheet 40 to sort and tally the coins. Find the frequency of each coin.

2 Use your chart to help you answer these questions.
(a) Which coin is the **mode** of Liz's collection?
(b) Which coin is the **least frequent**?

3 Look at the four diagrams below. Which diagram most accurately represents the data in your chart?

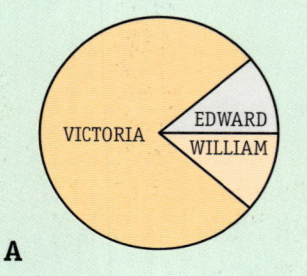

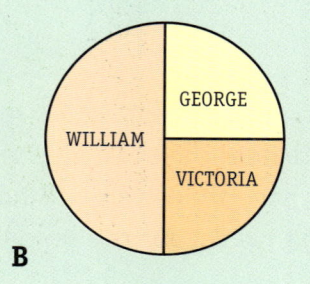

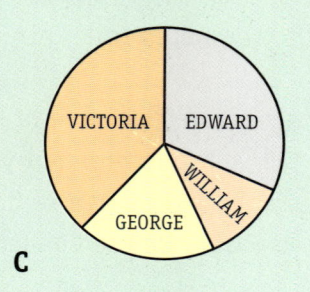

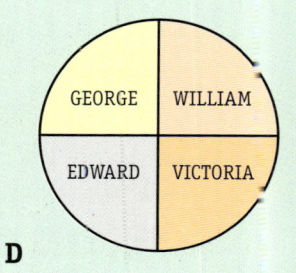

A   B   C   D

92 Chapter 13

Exercise 1

This is a list of the monarchs since 1485.

1485–1509	Henry VII
1509–1547	Henry VIII
1547–1553	Edward VI
1553–1558	Mary I
1558–1603	Elizabeth I
1603–1625	James I of England
1625–1649	Charles I
1649–1660	no ruling monarch
1660–1685	Charles II
1685–1688	James II
1689–1702	William III and Mary II
1702–1714	Anne
1714–1727	George I
1727–1760	George II
1760–1820	George III
1820–1830	George IV
1830–1837	William IV
1837–1901	Victoria
1901–1910	Edward VII
1910–1936	George V
1936	Edward VIII
1936–1952	George VI
1952 to date	Elizabeth II

1. Between which years did Queen Anne reign?
2. For how many years did Queen Anne reign?
3. Who reigned between 1625 and 1649?
4. Who reigned between George IV and Queen Victoria?
5. Which King came before George V?
6. How many Kings are there? How many Queens are there?
7. Which is the most popular name on the list?
8. Who reigned before Mary I?
9. Who reigned between Henry VIII and Mary I?
10. Who was on the throne for less than 1 year?

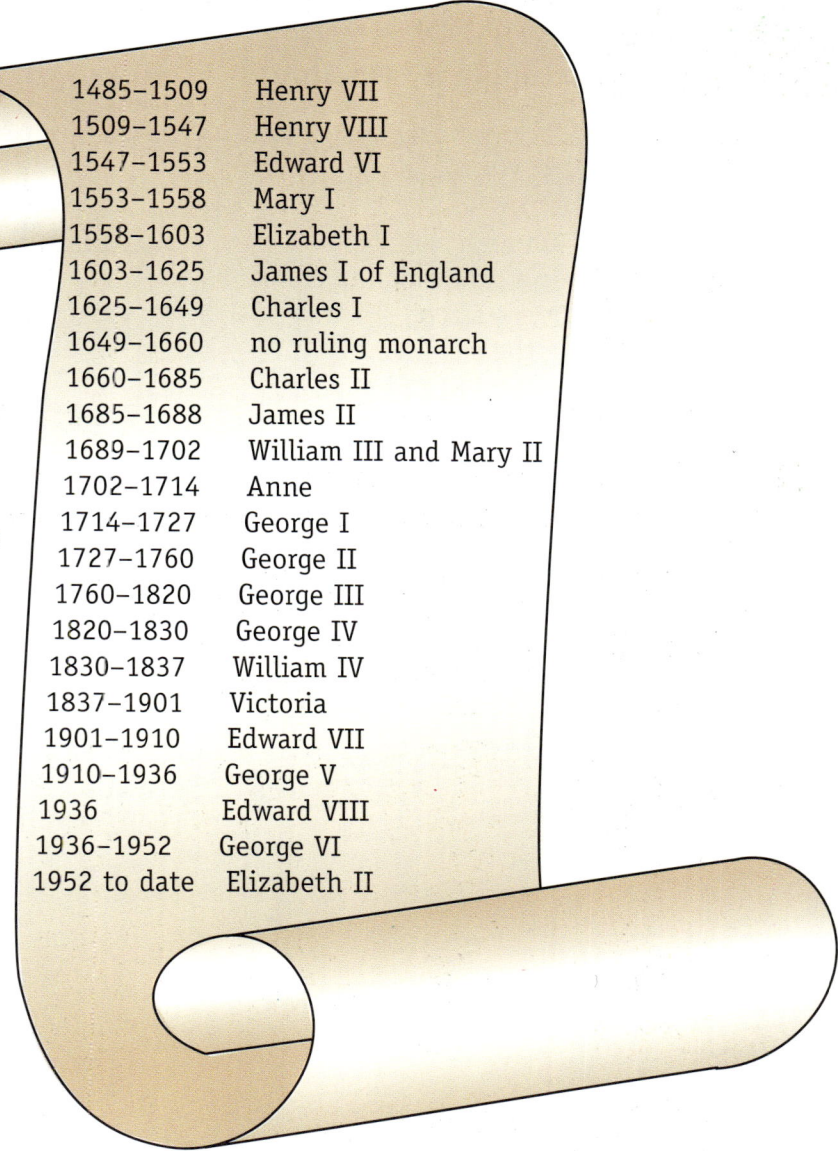

Exercise 2

The bar chart shows how many years some of the monarchs were on the throne.
Use it to answer these questions.

1. Which monarch reigned for almost 35 years?
2. Which monarch reigned for about 60 years?
3. Who reigned for the longest period of time?
4. Who reigned for the shortest period of time?
5. For approximately how many years did George I reign?
6. For approximately how many years did George V reign?
7. Two monarchs were on the throne for over 120 years between them. Who were they?
8. How many monarchs reigned for less than 20 years?

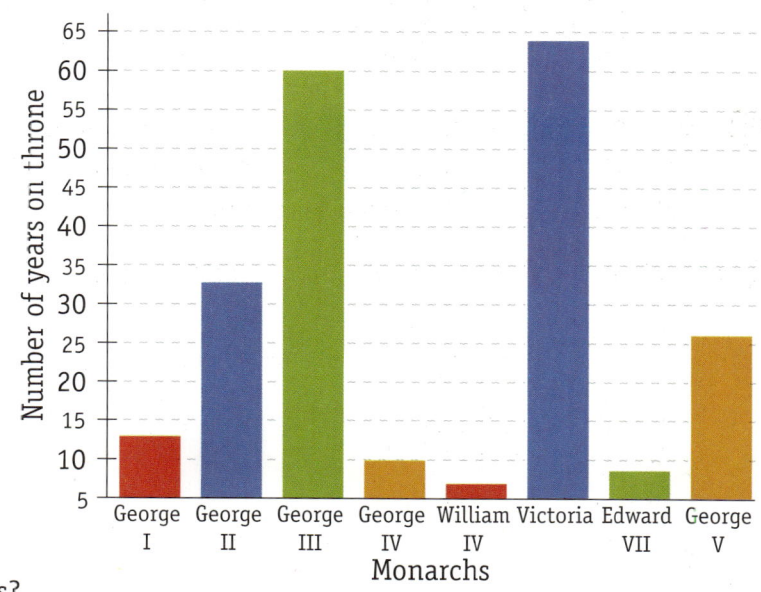

Data Handling 93

Putting data into groups

At Pinchfoot's shoe shop Henry has to sort boxes of shoes.
Here is this week's order.

On each shoe box is a card which tells him:
- the size;
- the colour;
- the price.

8 Brown £20	6 Black £12	7 Grey £30	8 Red £20	9 Brown £40	7 Brown £20	8 White £35
6 Red £10	12 Brown £48	8 Brown £45	11 Black £55	9 Red £15	10 Black £36	7 Brown £35
10 Black £38	8 Black £35	11 Black £48	10 Grey £35	8 Grey £30	7 Black £45	9 Black £28
8 Brown £48	9 White £48	7 Grey £25	7 Brown £59	9 Brown £57	8 Black £45	10 Red £25
7 Black £42	6 Brown £31	9 Brown £35	9 Brown £59	8 Red £30	7 Black £37	8 Brown £45

There are different ways that the boxes can be sorted.

Exercise 3

Discuss these questions with your partner or your teacher.

1. Which way has Henry chosen to sort the boxes?
2. Write down other ways the boxes can be sorted.
3. Using Henry's stack, which shoe size do you think the shop expects to sell the most of?
4. Why do you think that the shop ordered only one pair of size 12 shoes?
5. What does this display tell us about people's **average** shoe size?
6. Do you think that this is a children's shoe shop? Give a reason for your answer.
7. Which shoe size is the **mode**?

94 Chapter 13

Interval sizes

Henry's stack on page 94 is easy to make.
He has only 7 **different** shoe sizes (6, 7, 8, 9, 10, 11 and 12).
When he tries to sort the shoes by price he has trouble ...

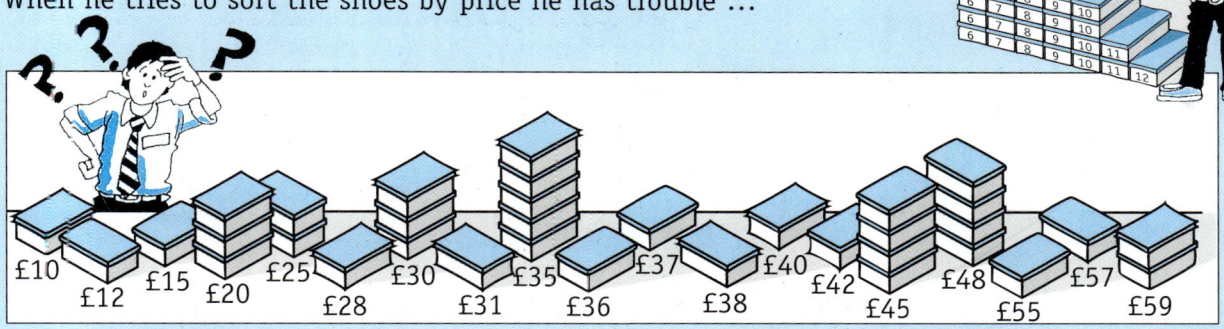

£10 £12 £15 £20 £25 £28 £30 £31 £35 £36 £37 £38 £40 £42 £45 £48 £55 £57 £59

There are 19 **different** prices, so he has 19 different piles. Henry decides that he needs to group the prices. He decides to group the prices into £10 **intervals**.

Exercise 4

Interval 1	£10–£19
Interval 2	?
Interval 3	?
Interval 4	?
Interval 5	?

1 What are the price intervals for the shoes shown on page 94?
   Remember that these prices go up in **intervals** of £10.
   Copy and complete the list alongside.

2 Why did Henry start at £10–£19?

3 What is the size of the interval?
   (Start at £10 and count to £19. Check each interval to see if they are all the same.)

4 Make a chart of price intervals then draw a diagram to show the shoes grouped by price.
   (Use Worksheet 41 for this task.)

5 Why would it be difficult to make an interval of shoe colour?

Exercise 5

This drawing shows a new delivery of Summer sandals.

1 Sort the sandals: **(a)** by size; **(b)** by price.
2 Decide if you need to group the values into intervals.
3 Make tally charts to show how you sorted the sandals.
   (Use Worksheet 42 for this task.)

Size 1 £14.00	Size 6 £13.00	Size 8 £8.00	Size 4 £9.50	Size 11 £20.99
Size 8 £16.00	Size 7 £31.99	Size 5 £26.00	Size 9 £4.50	Size 6 £36.00
Size 2 £40.99	Size 2 £55.00	Size 7 £67.99	Size 4 £43.99	Size 12 £59.99
Size 4 £17.00	Size 3 £29.99	Size 12 £48.00	Size 10 £8.00	Size 10 £13.50
Size 4 £19.99	Size 7 £50.99	Size 6 £60.99	Size 9 £72.00	Size 9 £9.99
Size 13 £11.99	Size 8 £44.99	Size 8 £54.99	Size 2 £16.99	Size 3 £14.50
Size 9 £69.99	Size 7 £74.99	Size 7 £43.50	Size 1 £3.50	Size 3 £24.99

Data Handling

Exercise 6

Look at the data below about collar sizes.

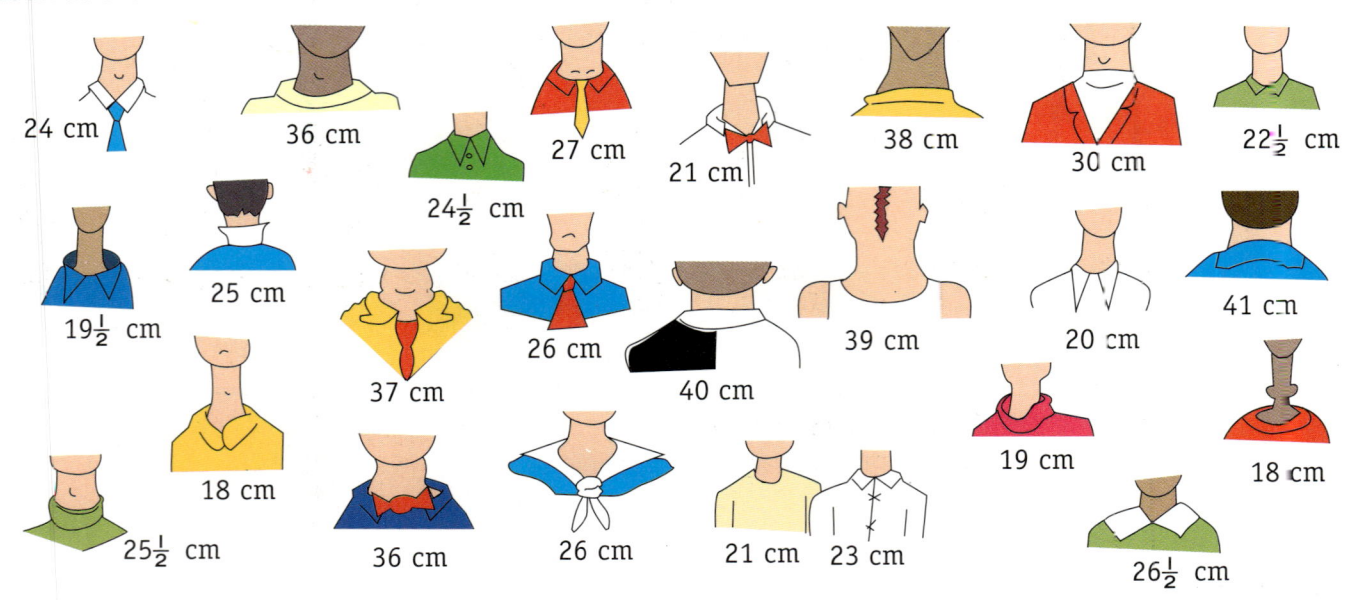

24 cm, 36 cm, 27 cm, 21 cm, 38 cm, 30 cm, $22\frac{1}{2}$ cm, $24\frac{1}{2}$ cm, $19\frac{1}{2}$ cm, 25 cm, 26 cm, 39 cm, 20 cm, 41 cm, 37 cm, 40 cm, 19 cm, 18 cm, $25\frac{1}{2}$ cm, 18 cm, 36 cm, 26 cm, 21 cm, 23 cm, $26\frac{1}{2}$ cm

1. Which are the smallest and largest collar sizes?
2. Sort the data into groups. Decide upon the interval size of the groups and make a tally chart using the intervals that you chose.
3. What is the **modal** group?

Exercise 7

1st Time: 21 mins	2nd Time: 21 mins	3rd Time: 24 mins	4th Time: 25 mins	5th Time: 28 mins	6th Time: 29 mins
7th Time: 31 mins	8th Time: 32 mins	9th Time: 34 mins	10th Time: 37 mins	11th Time: 40 mins	12th Time: 41 mins
13th Time: 42 mins	14th Time: 44 mins	15th Time: 44 mins	16th Time: 45 mins	17th Time: 48 mins	18th Time: 49 mins
19th Time: 50 mins	20th Time: 50 mins	21st Time: 52 mins	22nd Time: 53 mins	23rd Time: 54 mins	24th Time: 55 mins
25th Time: 56 mins	26th Time: 57 mins	27th Time: 58 mins	28th Time: 59 mins	29th Time: 63 mins	30th Time: 69 mins

Barrington keeps the times for an under 13's cross country run. He records the times (to the nearest minute) on the chart above.

1. Group the times into intervals of 10 minutes, starting at 21 minutes.
2. Use your tally chart to find the **modal** time taken by the runners.
3. If you drew a bar chart of these groups, which group would have the longest bar?
4. Show all of the groups on a bar chart. Check your answer to question 3.

Chapter 13

The median

The people in this line are all different heights, so there is no **mode**.
Can you think of another way to give an **average** height? Who would you choose?

| Tom | Fred | Kelvin | Brenda | Ayesha | Hannah | Surjit | Michael | Pauline |

Ayesha is in the middle of the line.
There are the same number of people taller than her, as there are shorter than her.
We can say that she is the **average** height for that line of people.
This type of average is called the **median**.

Exercise 8

Find the **median** in each display below.
You will have to write the shoe sizes in order before you try to find the **median**.

1. 8, 2, 11, 9, 3, 7, 5, 12, 6
   → 2, 3, 5, 6, 7, 8, 9, 11, 12

2. 5, 7, 8, 10, 11

3. 2, 9, 5, 4, 6, 9, 7, 3, 9

4. 6, 12, 13, 3, 11, 4, 9, 2, 10

5. 3, 12, 10, 9, 7, 3, 3, 12, 3

6. 7, 11, 6, 5, 7, 3, 9, 7, 7

7. 4, 13, 12, 4, 7, 5, 4, 11, 4, 11, 8

8. Some of the displays have **modes**. Say which type of average tells us the most about each display.

There is an **even number** of shoe boxes in this pile.

| 8 Brown £20 | 6 Black £12 | 7 Grey £30 |
| 6 Red £10 | 12 Brown £48 | 8 Brown £45 |

| 6 Red £10 | 6 Black £12 | 8 Brown £20 | 7 Grey £30 | 8 Brown £45 | 12 Brown £48 |

When the shoes are arranged in order of **price** there is no 'single middle' value. There are two prices in the middle: £20 and £30. The **median** is halfway between these two. The **median** is £25.

Exercise 9

1. Follow these instructions to find the median shoe **size** in the drawing above.
   - Write the shoe sizes in order (smallest to largest).
   - Find the two 'middle' sizes.
   - Find the halfway size between the two middle values. This is the median average.

2. Does this size really happen in this small display?

3. Would this value be useful as an average? Explain your answer in a short sentence.

Exercise 10

Find the median average of each display of numbers. For each display:
- write the numbers in order (smallest to largest);
- find the two 'middle' values;
- work out the halfway value. This is the median.

1. £15, £9, £10, £16, £31, £26, £25, £18

2. 2, 15, 8, 2, 20, 16, 2, 19, 17, 19

Exercise 11

8 Red £20	7 Brown £40	7 Brown £20	12 White £35
11 Black £55	9 Red £15	10 Black £36	7 Brown £37
10 Grey £34	6 Grey £30	7 Black £45	9 Black £28
7 Brown £59	9 Brown £57	8 Black £45	10 Red £25

1 Find the median and mode for the shoe **sizes**.

2 Which of these two averages gives us the more useful information?

3 Explain why your choice of average is the better one.

4 Find the median and mode for the shoe **prices**.

5 Does the median give us a good idea of the average price of the shoes on the shelf. Explain your answer.

Key ideas

An **average** is a **typical** value.
More people will be near the average shoe size than any other size.

The **mode** is a type of **average.** The mode is the value that occurs most often.
2, 3, 5, 2, 6, 8, 2   Here the mode is 2. There are more 2s than any other value.

The **median** is another type of **average.** It is the 'middle' value after they have been put in order of size. It is a useful average if there is no mode.
2, 3, 5, 2, 6, 8, 2 → 2, 2, 2, 3, 5, 6, 8   Here the median is 3.

When there are a lot of **different** values and we need to **sort** and **tally** them, we **group** the data into **equal intervals**.

Data Handling

Chapter 14 Large Numbers

Step-up

1. Copy the grid below. Write these numbers as figures onto the grid. The first is done for you.

	Thousands	Hundreds	Tens	Units
(a)	2	8	2	3
(b)				

   (a) Two thousand eight hundred and twenty-three.
   (b) Five thousand six hundred and nineteen.
   (c) One thousand eight hundred and thirty-seven.
   (d) Eight thousand five hundred and sixty.
   (e) Three thousand and fifty-seven.
   (f) Nine thousand seven hundred and two.
   (g) Two thousand and forty.
   (h) Four thousand and eleven.

2. Is the bold figure in each number in the **thousands**, **hundreds**, **tens** or **units** column?
   (a) **1** 5 7 9   (b) 5 4 2 **1**   (c) 6 **1** 3 4   (d) 2 0 **4** 8
   (e) 6 **4** 4 3   (f) 8 7 **3** 5   (g) 2 4 9 **8**   (h) 6 8 **3** 1

3. Thousands, hundreds, tens or units?
   (a) What does the figure 3 stand for in this number?   6375
   (b) What does the figure 7 stand for in this number?   7121
   (c) What does the figure 8 stand for in this number?   5083
   (d) What does the figure 2 stand for in this number?   6612
   (e) What does the figure 5 stand for in this number?   3581

4. Here is the number 2154 'broken up' into thousands, hundreds, tens and units.

   1000 1   10   10   1
   10   1   100 1   1000 10 10

   Break these numbers into thousands, hundreds, tens and units.
   (a) 3 4 4 1   (b) 2 5 3 5   (c) 1 3 5 5   (d) 3 2 6 4

5. These numbers have been 'broken up'. What numbers are shown here?

   (a)
   10 1 1
   1000 100
   10 100 10
   10 100

   (b)
   1000 1 100
   10 10 10 100
   1000 1000 100
   100 10

   (c)
   1 1 1000 100
   1000 100 10 10
   10 10 1 1 100
   100 10 10

100 Chapter 14

Tens of thousands

Here is the number twenty-three thousand:

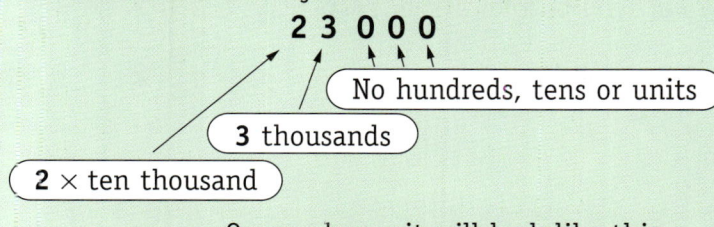

2 3 0 0 0

- 2 × ten thousand
- 3 thousands
- No hundreds, tens or units

On an abacus it will look like this:

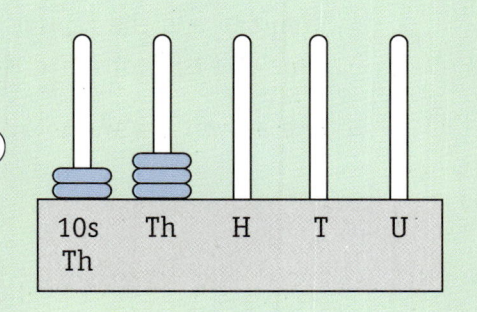

Exercise 1

How many thousands are shown in each of these numbers?
Match the figures with the written numbers, for example **1 (e)**

1. Forty-five thousand
2. Twenty-six thousand
3. Fifty-one thousand
4. Twelve thousand
5. Seventeen thousand
6. Thirty-four thousand
7. Eighteen thousand
8. Sixty-eight thousand

(a) 12 000   (b) 18 000   (c) 26 000   (d) 34 000
(e) 45 000   (f) 51 000   (g) 17 000   (h) 68 000

Exercise 2

Copy this grid. Copy the numbers below onto the grid. The first is done for you.

10s of thousands	Thousands	Hundreds	Tens	Units
3	5	2	4	6

1. 35 246
2. 25 639
3. 41 802
4. 54 148
5. 30 926
6. 16 574
7. 33 841
8. 87 448
9. 61 050

Exercise 3

Write down the number shown on each abacus.

1 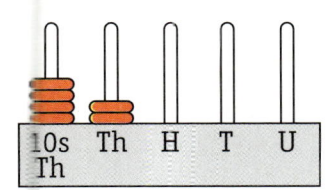
2 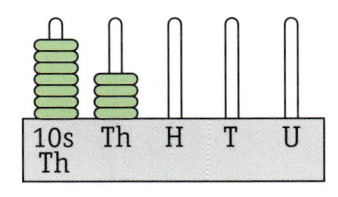
3 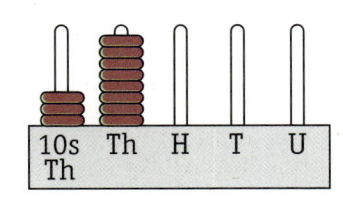
4 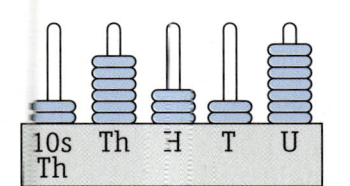
5 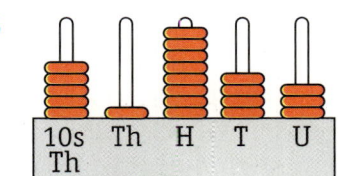
6

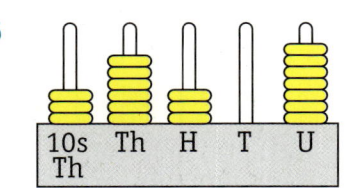

Large Numbers 101

This is a Magic Square.
(You can add the figures across, down or diagonally from one top corner to the opposite bottom corner.)

The answer is always 15.

4	3	8	= 15
9	5	1	= 15
2	7	6	= 15

15 15 15 15 15

Exercise 4

This Magic Square involves very large numbers.
Check that the Magic Square adds up to the same number, across, down and diagonally. Do four or five additions.

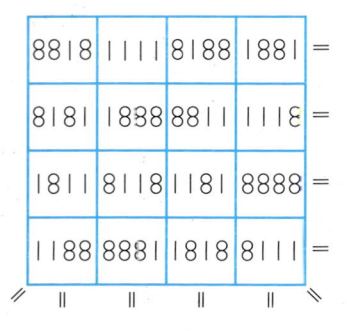

8818	1111	8188	1881	=
8181	1888	8811	1118	=
1811	8118	1181	8888	=
1188	8881	1818	8111	=

1 Do the numbers all add up to the same amount?
2 Turn the page upside down. Try two or three additions. What do you notice about your answers?

Exercise 5

Here is a list of soccer grounds and their capacities (the number of people the ground can hold).

Team	Ground	Capacity
Aston Villa F.C.	Villa Park	39 339
Blackburn Rovers	Ewood Park	31 367
Chelsea F.C.	Stamford Bridge	30 688
Huddersfield	Alfred McAlpine Stadium	19 600
Leeds United F.C.	Elland Road	39 896
Liverpool F.C.	Anfield	41 100
Manchester United F.C.	Old Trafford	55 300
Middlesbrough F.C.	Riverside Stadium	30 300
Millwall	The Den	20 146
Newcastle United F.C.	St. James's	36 563
Q.P.R.	Rangers Stadium	19 074
Stoke City	Britannia Stadium	26 000

1 What is the capacity at Leeds United?
2 What is the capacity at the Riverside Stadium?
3 Which club has the largest capacity?
4 Which ground has the smallest capacity?
5 How many grounds hold more than thirty thousand?
6 Which ground holds about fifty-five thousand?
7 Which ground holds about thirty-six thousand?
8 Which club has a capacity of almost 40 000?
9 How many grounds hold less than 35 000?
10 Order the clubs by capacity; smallest first.

George Parker (1806–1878) was known as Calculator Boy. He did not learn to read or write until he was 10 years old. He worked out this problem in his head!

$$257\,689\,435 \times 356\,875\,649$$

Answer: 91 963 084 356 068 315

It took him 6 minutes!

Addition Card One

See how many can you do in 6 minutes.

1	12 658 + 23 305	2	29 127 + 26 506	3	30 719 + 16 090
4	55 283 + 32 909	5	16 584 + 15 160	6	29 308 + 41 038
7	36 095 + 27 625	8	25 359 + 35 907		

Subtraction Card One

See how many can you do in 6 minutes.

1	64 862 − 23 560	2	35 673 − 15 301	3	54 898 − 30 825
4	85 682 − 35 156	5	47 180 − 17 024	6	51 880 − 26 419
7	38 516 − 18 076	8	70 859 − 47 369		

Hundreds of thousands

This number is two hundred and fifty thousand: **250 000**

(Two hundred and fifty) × (thousand)

Exercise 6

Read these numbers to yourself. Next, write them out in figures. The first is done for you.

1. Three hundred and fifty-six thousand.   356 000
2. Two hundred and sixty-seven thousand.
3. Five hundred and eighty-two thousand.
4. One hundred and seven thousand.
5. Nine hundred and fifty thousand.

These numbers are a little more complicated. The first is done for you.

6. Two hundred and fifty-eight thousand, three hundred and twenty-nine.   258 329
7. Five hundred and forty-nine thousand, six hundred and fifty-one.
8. Three hundred and eighty-two thousand, one hundred and sixty-three.
9. Seven hundred and twenty-two thousand, eight hundred and three.
10. Six hundred and five thousand, two hundred and twenty.

Large Numbers

Really big numbers!

This box contains 1000 dots (count them if you do not believe it!). If we had one thousand (1000) boxes like this we would have one million (1 000 000) dots. One million is a very big number.

One million is one thousand × 1000.

If you counted from 1 to a million, non-stop, counting one number each second, how long do you think it would take?

(a) 18 hours **(b)** 2 days and 13 hours **(c)** 6 days and 3 hours **(d)** 11 days and 14 hours

(The answer is at the bottom of the page.)

Exercise 7

There are 10 cities on the map. The **population** of the city is shown below each name.
Answer the questions about these populations.

1. Which city has the biggest population?
2. Which city has the smallest population?
3. Which city has a population of 446 000?
4. What is the population of Cardiff?

It is difficult to hold big numbers in your head, and to understand them. To make it easier, we 'round' to the nearest useful amount.
Dublin has a population of 1 100 000 – we could say that Dublin has a population of **about** one million.

5. To the nearest million, what is the population of London?
6. To the nearest million, what is the population of Birmingham?
7. Which three cities each have a population of about 450 000?
8. 'Round' the populations of: **(a)** Glasgow **(b)** Liverpool

Glasgow 690 000
Edinburgh 446 000
Belfast 280 000
Dublin 1 100 000
Liverpool 462 500
Leeds 740 000
Manchester 441 000
Birmingham 1 020 000
Cardiff 287 000
London 6 833 000

A computer gave the following problem to a Mrs Devi:
7 686 369 774 870 × 2 465 099 745 779
She worked out the answer in her head in 28 seconds!

Answer: 18 947 668 177 995 426 462 773 730

(The answer is **(d)** – just under 11 days and 14 hours.)

Chapter 14

Exercise 8

Here is some information about the population of eight countries.

Country	Population		
Australia	17 800 000	–	nearly 18 million people.
Brazil	174 200 000	–	over 174 million people.
Canada	28 800 000	–	nearly 29 million people.
China	1 185 200 000	–	over one billion people!
France	58 800 000	–	nearly 59 million people.
Great Britain	58 400 000	–	over 58 million people.
Japan	124 700 000	–	nearly 125 million people.
United States of America	263 400 000	–	over 263 million people.

1 Which of these countries has the smallest population?
2 Which two countries have a population that is almost the same?
3 Which country has the largest population?
4 Which country has a population of about 125 million people?
5 How many millions of people live in Canada?
6 How many millions of people live in Brazil?
7 Which country has a population between 25 and 30 million?
8 Which country has about two hundred and sixty-three million people?

> During one year, your heart beats about 30 million times (30 000 000!).

> In one year the planet Earth travels about 460 000 000 km in its journey around the Sun.

> The nearest star to our Sun is 4.25 light years away, or nearly 2 000 000 000 000 km away!

The population of planet Earth is about **6 billion** people (6 000 000 000).
If all the people in the world lined up, one behind the other, the queue would be 3 million kilometres long, and stretch 75 times around the world!
The population is increasing. By the year 2025 it is expected to be nearly **9 billion**.

What are we queueing for?

Key ideas

The value of a figure depends upon which column it is in.
If the figure **2** is in the hundreds column it stands for **two hundred**.
If the figure **2** is in the thousands column it stands for **two thousand**.
Here are some of the columns:

100s of thousands	10s of thousands	Thousands	Hundreds	Tens	Units	
					1	This stands for one
				1	0	This is ten
			1	0	0	This is one hundred
		1	0	0	0	This is one thousand
	1	0	0	0	0	This is ten thousand
1	0	0	0	0	0	This is one hundred thousand

Large Numbers

Chapter 15 Decimals

Step-up 1

1 What decimal part of each chocolate bar can be seen in each of these drawings? The first one has been done for you.

(a) 0.9   (b) 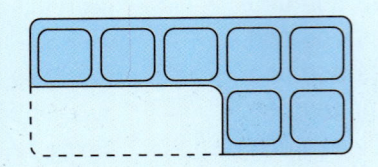   (c)

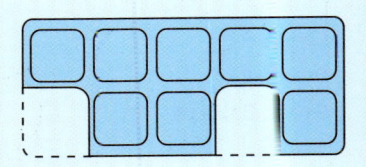

(d) 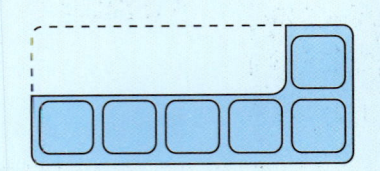   (e) 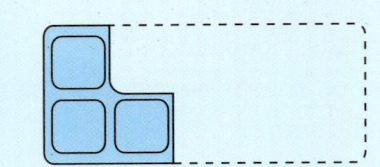   (f)

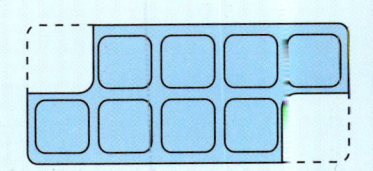

2 What are the readings on these decimal scales?

(a)   (b)    (c)    (d)

3 Complete these decimal additions.

(a) 0.4   (b) 1.3   (c) 6.4   (d) 1.6   (e) 5.4   (f) 3.7   (g) 6.9
   + 3.2   + 5.5   + 2.5   + 2.6   + 3.7   + 4.6   + 5.6
   ─────   ─────   ─────   ─────   ─────   ─────   ─────

4 When these boxes are put onto a scale, what weight will be shown for each group?

(a) 2.3 kg, 5.2 kg

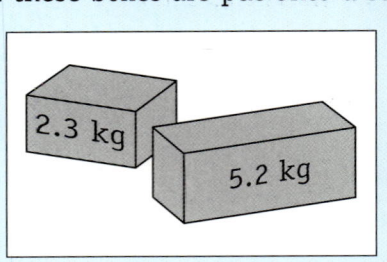

(b) 2.3 kg, 4.2 kg, 2.0 kg

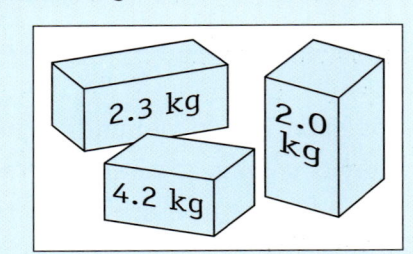

(c) 3.3 kg, 12.4 kg, 12.2 kg

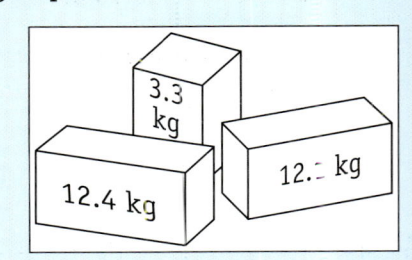

(d) 2.6 kg, 6.8 kg

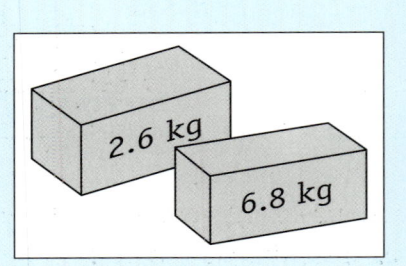

(e) 7.1 kg, 10.6 kg, 2.0 kg

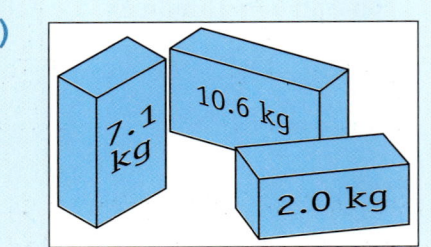

(f) 5.5 kg, 1.7 kg, 1.6 kg

106 Chapter 15

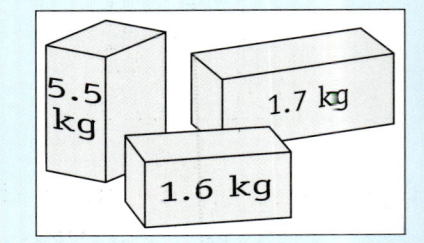

Step-up 2

1 (a) Which of these objects is the heaviest? (b) Which is the lightest?

2 Put the objects in weight order from the lightest to the heaviest.

3 Copy this number line and fill in the missing numbers for **A** to **E**.

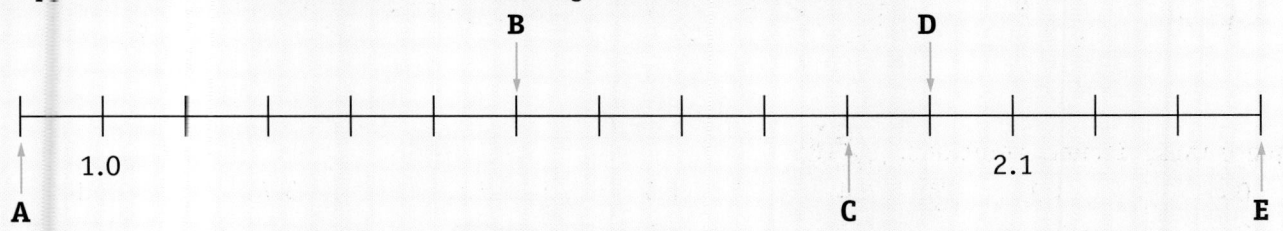

4 This symbol > means 'is greater than'. When it is turned around < it means 'is less than'.
5.1 > 4.9   This reads '5.1 is greater than 4.9'   4.9 < 5.1   This reads '4.9 is less than 5.1'

Use these signs between these pairs of numbers.
(a) 0.9   1.0   (b) 2.3   1.7   (c) 7.0   5.9   (d) 0.8   0.3
(e) 5.6   4.9   (f) 9.0   0.9   (g) 1.1   2.0   (h) 0.2   2.0

5 What numbers are shown on the abacuses?
(a)   (b)   (c)   (d)

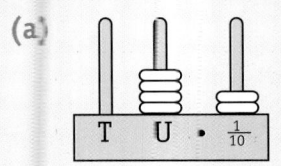

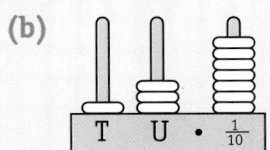

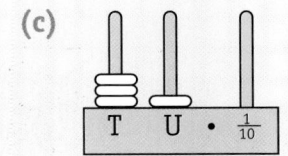

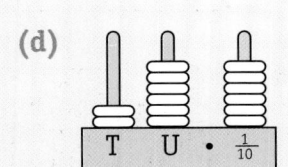

6 In a fishing competition Linda catches three fish: a pike, a tench, and a carp. Altogether, they weigh 8.5 kg. The tench weighs 1.5 kg and the carp weighs 2 kg. How much does the pike weigh?

Decimals   107

Two decimal places

We call the positions to the right of the decimal point: **decimal places.**
This decimal abacus shows
1 ten, 2 ones, and 5 tenths,
12.5 has **one decimal place**.

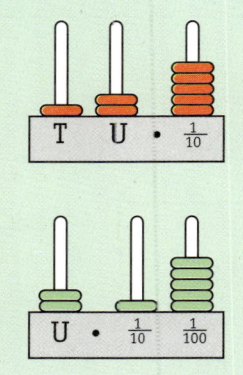

This abacus shows:
2 ones, one tenth and five hundredths,
2.15 has **two decimal places**.

Exercise 1

Write the decimal shown on each abacus. The first one has been done for you.

1. 1.53
2. 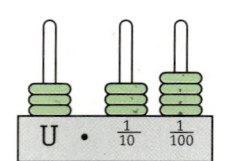
3. 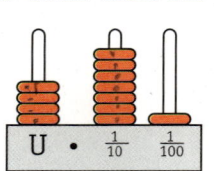
4. 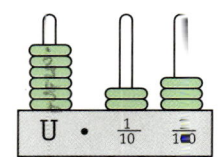
5. 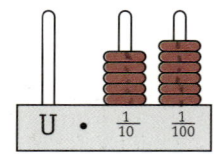
6. 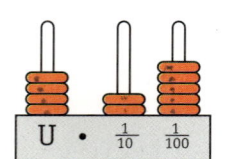
7. 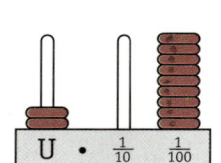
8.

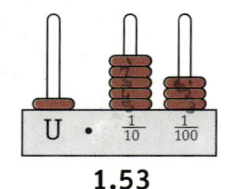

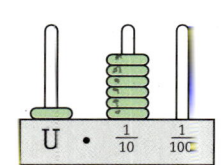

Decimal places and money

There are different ways to think of money and decimals.
One pound can be made of ten 10p coins   or   one hundred 1p coins.

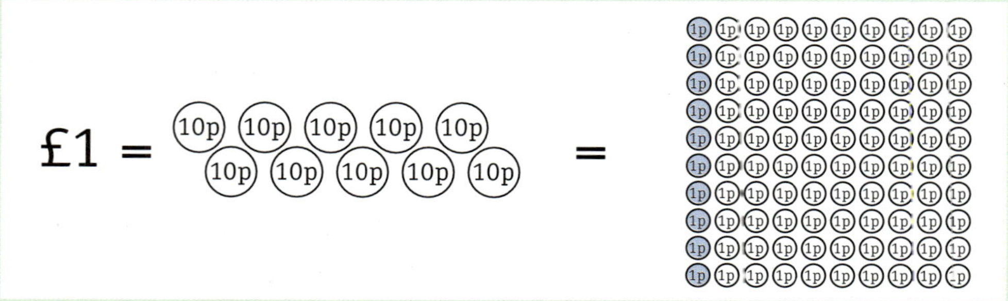

£1 = (ten 10p coins) = (one hundred 1p coins)

Each 10p coin is $\frac{1}{10}$ of a pound, or as a decimal, **0.1 of a pound**.

The shaded column is worth 10p or **0.1 of a pound**.
There are **100 1p coins**. Each 1p coin is **0.01 of a pound**.

108 Chapter 15

The decimal scale below shows pence as decimal parts of a pound. (0p to 25p)

0 0.01 0.02 0.03 0.04 0.05 0.06 0.07 0.08 0.09 0.10 0.11 0.12 0.13 0.14 0.15 0.16 0.17 0.18 0.19 0.20 0.21 0.22 0.23 0.24 0.25

Exercise 2

Write these sums of money as decimal parts of a pound (£).
You will need to think beyond the 25p marker. Questions 1 and 5 have been done for you.

1   2 pence = £0.02
2   4 pence = £ ?
3   7 pence = £ ?
4   9 pence = £ ?
5   10 pence = £0.10
6   19 pence = £ ?
7   60 pence = £ ?
8   82 pence = £ ?

This sum of money is £2.47. This is made from **2** whole pounds, **0.4** of a pound and **0.07** of a pound.

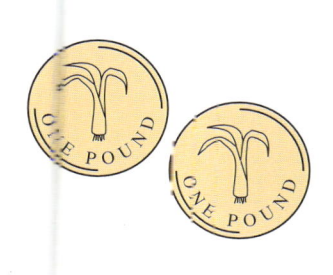

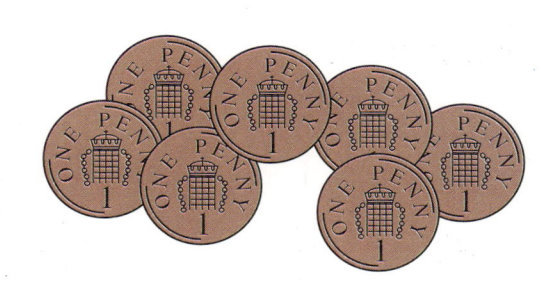

Exercise 3

Write these amounts in whole £s (pounds), and decimals.
Like this: '15 pence = £0.15' and '125 pence = £1.25'.

1   26 pence = £ ?
2   16 pence = £ ?
3   151 pence = £ ?
4   191 pence = £ ?
5   216 pence = £ ?
6   100 pence = £ ?
7   260 pence = £ ?
8   555 pence = £ ?
9   38 pence = £ ?
10 110 pence = £ ?
11 302 pence = £ ?
12 200 pence = £ ?

Exercise 4

Who has the larger sum of money?

1   Freya has £0.10
    Declan has £0.01
2   Ali has 20p
    Simeon has £0.21
3   Emma has £0.09
    Gill has 19p
4   Luke has £0.76
    Ella has 39p
5   Mahir has 11p
    Mina has £0.90
6   Penny has £1.15
    Tom has 121p

Exercise 5

This symbol > means 'is greater than'. When it is turned around < it means 'is less than'.
Use the two symbols to say which is the larger number in each pair.

1   0.1   0.01
2   1.01   1.10
3   2.00   0.02
4   0.19   0.09
5   6.08   6.1
6   0.07   0.2
7   0.03   0.29
8   0.13   0.3

Decimals

This is the world's biggest bar of chocolate.

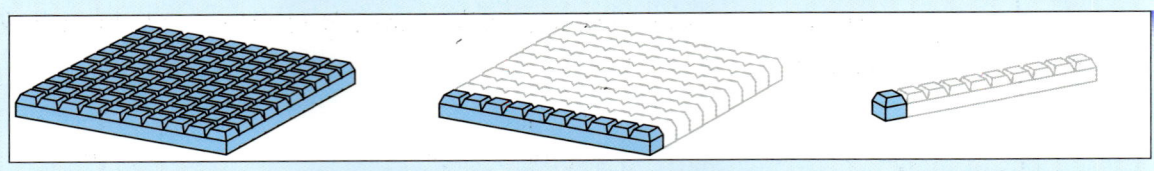

It has 100 pieces.
1 bar is one whole **1**.
This picture shows
1.23 bars

There are ten rows.
Each row is **0.1** of the bar.

Each row has ten pieces.
Each small piece is **0.01** of the bar.
This picture shows
0.13 bars

Exercise 6

How much chocolate is shown in each diagram below? Write your answer as a decimal.

1   2   3   4   5

6   7   8   9   10

Exercise 7

Show these amounts by using drawings like the ones above.

1   1.3 bars   2   1.03 bars   3   0.04 bars   4   0.4 bars   5   0.15 bars   6   2.30 bars

When 1 whole bar is broken into the small pieces, there are 100 × 0.01 pieces.

When a row is broken into the small pieces there are 10 × 0.01 pieces.

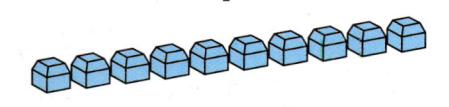

Exercise 8

When each of these is broken into the small 0.01 pieces, how many will there be?

1   2 bars
2   0.2 bars
3   0.15 bars
4   1.1 bars
5   0.5 bars
6   3 bars

110   Chapter 15

Get the point!

When we set out calculations using decimals, it is important to make sure that the **decimal points** are all in line, under each other.

```
   £ . p              £ . p              £ . p
   1.20               120                1 . 20
+  1.55         X  +  155       X     +  1 . 55     ✓
  ─────             ─────              ────────
   .355              275                2 . 75
```

Exercise 9

Use decimal addition or subtraction to solve these problems.

1. Simon buys a PC game that costs him £24.75. Then he finds out that he needs a new control pad which costs another £8.10. How much does he have to pay altogether?

2. Ray weighs 65.50 kg. He diets and loses 4.30 kg. How much does he weigh now?

3. Shannon jumps 3.25 metres for her school in the long-jump competition. She is beaten by Ella who jumps another 0.36 metres. How far did Ella jump?

4. The weight limit of a bridge is 12.50 tonnes. Two lorries weighing 7.75 tonnes and 4.50 tonnes cross the bridge at the same time. Should the bridge stand their weight?

5. Ajeeta's piano lesson costs £16.50. Her swimming lesson costs £8.50. How much does she spend on the two lessons?

6. Jeff has £1.96 in his pocket. He spends £0.86. How much does he have now?

7. Khalid is 2.07 metres tall. John is 1.97 metres tall. What is the difference in their heights?

8. Nick cycles 16.55 km to Anton's house. He then cycles another 20.56 km to Patrick's flat. How far has he cycled altogether?

Decimal Addition Card One

1. £2.50
  + £3.30

2. £3.20
  + £4.50

3. £6.70
  + £3.20

4. £5.40
  + £3.20

5. £3.51
  + £5.34

6. £1.42
  + £6.53

Decimal Addition Card Two

1. £2.24 + £3.03 = ?
2. £0.55 + £3.22 = ?
3. £6.11 + £3.26 = ?
4. £4.25 + £2.41 = ?
5. £5.64 + £2.09 = ?
6. £7.06 + £5.85 = ?
7. £1.84 + £9.23 = ?
8. £1.85 + £1.24 = ?
9. £3.64 + £5.06 = ?
10. £9.32 + £0.68 = ?

Decimals 111

Nick makes a triangle using straws. Each straw is 10.5 cm long. The perimeter of the triangle will be:

10.5 cm + 10.5 cm + 10.5 cm

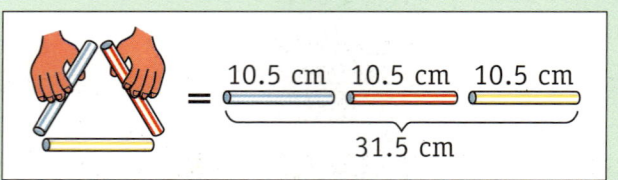

= 10.5 cm 10.5 cm 10.5 cm
   31.5 cm

Nick adds the lengths of the straws together.

```
  10.5
  10.5
  10.5
  ————
  31.5 cm
```

Exercise 10

Find the perimeters of these shapes by adding their lengths together.

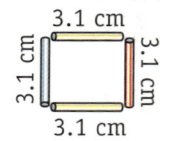

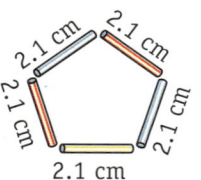

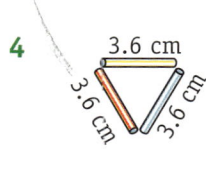

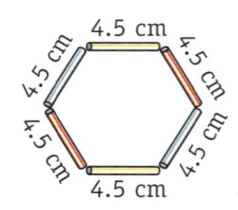

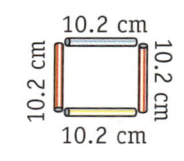

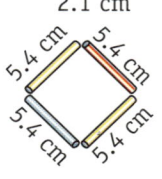

1. Triangle with sides 3.2 cm, 3.2 cm, 3.2 cm
2. Square with sides 3.1 cm
3. Pentagon with sides 2.1 cm
4. Triangle with sides 3.6 cm
5. Hexagon with sides 4.5 cm
6. Rectangle with sides 10.2 cm
7. Square with sides 5.4 cm
8. Pentagon with sides 4.5 cm

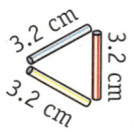

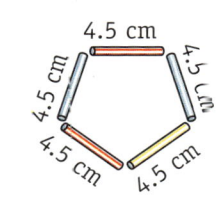

Multiplying decimals

A quicker way to find the perimeter of Nick's triangle would be to **multiply**.

```
    10.5
  ×    3
  ——————
    31.5 cm
```

3×10.5 We need to know where the **decimal point** is placed. We estimate the answer to 3×10 is 30, so we put the decimal point in a place so that the answer is close to 30 ... **31.5 cm**.

Exercise 11

Use multiplication to find the perimeters of these shapes.

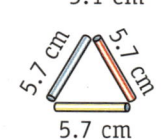

1. Square with sides 2.3 cm
2. Hexagon with sides 5.1 cm
3. Triangle with sides 10.6 cm
4. Pentagon with sides 3.4 cm
5. Triangle with sides 5.7 cm
6. Square with sides 5.6 cm

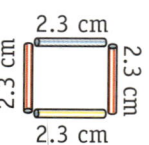

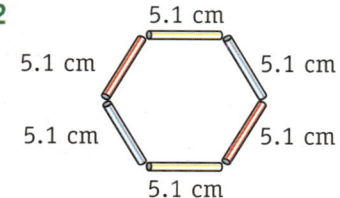

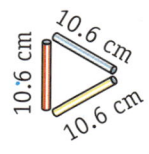

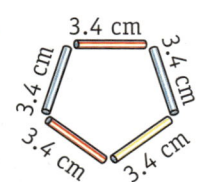

Chapter 15

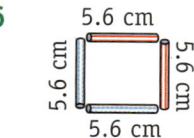

Exercise 12

Estimate the cost of the items below to the nearest whole pound (£).
Write: 'Three packets of Scrubo cost ... '

1 SCRUBO SOAP POWDER
£2.13 × 3

2 PRAWN AND CABBAGE SOUP
£1.21 × 4

3 BANANA AND TURNIP CAKE
£2.31 × 3

4 JELLY LOLLIES
£1.06 × 2

5 RUFF'S TOILET PAPER
£0.31 × 5

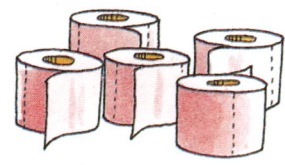

6 EGG, BEANS AND ONION PIZZA
£2.50 × 4

Calculating exactly
To calculate the exact cost of 3 packets of 'Scrubo' we need to **multiply** 3 × £2.13
We need to **estimate** the answer to the multiplication: roughly £6
Now we can place the decimal point so that the answer is close to £6: **£6.39**

£2.13
× 3
£6.39

Exercise 13

Calculate the exact costs of the groups of items in Exercise 12. Do not use a calculator.

Key ideas

1 divided by 10 = $\frac{1}{10}$. As a decimal this is written as 0.1.
1 divided by 100 = $\frac{1}{100}$. As a decimal this is written as 0.01.
100p = £1. 1p = £0.01 (£$\frac{1}{100}$).

When you put an arrow sign (<, >) between two numbers,
it always points to the smaller one, for example 5 < 6, 8 > 3.

Decimals

Chapter 16 Algebra
Step-up

1. Answer these questions about the group of shapes above.
   (a) There are ? squares.
   (b) There are ? circles.
   (c) There are ? triangles.
   (d) There are ? white shapes.
   (e) There are ? grey shapes.
   (f) There are ? green shapes.

2. Copy and complete these sentences. The first one is done for you.

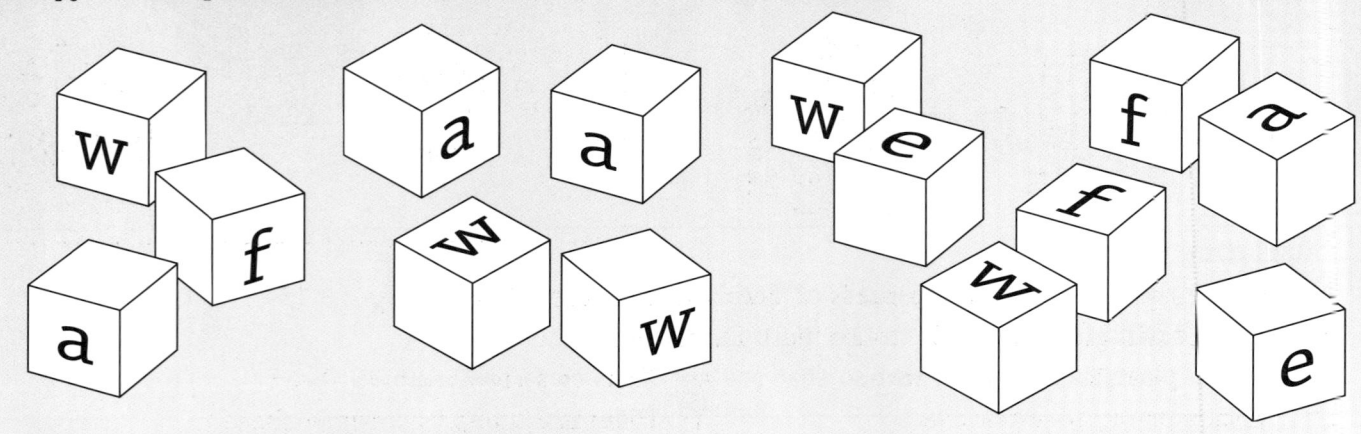

   (a) There are **4 a**s. We write it like this **4a**.
   (b) There are ? es. We write it like this ?.
   (c) There are ? fs. We write it like this ?.
   (d) There are ? ws. We write it like this ?.

3. Sort these letters into groups and say how many there are. The first one is done for you.

   $f \; f \; {}^y_c \; \chi \; {}^c_h \; f \; f \; {}^y_c \; \chi \; f \; {}^h_h \; f \; \chi \; h$

   (a) There are **2 y**s. We write **2y**.
   (b) There are ? hs. We write ?.
   (c) There are ? χs. We write ?.
   (d) There are ? fs. We write ?.
   (e) There are ? cs. We write ?.

4 Symbols are used to give information quickly and simply.
Which symbol matches which picture?

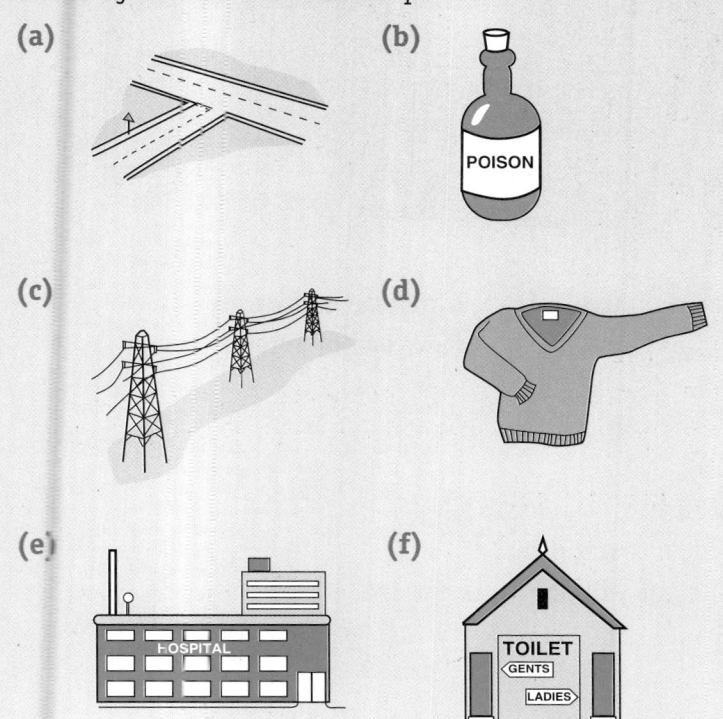

(a) (b) (c) (d) (e) (f)

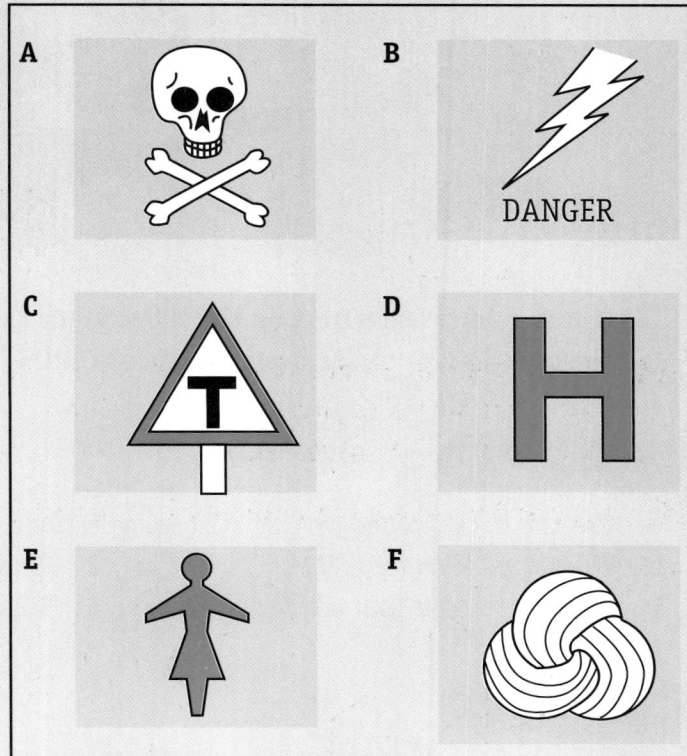

A B C D E F

5 Symbols and signs are used on the roads to give drivers information quickly.
Which symbol will give drivers the following information.

(a) You are about to go into a tunnel.
(b) There is a level crossing ahead.
(c) You are coming to a crossroad.
(d) There is a humpback bridge ahead.
(e) The road will bend to the left.
(f) The road will become narrow.
(g) You are coming to a roundabout.
(h) There is a school crossing ahead.
(i) Be alert for wild animals.
(j) You may see low flying aircraft.

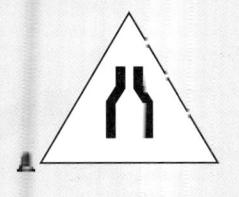

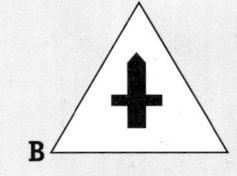

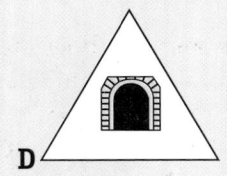

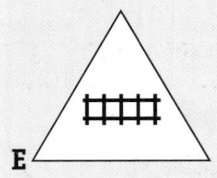

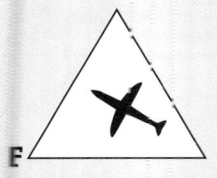

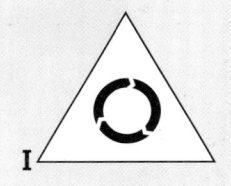

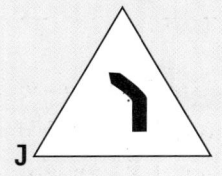

Algebra 115

Kim and John's diner

Kim and John use letters on the till to stand for words, like this: **b** instead of **burger**
The code list for the letters is beside the till. **f** instead of **fries**

b = burger
k = Kingburger
h = hot dog
v = vegetarian burger
f = fries
c = cola
l = lemonade
t = tea

Exercise 1

Use the list of codes to answer these questions. Write: 'k stands for ?.'
1. What does **k** stand for?
2. What does **f** stand for?
3. What letter will Kim use for cola?
4. What letter will John use for tea?

Exercise 2

Write out these orders using the letters on the list.
Write **and** between the letters, like this: 'f and b'.

1. Fries and a burger please!
2. A cola and a lemonade please.
3. One vegetarian burger and one tea please.
4. Could I have a cola and a hot dog please?
5. Kingburger and fries please.
6. Could I have a tea and a lemonade please?
7. A burger and a lemonade please.
8. Just two bags of fries please.

116 Chapter 16

Adding symbols

> Two portions of fries please.

Kim would not press the **f** button twice – there is a shortcut.
She puts **2f** into the till keyboard. **2f** means **2 × f**.

Exercise 3

Use Kim's shortcut to write out these orders.

1. 'Can I have three portions of fries please?'
2. 'Two lemonades please.'
3. 'Just two teas please Kim.'
4. 'Five cola drinks please.'
5. 'Three Kingburgers.'

These orders have more than one item so you have to use the **+** sign between each group of symbols.
So 'two burgers and three colas' will be written as: **2b + 3c**.

6. 'Three portions of fries and three hot dogs.'
7. 'Two burgers and one Kingburger please.'
8. 'Six colas, two portions of fries and three hot dogs please.'
9. 'One tea, one lemonade and four vegetarian burgers please.'
10. 'Burger and fries, three times please Kim.'

Exercise 4

Use Kim's shortcut to re-write these long orders.

1. c + c + c + c + f + f + f = **4c + 3f**
2. k + b + b + b + f + f + f + f = ?
3. v + v + f + f + f + v = ?
4. t + t + t + k + k + b + f + k = ?
5. f + f + f + f + f + c + t + c = ?
6. b + h + h + f + f + k + b + b = ?

John has started to write out these orders. Finish them for him.

7. 2b + b = ?
8. k + 3k + f + f + f = ?
9. 3c + b + 2c + b = ?
10. l + 2v + 3l + v + h + h + v = ?

Algebra

Working with symbols

When the till is broken, Kim and John have to find the cost of the food orders by adding.

They make the bills from this price list.

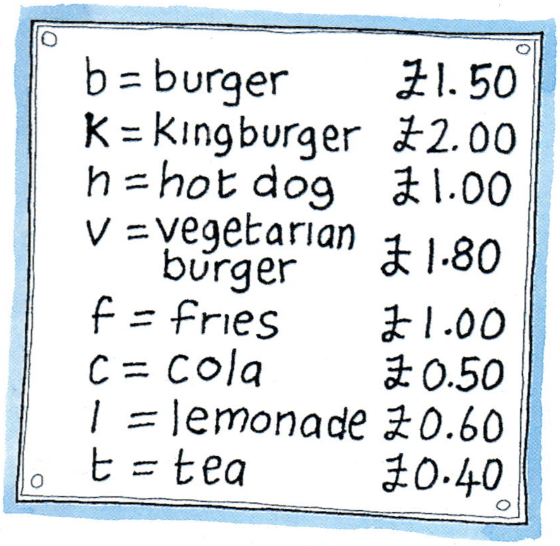

b = burger £1.50
K = Kingburger £2.00
h = hot dog £1.00
v = vegetarian burger £1.80
f = fries £1.00
c = cola £0.50
l = lemonade £0.60
t = tea £0.40

They calculate the bills like this:

Burger and fries please.

b = £1.50
f = £1.00
b+f = £2.50

Exercise 5

Use the price list to calculate these bills. Write: 'c and b = £ ?'

1. c and b = ?
2. k and f = ?
3. h and l = ?
4. b and b = ?
5. t and l and c = ?
6. f and v and f = ?
7. k and k and f = ?
8. v and c and f = ?
9. k and f and b = ?
10. h and f and t = ?
11. c and f and f = ?
12. f and f and v = ?

Exercise 6

These bills have been written using the + symbol instead of the word **and**.
Find the cost of each bill. Write: '2c + b = £2.50.'

1. c + c + b = ?
2. k + k + t = ?
3. h + h + f = ?
4. v + v + f + f = ?
5. c + c + c + k = ?
6. f + f + f + k = ?

Exercise 7

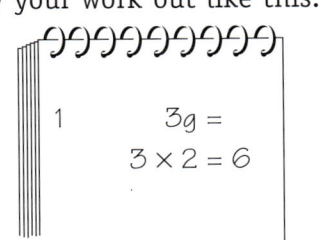

a = 2   b = 5   c = 1   d = 4

Use these values to answer the problems below.

Lay your work out like this:

1   a + b =
    2 + 5 = 7

1   a + b = ?
2   a + d = ?
3   c + a = ?
4   b + c = ?
5   d + b = ?
6   d + c = ?
7   b − c = ?
8   d − a = ?
9   b − d = ?
10 b − a = ?
11 a − c = ?
12 d − c = ?

Exercise 8

q = 10   r = 3   s = 7   t = 2   u = 5

Use these values to answer the problems below.

Lay your work out like this:

1   r + t + u =
    3 + 2 + 5 = 10

1   r + t + u = ?
2   q + r + t = ?
3   s + t + u = ?
4   r + s + t = ?
5   q + r + s = ?
6   u + q + r = ?

Exercise 9

d = 3   e = 5   f = 4   g = 2

Use these values to answer the problems below.

Lay your work out like this:

1   3g =
    3 × 2 = 6

1   3g = ?
2   2d = ?
3   2e = ?
4   3d = ?
5   4g = ?
6   2f = ?

Codes

Exercise 10

Here is a simple code. Each number stands for a letter. Use the code to work out what each message says.

1	2	3	4	5	6	7	8	9
⇕	⇕	⇕	⇕	⇕	⇕	⇕	⇕	⇕
T	E	I	S	H	O	N	D	A

1. 4, 5, 2 – 5, 9, 4 – 9 – 5, 9, 1.
2. 5, 3, 4 – 5, 2, 9, 8 – 3, 4 – 5, 6, 1.
3. 4, 3, 1 – 6, 7 – 1, 5, 2 – 4, 2, 9, 1.

Put these messages into code.

4. She had to see the dish.
5. He hid in the tent.

Exercise 11

Decode this tongue-twister and say it 10 times.

2, 3, 7 – 1, 4, 2, 2, 5
5, 3, 1, 1, 4, 6 – 1, 4, 2, 2, 5.

1	2	3	4	5	6	7
⇕	⇕	⇕	⇕	⇕	⇕	⇕
L	R	E	O	Y	W	D

Exercise 12

Use the code to work out this tongue-twisting football result.

1, 3, 5, 1, 7, 5 – 1, 3, 9, 5.
10, 7, 8, 6 – 1, 4, 1, 10 – 1, 4, 2, 10.

1	2	3	4	5	6	7	8	9	10
⇕	⇕	⇕	⇕	⇕	⇕	⇕	⇕	⇕	⇕
F	V	O	I	R	T	A	S	U	E

Exercise 13

On the next page is the Monks' Maze.

Step 1 Start at the bottom of the page.
Step 2 Decode and write out each yellow bubble to describe your journey through the maze.
The code is written on the castle wall.
Step 3 You will find four red bags on your journey.
Decode the word in the green box to discover what you have found.
Step 4 Which door do you go through to escape from the maze?

120 Chapter 16

The Monks' Maze

9: 9 – 5, 19, 3, 1, 16, 5 – 20, 8, 18, 15, 21, 7, 8 – 20, 8, 5 – 7, 18, 5, 5, 14 – 4, 15, 15, 18

1 = A 2 = B 3 = C 4 = D 5 = E 6 = F 7 = G 8 = H 9 = I 10 = J
11 = K 12 = L 13 = M 14 = N 15 = O 16 = P 17 = Q 18 = R 19 = S 20 = T
21 = U 22 = V 23 = W 24 = X 25 = Y 26 = Z

4, 9, 1, 13, 15, 14, 4, 19

7: 14, 5, 24, 20 – 9 – 3, 12, 9, 13, 2 – 4, 15, 23, 14 – 20, 8, 5 – 18, 15, 16, 5

6: 9 – 7, 15 – 21, 16 – 20, 8, 5 – 19, 16, 9, 18, 1, 12 – 19, 20, 1, 9, 18, 19

5: 20, 8, 5, 14 – 3, 18, 15, 19, 19 – 20, 8, 5 – 2, 18, 9, 4, 7, 5

8: 9 – 18, 21, 14 – 21, 16 – 20, 8, 5 – 19, 20, 5, 16, 19

4: 3, 12, 9, 13, 2 – – 20, 8, 5 – 12, 1, 4, 4, 5, 18

19, 23, 15, 18, 4

3: 14, 5, 24, 20 – 9 – 8, 1, 22, 5 – 20, 15 – 10, 21, 13, 16 – 20, 8, 5 – 7, 1, 16

11, 5, 25

2: 20, 8, 5, 14 – 9 – 7, 15 – 21, 16 – 20, 8, 5 – 19, 20, 5, 16, 19

7, 15, 12, 4 – 18, 9, 14, 7

1: 9 – 7, 15 – 14, 15, 18, 20, 8

North
W — E
S

Key ideas

Symbols are used to represent ideas. They can represent objects and numbers.

Codes are used as a 'shorthand' in algebra.

In Algebra, letters are used to stand for numbers. Usually we use lowercase letters as symbols (not capitals).

You can only add or subtract symbols that are the same, for example: $a + a = 2a$ ✔ $a + b = ab$ ✘

Algebra 121

Chapter 17   Fractions, Decimals and Percentages

Step-up

1 From the drawings below:
  (a) Find the litre jars that are marked in tenths ($\frac{1}{10}$s).
  (b) As a fraction, how full are these tenth jars?
  (c) As a fraction, how much space is left in each tenth jar?

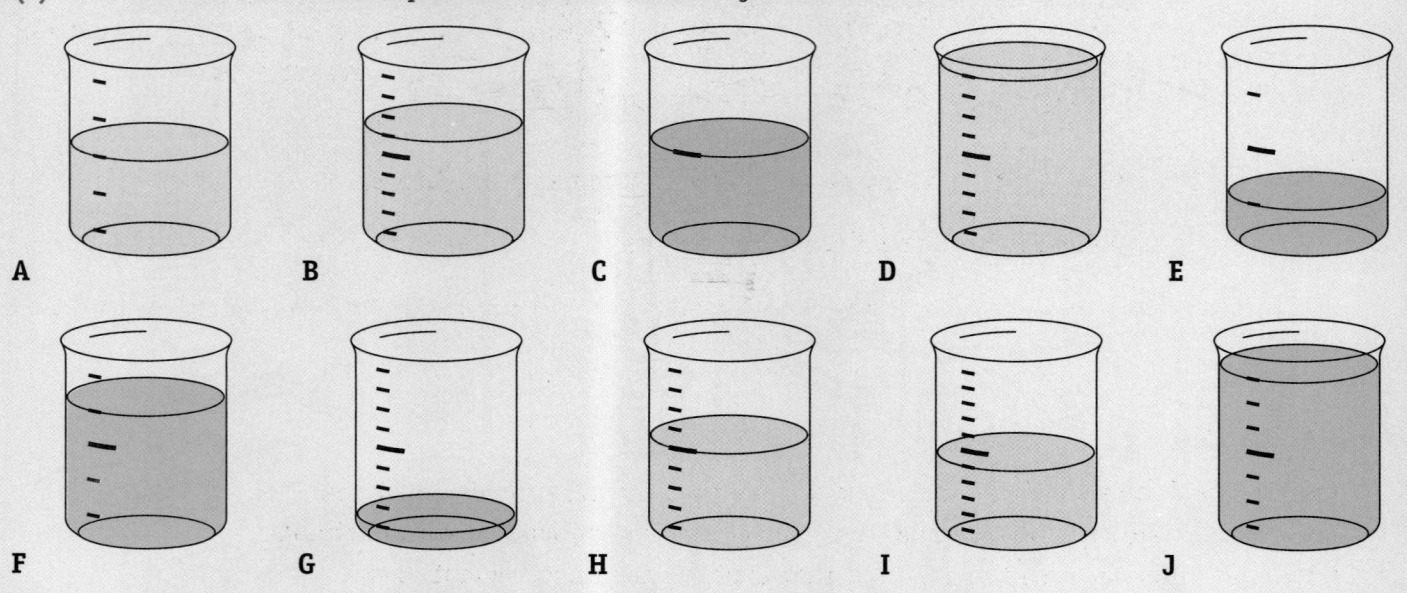

A   B   C   D   E

F   G   H   I   J

2 How much liquid is there in each picture below?
  (a) Write your answers as decimals.
  (b) Put your answers in order. Start with the smallest amount.

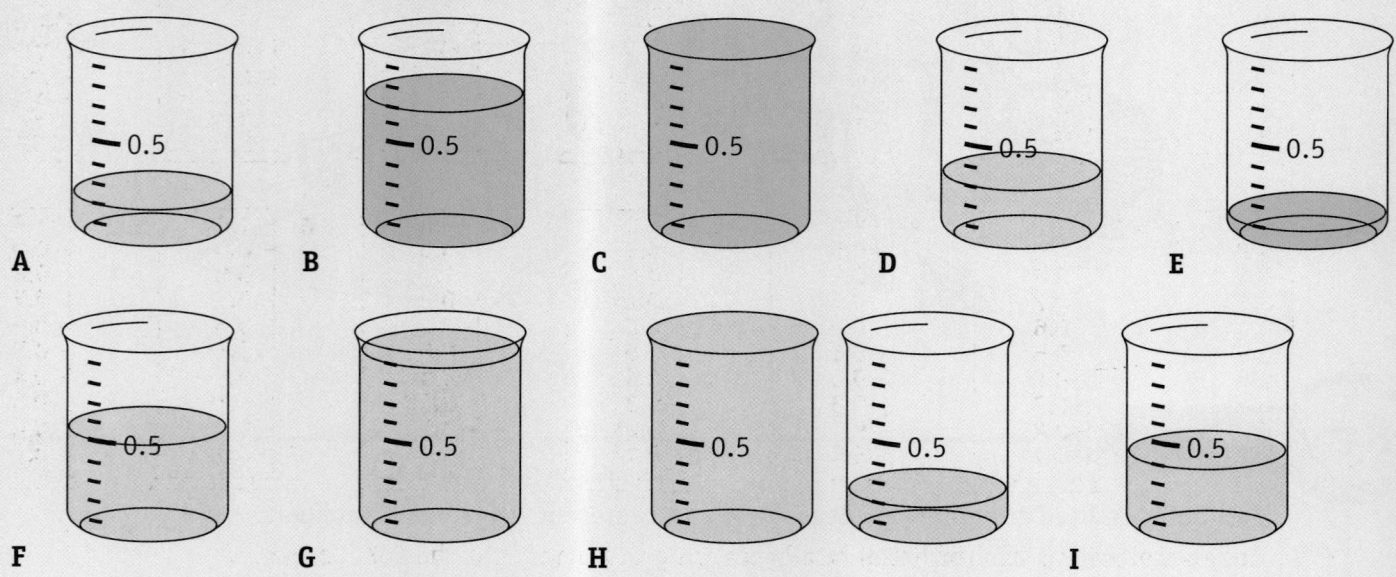

A   B   C   D   E

F   G   H   I

3 (a) If you empty all the jars from question 2 into one big container, how many litres will there be?
  (b) Round your answer to the nearest whole litre.

Doctor Notwot and Professor Eclare are two of the world's greatest fizzologists. They work for the Polar Cola company. They are inventing a new fizzy drink. They have to measure their ingredients very carefully.

Dr Notwot works in **fractions**. Prof. Eclare measures in **decimals**.

$\frac{5}{10}$ and **0.5** are the same. Check the two jars.

Exercise 1

Look at the two sets of jars. One set holds grey fizz, the other holds green fizz.
The **grey** jars are marked with **fractions**, the **green** jars are marked with **decimals**.

1. Match each grey jar with the green jar that contains the same amount of fizz.

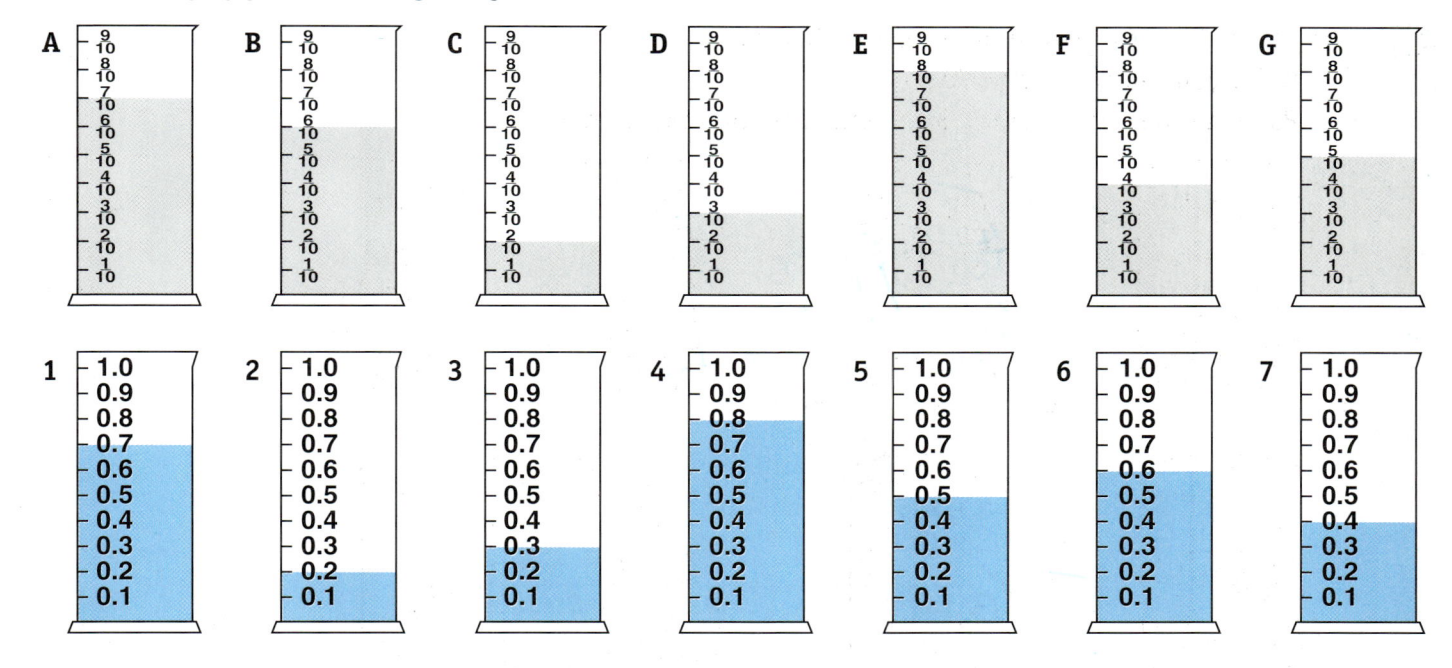

You can make exactly 1 litre of green fizz by pouring 0.3 litres into the 0.7 litre jar.

2. (a) Which other pairs of green jars will come to exactly 1 litre when poured together?
   (b) Which pairs of grey jars will combine to make exactly 1 litre when poured together?

3. Look at all the jars and find any pairs that will make exactly one litre of liquid.

Fractions, Decimals and Percentages

Exercise 2

The Doctor and the Professor mix another new drink. Notwot reads the mixture to the Professor.

1. Take $\frac{2}{10}$ l of A.
2. Add $\frac{1}{2}$ l of bottle B.
3. Finally add $\frac{3}{10}$ l of bottle C.

1 What decimal amounts will Professor Eclare add to the litre jar?
Write: 'A ⟶ 0.2 litre.'

This time Eclare reads the instructions to the Doctor.

1. Pour 0.1 l from bottle W.
2. Add 0.4 l of bottle X.
3. Next add 0.3 l of bottle Y.
4. Finally add 0.2 l of bottle Z.

2 What fractions will Dr Notwot add to his litre jar?
Write: 'W ⟶ $\frac{1}{10}$ litres.'

3 How much liquid is shown in each jar below?
Give your answers as **fractions** then as **decimals**.

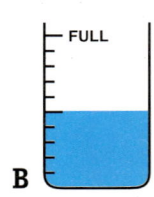

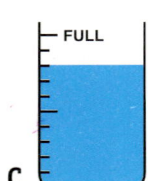

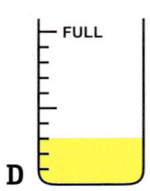

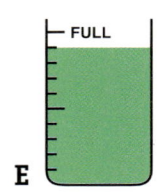

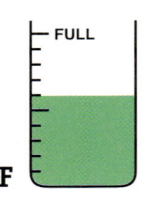

A   B   C   D   E   F

Exercise 3

Now they come up with a top-secret recipe for the 'new' Polar Cola. "The world's coolest cola!"
The jar shows how they mixed their latest drink.
Make a table like this and write the secret mixture onto it as fractions and then as decimals.

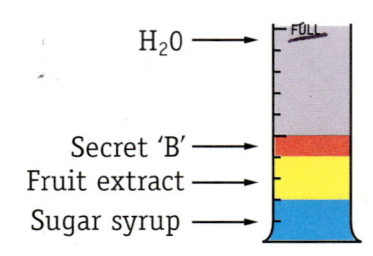

H_2O
Secret 'B'
Fruit extract
Sugar syrup

Ingredients	Fraction	Decimal
H_2O		
Secret 'B'	$\frac{1}{10}$	0.1
Fruit extract		
Sugar syrup		

C'est horrible !
Gadzooks It's disgusting!

Disaster! New Polar Cola tastes awful. What's the solution?
Professor Bud flies in from America specially to help. See the next page!

Percentages

Professor Bud arrives and tells the two fizzologists that their **percentages** are all wrong. She shows them the connection between their **fractions** and **decimals**, and **percentages**.

She shows them that $\frac{1}{10} = 0.1 = 10\%$.

Dr Notwot quickly works out that 1 whole unit must be the same as $10 \times 10\% = 100\%$.

Shortly after, Professor Eclare works out that $\frac{1}{2} = 0.5 = 50\%$.

Per cent means 'parts out of a hundred'. 20% would be 20 parts out of a hundred.

Exercise 4

They try another mixture. Draw another table like this and transfer the readings from the jar to the table.

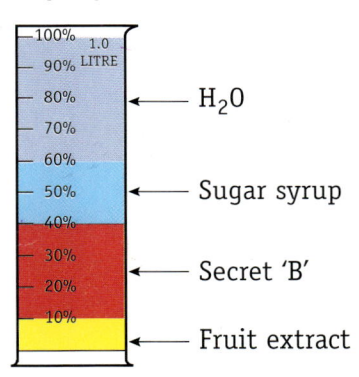

Ingredients	Fraction	Decimal	Percentage
Fruit extract			
Sugar syrup	$\frac{2}{10}$	0.2	20%
Secret 'B'			
H_2O			

Exercise 5

There should be three jars in each picture, each with the same amount of liquid (as shown in question 1). Write the amounts shown on the jars, then write the amount that will be in the missing jars. You must have three answers – a fraction, a decimal and a percentage – for each question.

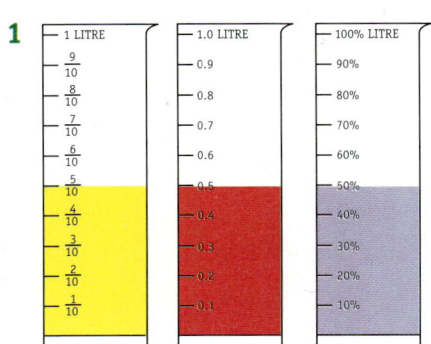

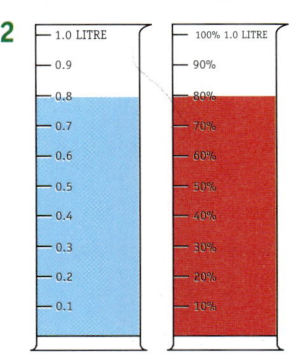

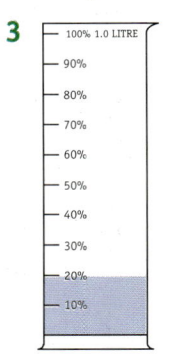

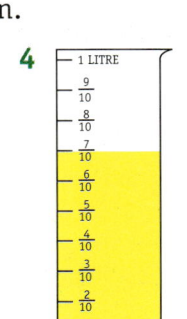

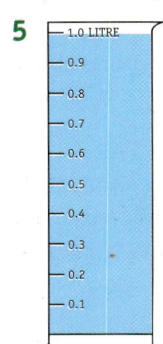

Fractions, Decimals and Percentages

Exercise 6

The table holds recipes from some of Professor Bud's top-secret experiments with Polar Cola.
Some of the recipes are not complete.

1. Copy the table and fill in the missing amounts for the five ingredients.

Experiment code Recipes	H_2O	Sugar syrup	Secret 'B'	Fruit extract	Root extract
Ver 1.0	40%	20%	10%	20%	?
Ver 1.2	50%	15%	20%	5%	?
Ver 2.1	30%	10%	10%	?	40%
Ver 2.5	45%	5%	?	20%	10%
Ver 3.0	?	20%	10%	5%	5%
Ver 3.6	50%	20%	10%	10%	?
Ver 5.1	70%	?	0%	15%	15%
Ver 6.0	65%	5%	10%	?	5%
Ver 6.2	50%	10%	?	25%	15%
Ver 6.9	90%	5%	?	5%	?

2. When you add up the percentages for each of the recipes above, what would you expect the total to be?

These three scales show fractions, decimals and percentages.

Fractions	$\frac{0}{10}$	$\frac{1}{10}$	$\frac{2}{10}$	$\frac{3}{10}$	$\frac{4}{10}$	$\frac{5}{10}$	$\frac{6}{10}$	$\frac{7}{10}$	$\frac{8}{10}$	$\frac{9}{10}$	1
Decimals	0.0	0.1	0.2	0.3	0.4	0.5	0.6	0.7	0.8	0.9	1.0
Percentages (%)	0	10	20	30	40	50	60	70	80	90	100

Exercise 7

Use the scales above to answer these questions.

1. Arrange these numbers into size order, smallest first.
   (a) $\frac{3}{10}$ 0.4   45%
   (b) $\frac{1}{2}$ $\frac{3}{10}$ 90%
   (c) 25% $\frac{1}{10}$ 0.3
   (d) $\frac{7}{10}$ 60%   0.1
   (e) 35% $\frac{3}{10}$ 0.2
   (f) 1.0   0.1 $\frac{3}{10}$

2. In a survey about whether or not they liked 'the world's coolest cola' people were asked to answer **yes** or **no**. 80% said **no**.
   What fraction of people liked the new drink?

The Polar Company tried out their new line of drinks in schools. They asked 10 pupils from Year 8 to help. If a pupil liked a drink they raised their hand to vote for it.

Exercise 8

Use the drawings to answer these.
1. Which drink was the most popular?
2. Which drink did pupils like the least?
3. List the percentage of votes for each drink in order of popularity.
4. Which drink got exactly 50% of the votes?

Key ideas

Fractions, **decimals** and **percentages** are all ways of writing numbers that are **less than 1 whole**.

% This sign means 'percentage' – **parts out of one hundred**.

When fractions are written as tenths ($\frac{1}{10}$s) they are easily written as decimals and percentages. See the scales below.

Fractions	$\frac{0}{10}$	$\frac{1}{10}$	$\frac{2}{10}$	$\frac{3}{10}$	$\frac{4}{10}$	$\frac{5}{10}$	$\frac{6}{10}$	$\frac{7}{10}$	$\frac{8}{10}$	$\frac{9}{10}$	1
Decimals	0.0	0.1	0.2	0.3	0.4	0.5	0.6	0.7	0.8	0.9	1.0
Percentages (%)	0	10	20	30	40	50	60	70	80	90	100

(Later you will work with decimals and percentages that are not always organised in divisions of 10.)

Fractions, Decimals and Percentages

Chapter 18 Rules

Step-up

Which is the odd-one-out in these sets of drawings?

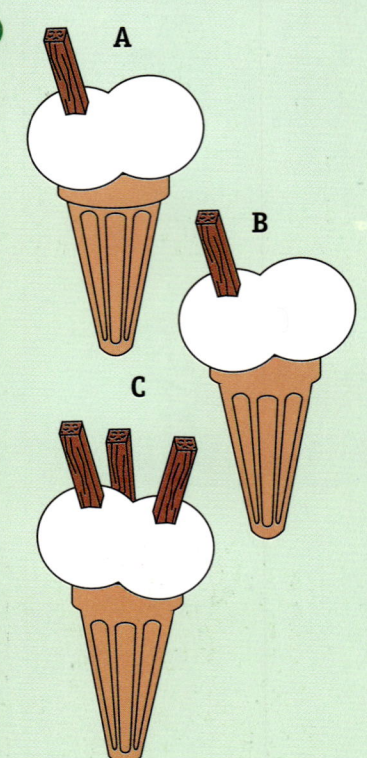

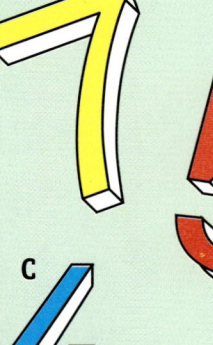

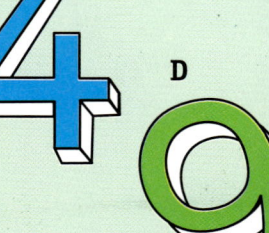

1 A, B, C

2 A, B, C, D, E

3 A, B, C, D

4 How did you decide which was the odd-one-out in each question?

5 Find the missing numbers or symbols (+ or −).
(a) 7 + 5 = ?
(b) 4 − 4 = ?
(c) 10 − ? = 7
(d) 6 ? 4 = 2
(e) ? − 5 = 19
(f) 11 ? 4 = 15
(g) 13 − 6 = ?
(h) 22 + 13 = ?

6 Answer these multiplication and division questions.
(a) 4 × 5 =
(b) 4 × 4 =
(c) 30 ÷ 6 =
(d) 6 × 4 =
(e) 20 ÷ 5 =
(f) 40 ÷ 4 =
(g) 3 × 6 =
(h) 36 ÷ 6 =

7 Write down the outputs for these 'rule machines'.
(a) 4 → × 3 → ?
(b) 7 → + 7 → ?
(c) 20 → ÷ 5 → ?
(d) 30 → − 13 → ?

8 Find the value of the question marks in each 'machine'.
(a) 6 → + ? → 11
(b) 4 → × ? → 16
(c) 10 → ÷ ? → 5
(d) 30 → − ? → 21
(e) 5 → × ? → 20
(f) 18 → ÷ ? → 2
(g) 21 → ÷ ? → 7
(h) 6 → × ? → 24

This is a ventriloquist's dummy.
This head is 4 centimetres long.
The body that matches this head will be 2 times longer than the head. The body will be 8 cm long.

The total height of the dummy will be 12 cm.

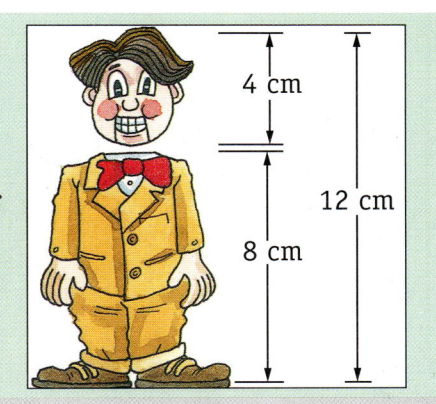

Exercise 1

Which dummy's head goes with which body?
Remember, the body is always twice the length of the head.

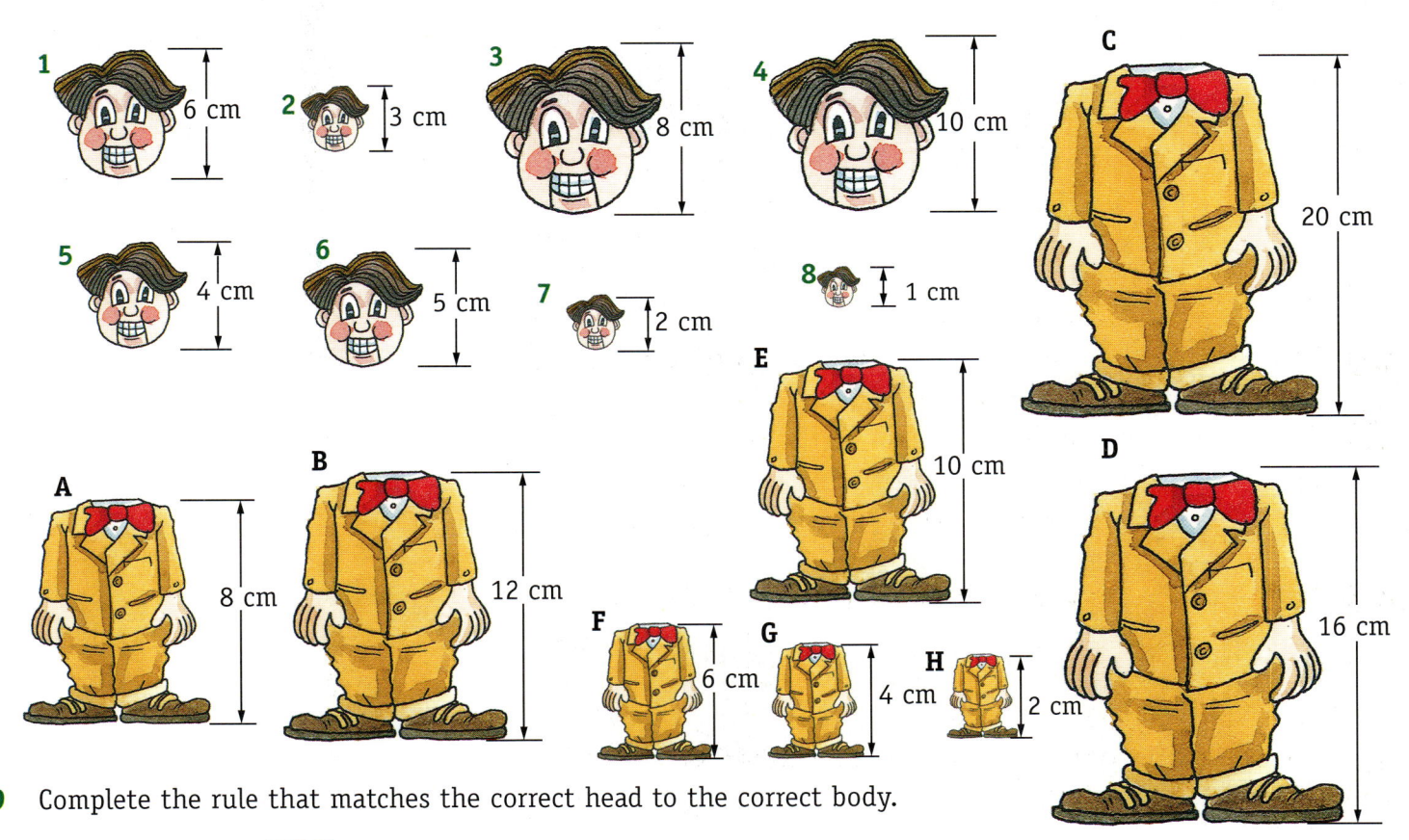

9 Complete the rule that matches the correct head to the correct body.

Length of head —[?]— **Length of body**

10 Can you think of a **different type of rule**, that will calculate the full height of a dummy?
Fill in the missing sign using one of these symbols: ÷ × − +

Length of head [?] **Length of body**

11 Use the rule to calculate the total height of each dummy.

Rules 129

Exercise 2

On an adult the body is 7 times the length of the head.

A 10 cm   B 2 cm   C 5 cm   D 3 cm   E 6 cm

The rule is: h (head) —[×7]— b (body)

1. Work out the length of the body for each head.
2. Add the length of the body to the length of the head to find the total height of each figure.
3. Does the rule h —[×8]— give you the total height of each figure?

Exercise 3

Here is a group of puppets. Which of the rules below matches each of the puppets, so that you can calculate the **total height** from the length of the head?

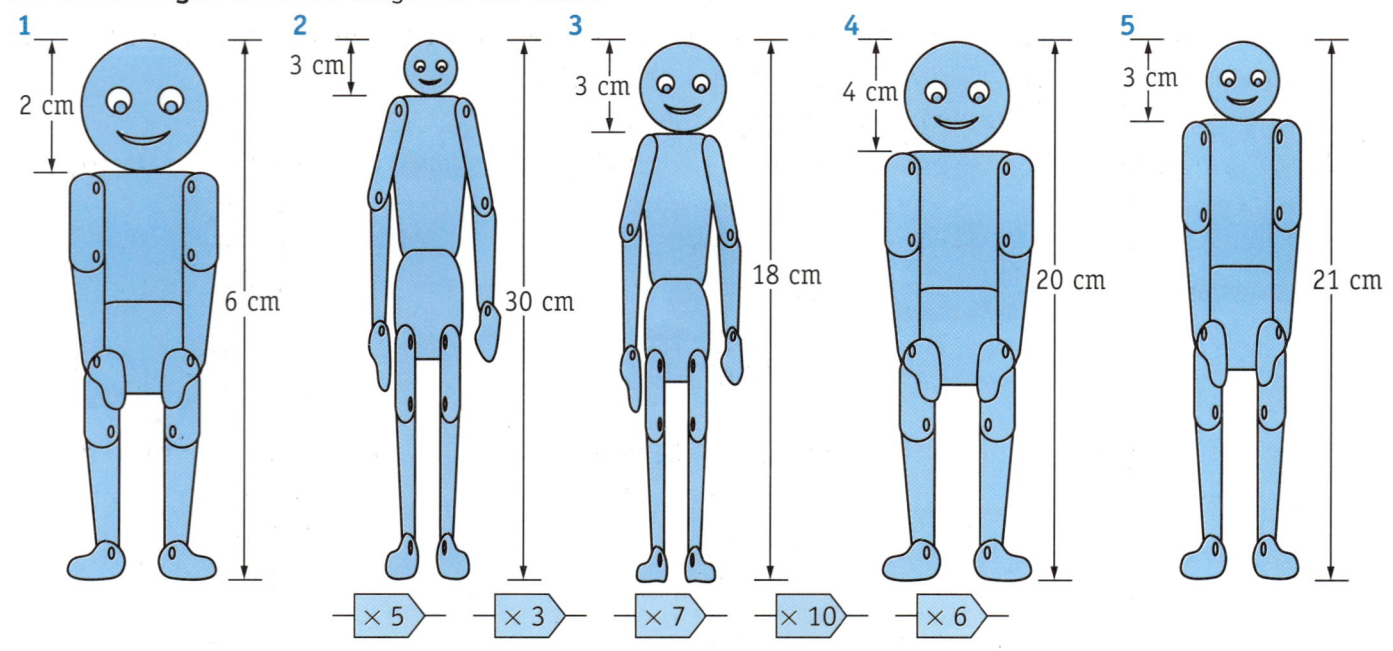

1. 2 cm, 6 cm
2. 3 cm, 30 cm
3. 3 cm, 18 cm
4. 4 cm, 20 cm
5. 3 cm, 21 cm

—[×5]— —[×3]— —[×7]— —[×10]— —[×6]—

The rule is: h (head) —[×?]— h (height)

130 Chapter 18

Mappings

The rule for this puppet is ×5

Below is a **mapping**.
It shows three of the head and height measurements that would fit **the rule** for this puppet.

head   height
4 ⟶ 20
2 ⟶ 10
3 ⟶ 15

head -×5- height

Exercise 4

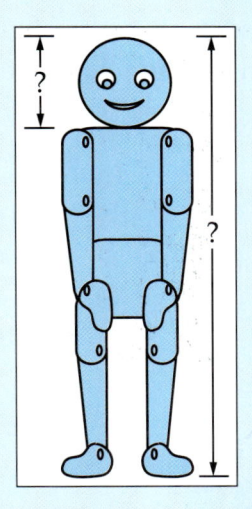

Use these mappings to find the rules that connect head size and height.

1
head   height
4 ⟶ 8
10 ⟶ 20
2 ⟶ 4

head -{?}- height

2
head   height
3 ⟶ 18
2 ⟶ 12
5 ⟶ 30

head -{?}- height

3
head   height
1 ⟶ 10
6 ⟶ 60
10 ⟶ 100

head -{?}- height

Exercise 5

Mappings can be used to show addition, subtraction and division as well as multiplication. Find the rules to fit these mappings. These mappings connect **input** and **output**.
If there is a ? in the mapping find the missing number.

1
Input   Output
5 ⟶ 10
4 ⟶ 9
25 ⟶ 30

-{?}-

2
Input   Output
9 ⟶ 6
15 ⟶ 12
3 ⟶ 0

-{?}-

3
Input   Output
5 ⟶ 10
3 ⟶ 6
50 ⟶ ?

-{?}-

4
Input   Output
8 ⟶ 4
20 ⟶ 10
? ⟶ 25

-{?}-

5
Input   Output
14 ⟶ 7
21 ⟶ 14
12 ⟶ ?

-{?}-

6
Input   Output
60 ⟶ 6
100 ⟶ ?
50 ⟶ 5

-{?}-

Rules

Exercise 6

In each of these mappings there is one pair of values that does not seem to follow the rule.
Find the rule and write it into your book.
Write down the pair of values that does not follow the rule properly.

1
In	Out
3 →	9
2 →	8
1 →	4
5 →	20

2
In	Out
9 →	13
2 →	6
10 →	15
3 →	7

3
In	Out
16 →	4
20 →	4
10 →	2
50 →	10

4
In	Out
3 →	15
5 →	17
8 →	20
4 →	48

Exercise 7

These mappings have values missing. Copy the mappings and fill in the missing numbers.

1
In	Out
4 →	12
2 →	?
10 →	30
5 →	15

2
In	Out
15 →	9
20 →	14
10 →	?
6 →	?

3
In	Out
5 →	20
? →	8
? →	40
3 →	12

4
In	Out
16 →	8
20 →	?
30 →	15
? →	20

The rule is **'multiply by two'**. You can make up a mapping as long as it obeys the rule **'multiply by two'**.

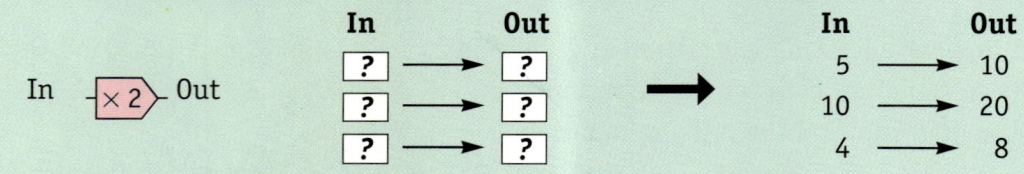

In —[× 2]— Out

In	Out
? →	?
? →	?
? →	?

➡

In	Out
5 →	10
10 →	20
4 →	8

Exercise 8

Make up a mapping for each of the rules below. Your mapping should have at least 3 pairs of values.

1 —[× 4]—

2 —[− 7]—

3 —[÷ 5]—

4 —[+ 11]—

132 Chapter 18

Exercise 9

1. In this café there is a house rule about seating arrangements. What do you think it is?
2. How many chairs will be needed if the café has:
   - (a) six tables
   - (b) 10 tables
   - (c) 20 tables
3. The owner decides to buy new furniture. He wants to seat 30 people; how many tables will he need?
4. To find the rule that links the number of chairs with the number of tables, do you:
   - (a) multiply by 3
   - (b) take away 3
   - (c) divide by 3
   - (d) subtract 3
5. This mapping shows the number of tables and chairs.
   ('**t**' stands for tables, '**c**' stands for chairs)

t	c
1	3
2	6
3	9
4	?
5	?
6	?

   (a) Complete the mappings in your book.

   (b) Write the mapping as a rule t —[× ?]— c

Exercise 10

1. There are 6 glasses on each table. Complete this mapping to show the number of tables and glasses.

2. Write the mapping as a rule   tables —[× ?]— glasses

tables	glasses
1	6
2	12
3	?
4	?
5	?
6	?
7	?
8	?

3. (a) There are 10 flowers on each table. Draw another mapping of tables to flowers.
   (b) Write the mapping as a rule.

Rules

> **Finding rules**
>
> These are the steps that we need to make when we are finding mathematical rules.
>
> 1 We need to LOOK or observe. 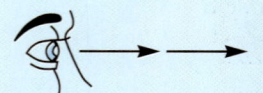
> 2 Next we RECORD the information in a **mapping**.
> 3 Check the mapping for number patterns and FIND 'the rule'.
>
> matches ⟶ triangles   matches –⟨ Rule? ⟩– triangles

Exercise 11

These shapes are made from matchsticks. The **matches** are arranged into patterns of **triangles**.

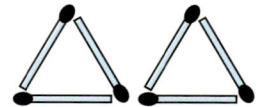

Find the rule that links the number of **triangles** with the number of **matches**. Follow the steps below.

1 Draw the next two patterns.

2 (a) Record the number of matches and triangles for each pattern on a mapping.
   t = number of triangles   m = number of matches
   (b) Add your two other results for 4 triangles and then 5 triangles.

t	m
1 ⟶	3
2 ⟶	6
3 ⟶	9
4 ⟶	?
5 ⟶	?

3 Find the rule that links the number of triangles and the number of matches needed. Give your answer in a 'machine' like this:

triangles –⟨ ? ⟩– matches

4 Use your rule to find the number of matches needed to make:
   (a) 10 triangles   (b) 11 triangles   (c) 20 triangles   (d) 100 triangles

5 If you use 45 matches in a pattern, how many triangles will you have made?

Exercise 12

Find the rule that links the number of pegs and the number of shirts on this washing-line.

1 Draw the next 2 patterns on the line.

pegs	shirts
2 ⟶	1
3 ⟶	2
4 ⟶	3
5 ⟶	?
6 ⟶	?

2 Record the number of pegs and shirts on a mapping.
3 Complete this rule: pegs –⟨ ? ⟩– shirts

Exercise 13

Each page on the message-board needs 4 pins. Here are the first two drawings showing pages and pins.

drawing 1   drawing 2

Find the rule that connects the number of pages with the number of pins.

1 Make the next two drawings in the pattern. They will show 3 pages and 4 pages.
2 The mapping shows the numbers of pins that are needed for each drawing. Copy the mapping and fill in the missing values.

   pages   pins
   1 ⟶ 4
   2 ⟶ 8
   3 ⟶ ?
   4 ⟶ ?

3 Write the rule that connects the number of pages with the number of pins.

   pages ─⟨?⟩─ pins

4 With your partner, discuss how you can test your rule to see if it is correct.
5 Use the rule to find how many pins will be needed for **(a)** 6 pages **(b)** 10 pages.

Key ideas

To find a **rule** we need to: **LOOK, RECORD, FIND A RULE.**

LOOK: Look at information or drawings.
RECORD: Make a record of your observations. A mapping is a good way to do this.
FIND A RULE: Use your mapping to find a number pattern. The pattern is the **RULE**.

MAPPING: triangles   matches
                   1   ⟶   3
                   2   ⟶   6

MACHINE: ─⟨× 3⟩─ ⟵ The 'rule' is you multiply the number of triangles by 3 to find the number of matches.

Rules 135

Chapter 19　Work Out 2　The Magic Shop

A Roy and Meera visit Max's Magic Shop. The first things they see are horror masks. Which of the masks are symmetrical?

A　B　C　D

E　F　G　H

MAX'S MAGIC SHOP
All masks
£15.99

B Next they walk into the Hall of Mirrors. Which of these images are **not** symmetrical?
For each mirror that does not give a symmetrical image, list three things that are not symmetrical.

A　B　C　D

C

Max greets Roy and Meera at the Magic Wall.

Welcome my friends.

1 Look at the people. If you were to measure each person in the picture, who do you **think** would be the tallest?

2 Measure the people. Was your guess correct?

D

1 You cannot always believe your eyes, says Max. Are these two lines **parallel**? How can you check them?

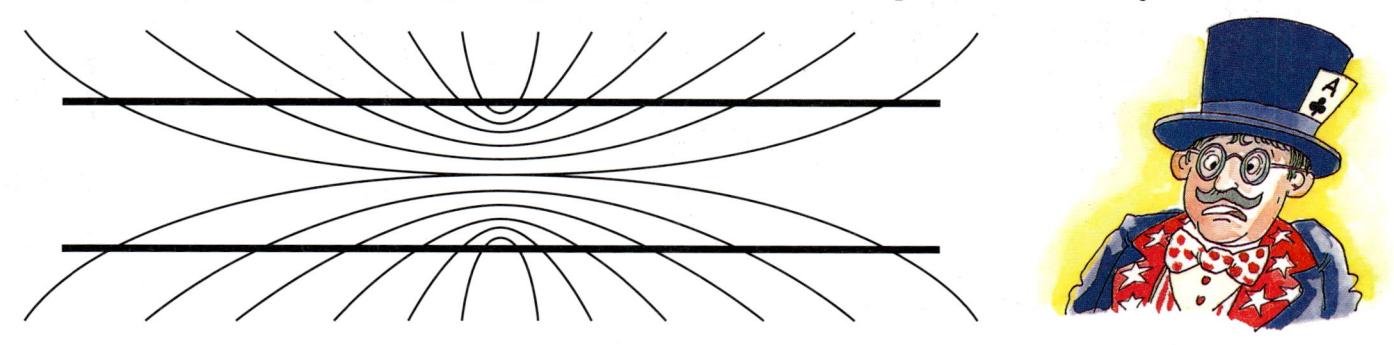

2 Are these lines **parallel** with each other? Use your ruler to see which lines are parallel with each other.

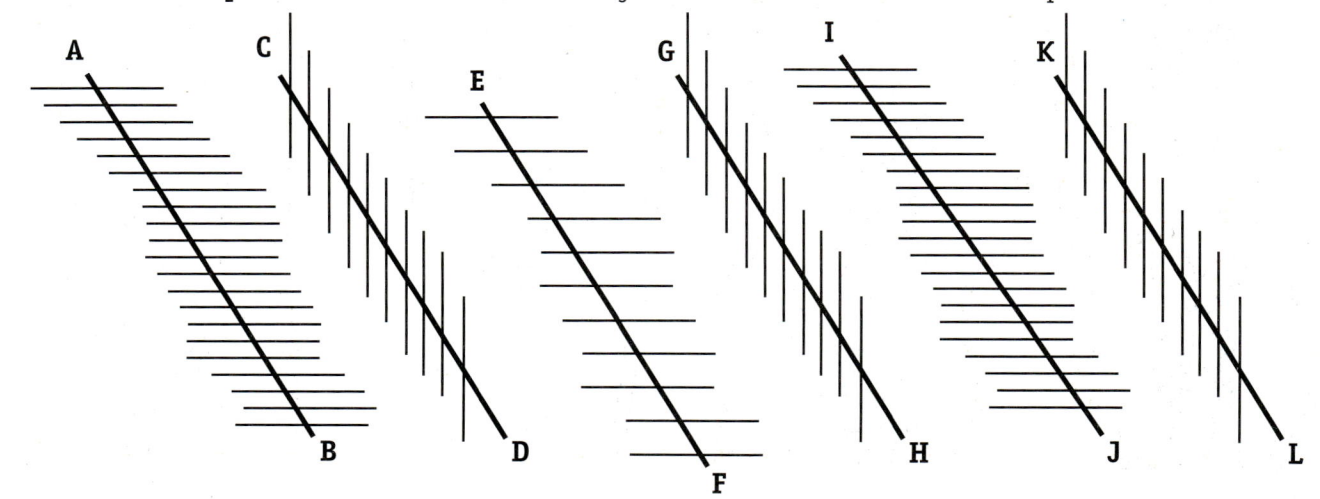

Work Out 2   137

E

Not everything is as it appears. What is odd about these two shapes?

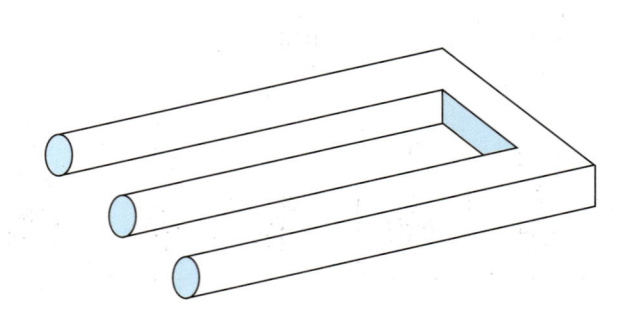

F

Which line is longer: **A**, **B** or **C**?

1

2

G

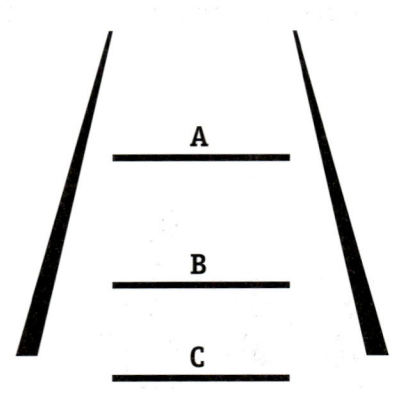

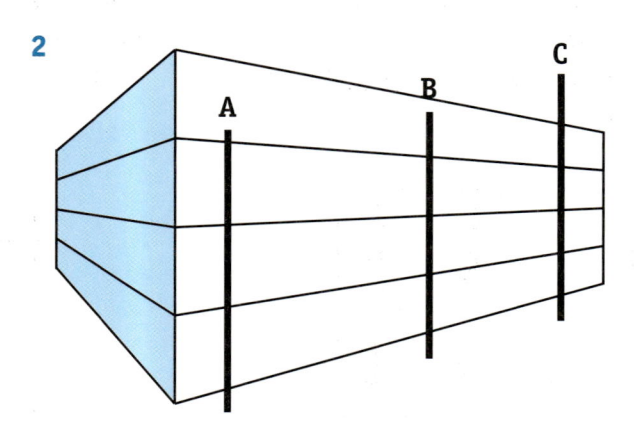

1   Describe how you are going to check that these two shapes are a square and a circle.

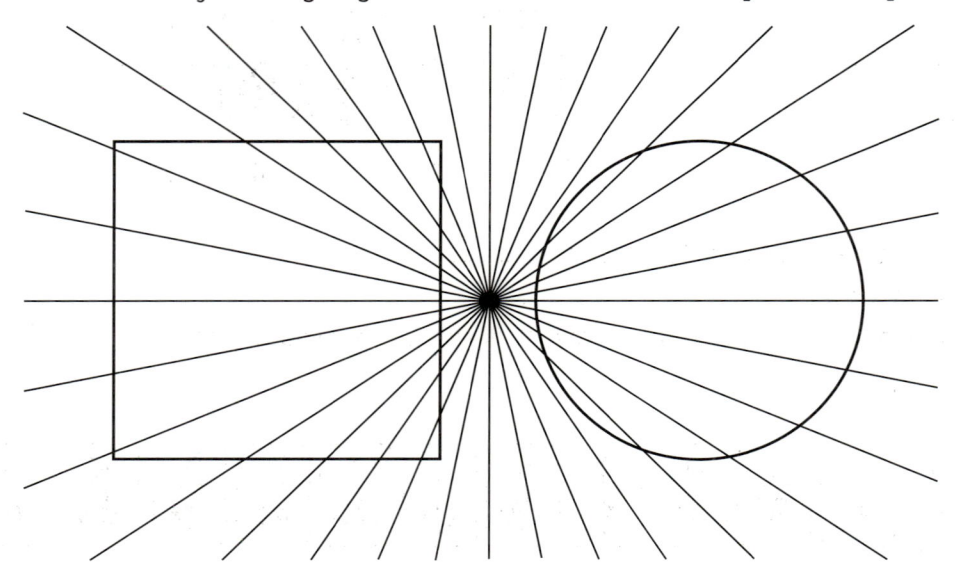

2   Is this a proper circle? Is this a proper square?
3   Explain what equipment you used and how you checked them.

138   Chapter 19

H

Max shows Roy and Meera a card trick.

Step 1 First they choose a card from the group below.

8♠ 5♣ 3♦ 10♥ 4♠ K♣ Q♦ 2♠ 7♣ 9♦ A♠

Step 2

The cards are then laid out on a grid.
They write down the co-ordinate of their chosen card as a number.
The co-ordinate for the ace of spades is (2, 1).
This is written as 21.

Step 3

The cards are shuffled on the grid.
They write down the new co-ordinate as a number.
The co-ordinate for the ace of spades is now (1, 1).
This is written as 11.

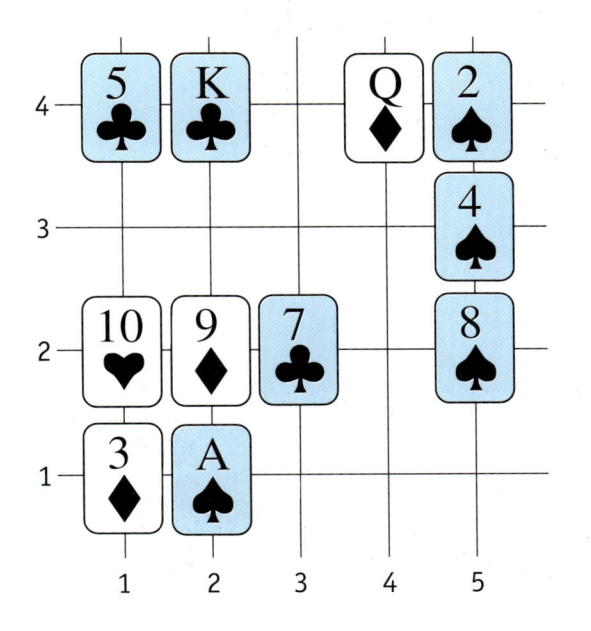

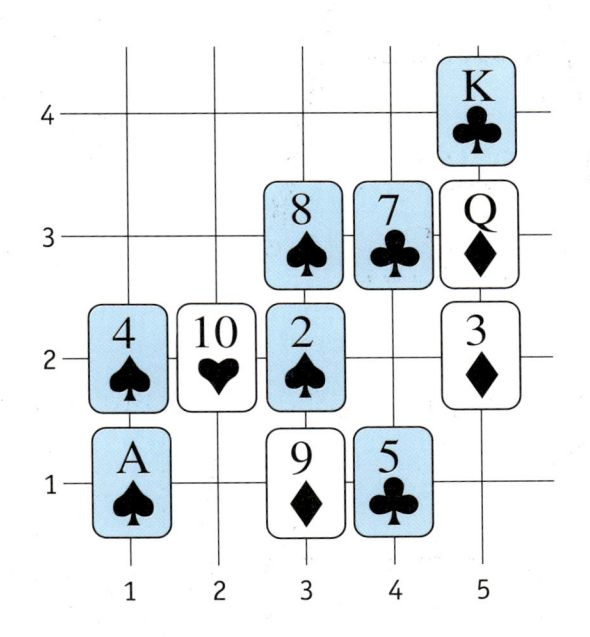

Step 4 Next they add the two co-ordinates – 21 and 11. The total is 32.
Step 5 Add 3 and 2 together. This makes 5.
Step 6 Look at the group of cards below. Count along five cards. It is the ace of spades; the card that Roy and Meera chose.

7♦ 5♥ 6♣ 3♥ A♠ J♥ 10♥ 9♥ 3♦ 5♦ 4♣ 7♠ 8♠ 2♠ K♣ Q♦

Go to Step 1 and choose your own card, and see if the trick works for you.
Do you know any card tricks? Can you explain how they are done?

Work Out 2   139

I

I love numbers.
My favourite number is 9.
Here is the 9 times table.

$1 \times 9 = $ **9**
$2 \times 9 = $ **18**
$3 \times 9 = $ **27**
$4 \times 9 = $ **36**
$5 \times 9 = $ **45**
$6 \times 9 = $ **?**
$7 \times 9 = $ **?**
$8 \times 9 = $ **?**
$9 \times 9 = $ **?**
$10 \times 9 = $ **?**

Notice that the answers add up to 9!
18 becomes $1 + 8 = 9$.
27 becomes $2 + 7 = 9$.

If you look down the answers column you find another pattern:
- the figure in the tens column **increases** by one each time;
- the figure in the units column **decreases** by one each time.

1 Use this pattern to copy and complete the 9 times table.

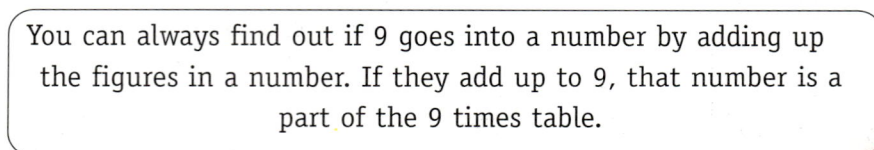

You can always find out if 9 goes into a number by adding up the figures in a number. If they add up to 9, that number is a part of the 9 times table.

Yes, but what about 11×9. That makes 99.
When you add 9 and 9 you get 18.

You simply add the 1 and the 8.
$1 + 8 = 9$!

2 Use this rule to see which of these numbers are part of the 9 times table.
You can check your results with a calculator.

(a) 405   **(b)** 634   **(c)** 711   **(d)** 525   **(e)** 5121   **(f)** 1058
(g) 855   **(h)** 6642   **(i)** 5845   **(j)** 7128   **(k)** 8476   **(l)** 6993

3 Look at the 5 times table.
Can you see any patterns or rules?

$1 \times 5 = 5$
$2 \times 5 = $?
$3 \times 5 = $?
$4 \times 5 = $?
$5 \times 5 = $?
$6 \times 5 = $?

J

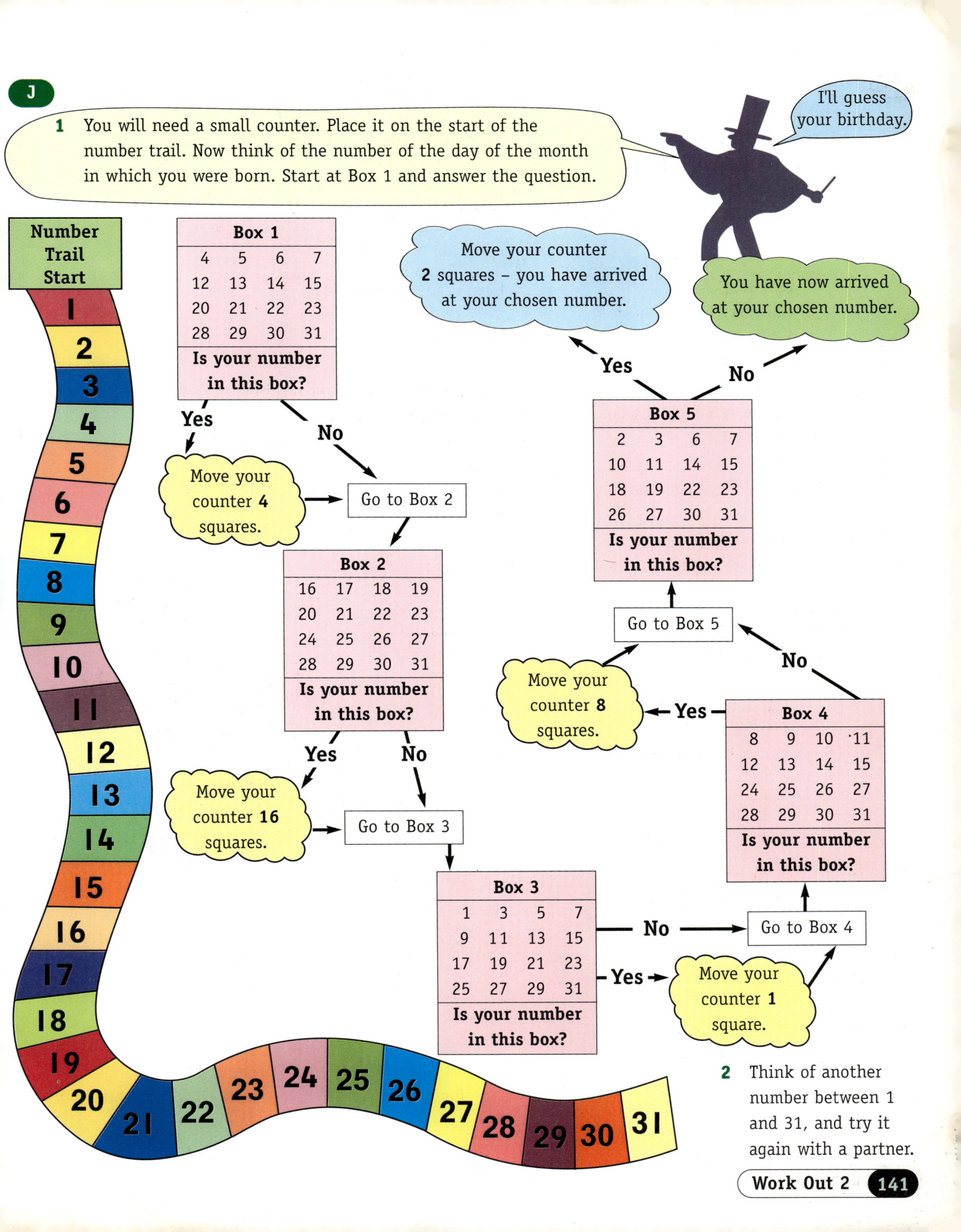

1. You will need a small counter. Place it on the start of the number trail. Now think of the number of the day of the month in which you were born. Start at Box 1 and answer the question.

I'll guess your birthday.

Number Trail Start → 1, 2, 3, 4, 5, 6, 7, 8, 9, 10, 11, 12, 13, 14, 15, 16, 17, 18, 19, 20, 21, 22, 23, 24, 25, 26, 27, 28, 29, 30, 31

Box 1

4	5	6	7
12	13	14	15
20	21	22	23
28	29	30	31

Is your number in this box?

- Yes → Move your counter **4** squares. → Go to Box 2
- No → Go to Box 2

Box 2

16	17	18	19
20	21	22	23
24	25	26	27
28	29	30	31

Is your number in this box?

- Yes → Move your counter **16** squares. → Go to Box 3
- No → Go to Box 3

Box 3

1	3	5	7
9	11	13	15
17	19	21	23
25	27	29	31

Is your number in this box?

- No → Go to Box 4
- Yes → Move your counter **1** square. → Go to Box 4

Box 4

8	9	10	11
12	13	14	15
24	25	26	27
28	29	30	31

Is your number in this box?

- Yes → Move your counter **8** squares. → Go to Box 5
- No → Go to Box 5

Box 5

2	3	6	7
10	11	14	15
18	19	22	23
26	27	30	31

Is your number in this box?

- Yes → Move your counter **2** squares – you have arrived at your chosen number.
- No → You have now arrived at your chosen number.

2. Think of another number between 1 and 31, and try it again with a partner.

Work Out 2 141

K

Finding your magic number

Step 1   Write these numbers down.
- (a) The number of the day of the month in which you were born.
- (b) The number of letters in the month in which you were born.
- (c) The door number of your home.
- (d) Your lucky number.
- (e) The number of letters in your favourite colour.
- (f) The last four digits in your school phone number.
- (g) The number of people in your family, including yourself.

Step 2   Now add all these numbers together.

Step 3   Now add the figures in your answer together. (If the total comes to two figures, add again.)

Meera's list

Step 1
- (a) Birthday — 27th
- (b) October — 7 letters
- (c) Number — 137
- (d) Lucky number — 10
- (e) Green — 5
- (f) Phone number — 3617
- (g) Family — 2

Step 2   Total   3805

Step 3 $3 + 8 + 0 + 5 = 16$
          $1 + 6 = 7$

You now have your **magic number**. Find out more about yourself below.

1 You work very hard at everything you do. This will bring you success in the future. But you must remember to enjoy life as well.

2 You have many talents that you have yet to discover. Do not waste these gifts; work hard and you will be rewarded.

3 You often appear to take life too seriously, and worry about little things. Relax. Let the real you shine out, and go out and achieve your aims.

4 You get on well with people and this will be of value to you in your future life. Keep showing the best side of your nature to the world!

5 Your life is busy and hectic and at times disorganised. Slow down a little and learn to plan your life. Think ahead.

6 You tend to be a thoughtful person, and others recognise this quality in you. Be patient with those people who do not yet value your talents.

7 You tend to be a day-dreamer. However, there are times when you have to turn your plans and dreams into reality. This requires hard work and effort.

8 People think you waste much of your time on unimportant things. Perhaps it is time to decide if you are wasting time, or developing a talent?

9 Sometimes you can take yourself too seriously and forget about the feelings of others and the important things in life. Be more thoughtful and you will be rewarded.

L

> Ladies and Gentlemen, now for my hardest trick! You are going to work out a problem. I have already predicted your answer on page 144!

> Roy and Meera are also going to try this. Do not choose the same numbers as them; try this piece of magic using your own numbers.

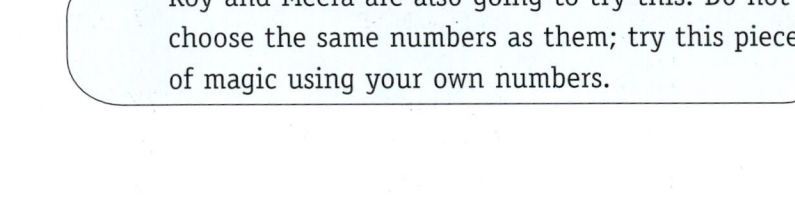

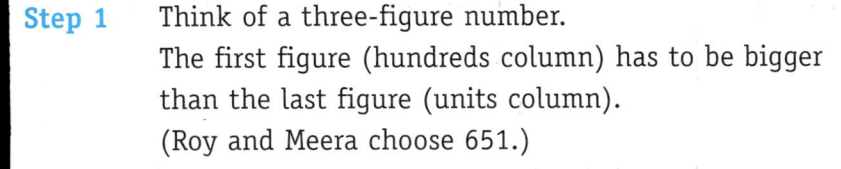

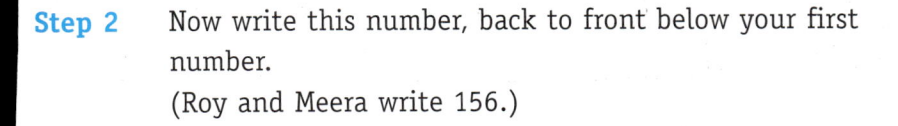

Step 1 Think of a three-figure number.
The first figure (hundreds column) has to be bigger than the last figure (units column).
(Roy and Meera choose 651.)

Step 2 Now write this number, back to front below your first number.
(Roy and Meera write 156.)

Step 3 Subtract the bottom number from the top number.
(Roy and Meera have 495 as their answer.)

Step 4 Write this answer out and below it write it out again, back to front.
(Roy and Meera write 594.)

Step 5 Now add the two numbers together.

Step 6 If you turn over the page you should see something interesting.

Work Out 2 143

1089

AMAZING!

Try this with another three-figure number.

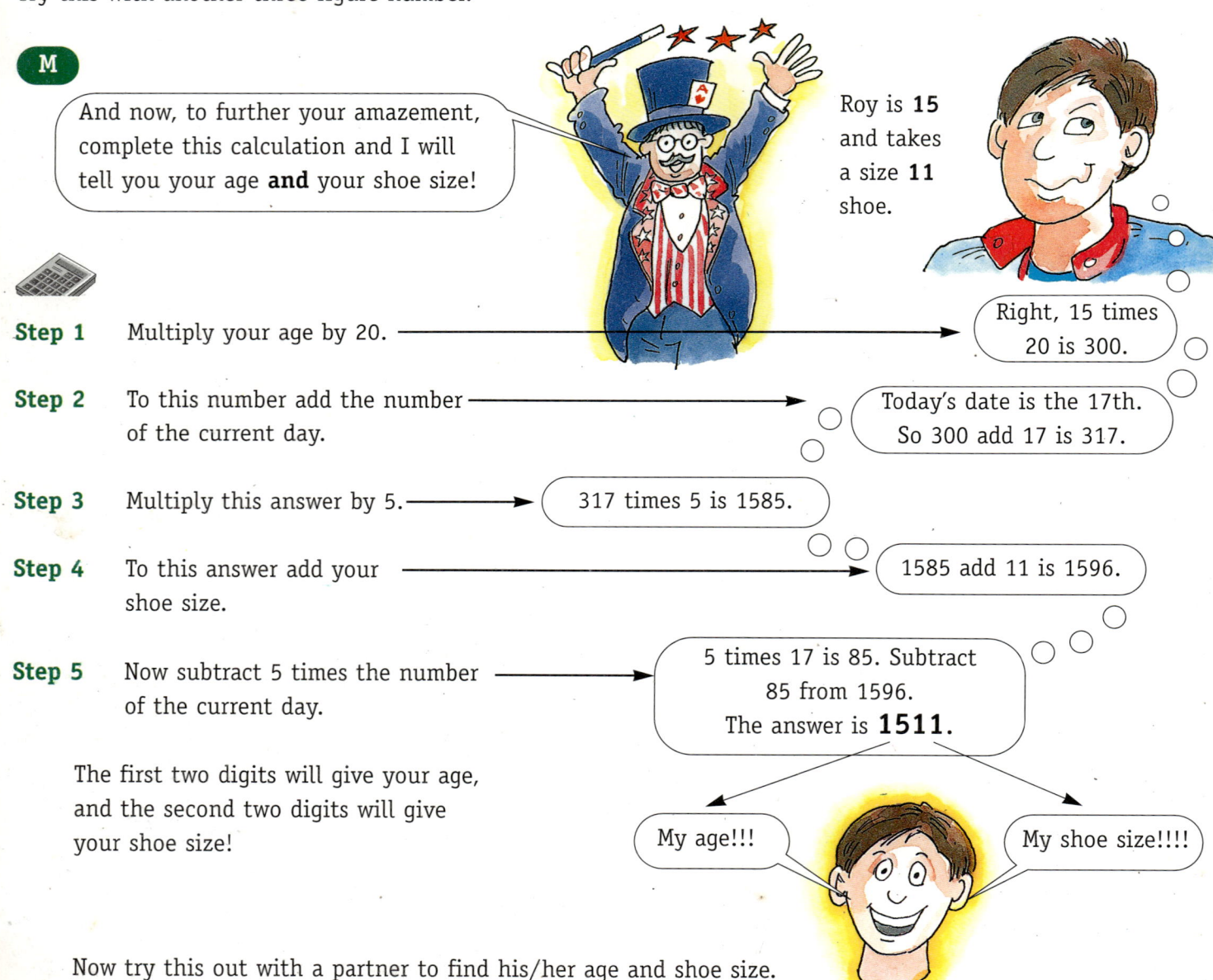

M

And now, to further your amazement, complete this calculation and I will tell you your age **and** your shoe size!

Roy is **15** and takes a size **11** shoe.

Step 1 Multiply your age by 20. — Right, 15 times 20 is 300.

Step 2 To this number add the number of the current day. — Today's date is the 17th. So 300 add 17 is 317.

Step 3 Multiply this answer by 5. — 317 times 5 is 1585.

Step 4 To this answer add your shoe size. — 1585 add 11 is 1596.

Step 5 Now subtract 5 times the number of the current day. — 5 times 17 is 85. Subtract 85 from 1596. The answer is **1511**.

The first two digits will give your age, and the second two digits will give your shoe size!

My age!!!   My shoe size!!!!

Now try this out with a partner to find his/her age and shoe size.

144 Chapter 19